THE ANSWER
TO ASTHMA

"THE ESSENTIAL ASTHMA BOOK helps to bridge the gap between what doctors know about asthma and what patients need to know to cope with their disease intelligently. It is well organized, cogently phrased, comprehensive, and, most important, accessible to the layman.

"Asthma has no cure. But it can be treated and controlled. Information is the key to living with asthma. And today, finally, that information is available."

Peter Salgo, M.D.

THE ESSENTIAL ASTHMA BOOK

A Manual for Asthmatics
of All Ages

Drs. Francois Haas and Sheila Sperber Haas

Illustrated by Dr. Kenneth Axen

IVY BOOKS • NEW YORK

Ivy Books
Published by Ballantine Books
Copyright © 1987 by Francois Haas and Sheila Sperber Haas

This book is not intended as a substitute for the medical advice of
physicians. The reader should regularly consult a physician in matters
relating to his/her health and particularly with respect to any symptoms
that may require diagnosis or medical attention.

Library of Congress Catalog Card Number: 86-26054

ISBN-0-8041-0287-2

This edition published by arrangement with Charles Scribner's Sons, a
Division of The Scribner Book Companies, Inc.

Manufactured in the United States of America

First Ballantine Books Edition: September 1988

To Albert Haas, M.D.,
the father of pulmonary rehabilitation

To our children and his grandchildren,
Alexander and Ariane

Contents

List of Illustrations

ix

Foreword

It was quite early one Wednesday morning several years ago that I received the phone call. A close friend of mine in New York had reached me in the operating room in Boston. His young daughter Katie was sick. In fact, she was in the hospital. She could not breathe well and was, at that moment, lying in an oxygen tent. Her doctors were considering placing a tube into her windpipe to help her breathe better.

I had known Tom, his wife, Nancy, and Katie for years, and I had studied the standard texts about asthma. But it was not until I heard Tom's voice on the telephone that I recognized the true impact the disease can have, both on the sufferer and upon those close to her. More importantly, I realized that although Tom and Nancy were living with Katie's asthma minute by minute, there were still scores of unanswered questions about the disease in their minds. They were questions that I thought Katie's doctor might have answered for them, but had not.

Since I am an internist, asthma and its complications had always played a large part in my practice. And yet, I had viewed it from a distance, with a clinician's cool and largely detached attitude. Patients would tell me that they "could not breathe out." I told them they had asthma. We embarked upon a search for the things around them that could provoke attacks. Then they tried to avoid them. I prescribed medication. They usually tried to take it properly.

All told, I felt pretty good about modern medicine and the tools it had given me to help asthmatics fight their disease. But now, Katie was sick. This was no distant doctor-patient dialogue. This was a desperate call for help from a friend. I flew to New York. On the airplane I began to wonder why Katie had gotten into trouble. I asked why Tom and Nancy needed me in addition to the excellent doctors they already knew quite well. And I wondered how much the average asthmatic and his or her family knew about the disease. I began to suspect the answer to that question was simple—not enough.

There are at least 9 million people in the United States who suffer from asthma. The true number of asthma victims is probably greater than that, because many people with the disease avoid seeing doctors. Some people estimate that as many as 20 million Americans suffer from the disease. It affects people of all ages, of both sexes. And the problem seems to be growing. There are new asthmatics every day.

And yet, in my experience, most asthmatics understand their disease quite poorly. It's not their fault. Until now, there was simply no source a patient might refer to for a comprehensive and intelligible discussion of the disease. Medical texts devote thousands of words to the subject, but medical texts are not written in English. They are written in a subspecies of the language—intelligible to doctors, but to few others.

Most patients don't ask their doctors the right questions about asthma. And for all their training and skill, doctors tend not to answer patients' questions very well. Effective communication is one course not taught in medical school. Patients today often find doctors imposing and inaccessible.

And so, without hard information to guide them, many asthmatics fall back upon the least reliable sources of information—gossip, rumor, folklore, and superstition. Some actually believe that asthma isn't a real disease at all but, rather, that it is a set of imagined symptoms.

Many asthmatics think it is dangerous to engage in sex. Others fear wet climates, flowers, and trees, or even household dust. They fear these things not so much because they know they are dangerous, but because they have heard, somewhere, that they might be dangerous.

We know far too much about asthma to leave a patient's well-being to chance. We know enough to advise parents about the best environments for their asthmatic children. We know enough about adult asthma to fill a library. We know enough about asthma-fighting drugs to give patients precise instructions for their use.

Most importantly, we know that asthma is a real disease, with real symptoms. It is not, as many asthmatics believe, a psychosomatic problem. Asthma is not "all in a patient's head." One look at little Katie, lying in a hospital bed, struggling to breathe, her lips blue and her chest heaving with each effort, would convince anyone that the disease can be a real, and violent, killer.

This information does no good locked inside a physician's mind, or sitting, unread, on a library shelf. It must reach the asthmatic and the asthmatic's family.

The Essential Asthma Book, written by Dr. Francois Haas and Dr. Sheila Sperber Haas, is an excellent attempt to bridge the gap between what doctors know about asthma and what patients need to know to cope with their disease intelligently. It is well organized, cogently phrased, comprehensive, and, most important, accessible to the layman.

All the same, it is not—nor can any book ever be—a substitute for concerned, intelligent medical care. Instead, it should serve as a guide. It should help the reader discover what he or she knows about asthma. It should help correct misinformation and stimulate questions about the disease, questions that any doctor should be happy to answer.

Perhaps the greatest benefit this book offers the careful

reader is an overall sense of order and organization. The book suggests that managing asthma is more a matter of common sense than of medical miracles. It proposes that asthmatics treat their attacks in an orderly and calm fashion. It urges asthmatics to recognize that panic is their chief enemy. The cure for panic is sound information, and that's what this book provides.

Four years have passed since I saw Katie struggle to breathe in her oxygen tent. And since that time, something her parents had never expected to happen has occurred. Her asthma has gone away. At some point, the wheezing, the coughing, and the sleepless nights stopped. Katie, at least for the time being, is asthma-free. And that, too, is a part of asthma. It often goes away, occasionally to return in later life.

Katie's problems emphasize the essential facts about asthma. The disease follows no set course. It often waxes and wanes throughout a lifetime. The disease has no cure. But it can be treated and controlled. Information is the key to living with asthma. And today, finally, that information is available.

PETER SALGO, M.D.

Preface

Nine million Americans reportedly suffer from asthma. That is the approximate number of asthmatics actually documented in this country, but professionals suspect it is really just the tip of the iceberg. Some people with asthma or asthmalike symptoms do not bring their complaints to a doctor. With others, the disease is never correctly diagnosed. (As you will learn, this diagnosis is not easy to make.) A more realistic estimate of the number of asthmatics in the United States is 15 to 20 million.

In September 1983, one of us—Francois—began a three-year research project investigating how exercise affects asthma. This work required close and prolonged contact with the asthmatics who volunteered to be subjects. As time passed, all these volunteers brought in many, many questions about their disease. And though these volunteers were only a tiny fraction of the asthmatics in this country, a great number of their questions were the same.

Our book had its origin in these questions. It became obvious to us that asthmatics face a major problem that has nothing to do with the disease itself. It is the serious lack of public information about their disease, the kind of information that would allow asthmatics to take effective control of their disease and achieve the best that life has to offer them.

Without this information, most asthmatics are severely handicapped in dealing with their disease. They do not understand enough about asthma to be able to ask their doctors the kinds of questions that would allow them to participate actively—and therefore effectively—in their own treatment. We believe that achieving the most effective treatment requires participation by both doctor *and patient*, and this book is meant to provide the information that asthmatics must have. It is a comprehensive lay handbook for adult asthmatics and parents of asthmatic children (whom we call "asthma parents").

Within the overall aim of producing as comprehensive a book as possible, we had several goals in mind—both formal and informal—when we began work. We will list them all now, then explain them below. One: This book will *not* be a substitute for a well-trained physician; its aim is to educate asthmatics, not treat them. Two: The book should be objective. Three: The book should be clearly written, enjoyable to read, and a pleasure to look at. Four: The book should go beyond the medical aspects of asthma to include everything relevant to handling the disease. Five: The book should be fun to write. Now that we have finished, we know we have succeeded in the last goal, and we feel we have done a good job in reaching the other four.

One: One of our biggest objections to most popular medical books is their strong implication, "Follow these rules and you will be cured." Some books give treatment rules, telling readers what drugs and doses to take. Once an ill person is diagnosed, however, he needs to be treated by a competent professional who knows his particular case. Each patient is an individual, and no two individuals should be treated exactly alike just because they have the same disease. Otherwise, doctors would be needed only to make diagnoses, and treatment could be dealt with at mass dispensaries. Any book that gives drug dosages applicable to everyone borders on the irresponsible. Other books promise an easy cure for asthma. This is equivalent to promising quality nutrition from junk food. To the extent they claim that their cure permits an asthmatic to throw away his medication, these easy-cure books are also irresponsible. The need for any element of antiasthma therapy, including drug type and dose, must be determined in the context of the whole person. This requires a qualified physician. Anyone looking for a cure or a recipe for treatment will find this book disappointing.

Two: We have not emphasized information because it agrees with our point of view, nor have we omitted information we disagree with. Our concerns are accuracy and fairness. We also do not ignore controversy when it exists, because we believe it is important for the reader to know when and why the professionals disagree. This means that differing points of view—and the basic reasons for them—appear whenever there is significant disagreement on an aspect of asthma or its treatment. Honesty, rather than artificially easy answers, is what every patient deserves. Despite our objective approach overall, though, we have not always kept our opinions and prejudices at a distance. When we have been unable to hold our peace, the reader has been so advised.

Three: The goal of writing a book that is easy and enjoyable to read does not need much explanation. Making information accessible involves more than just putting it all together in one place. And judging from our test readers' comments, we have succeeded in writing a book that is understandable to any reasonably literate person. Readers will notice some repetition every so often in defining certain technical terms. There are two reasons for this. One is that people differ in their capacity to retain relatively technical information. Readers who do not retain these facts easily will not have to hunt around for definitions when technical words and concepts reappear. The second reason is that some readers prefer to skip around instead of reading a book by chapter order. We do not want information to be incomprehensible because a reader has not yet read preceding sections.

We think the illustrations in this book are unique, and they are certainly a pleasure to look at. For this success we thank our friend and colleague of many years, Kenneth Axen, Ph.D. He shares our conviction that illustrations should combine clearly presented information with visual beauty. And because he is a scientist who studies breathing, he was able to develop these illustrations on his own, freeing us to concentrate on the research and writing.

Four: Socioeconomic factors are not usually discussed in this kind of medical book. The sad fact is, though, that poor people often do not get the best medical care. Poor asthmatics are no exception. Both the treatment of asthma and its impact on the individual and his family are frequently determined by a patient's economic circumstances. Where it is relevant we discuss the influence of poverty on this disease, on its medical care, and on appropriate treatment choices. We also note the politics of medicine and medication as they affect asthma patients.

Another aspect of looking beyond immediate medical concerns is our inclusion of a fair amount of the history of asthma and asthma treatment. Although this strongly reflects personal interests, we hope this material helps the reader realize that the state of medicine at any given time cannot be divorced from the society and technology in which it exists. What appears a valid treatment today may be dismissed as humbug tomorrow, possibly to reappear to acclaim the day after in a modestly different guise. Accepted medical treatments, like clothes, often depend on what is considered fashionable. We should not be too quick to dismiss therapies simply because they are considered passé.

Two elements of our writing style deserve some comment. We feel that the different subjects presented in the book require two different ways of addressing the reader. When we present background or technical information, we address the reader impersonally. In talking about experiences that most or all readers have, or will have, we address you personally. You will also notice that we consistently use the pronouns ''he'' and ''him.'' This does not reflect any sexist bias, but simply our strong distaste for the awkward "he/she." It substantially breaks up the flow of a sentence. So when you read these masculine pronouns, please picture male and female doctors and patients.

One last thought concerns our qualification for producing this book. We saw our education and experience as in our favor. We each have a Ph.D. (Francois in biophysics and physiology, Sheila in psychology). For the past ten years we have been intensely involved in studying various aspects of asthma. Further, we believed our scientific training would allow us to be objective in reviewing the scientific literature, and able to provide an overview of research findings rather than—as too often happens in popular medical books—the authors' personal opinions. Last but not least, one of us (Sheila) is a successful medical and science writer with a passion for simplicity and clarity in her work.

These advantages were offset by our lack of hands-on experience with the daily medical management of asthma patients. We overcame this limitation through the good fortune of our close association with two highly gifted physicians who specialize in treating respiratory diseases. We thank Frederick Bevelaqua, M.D., for taking time from his busy schedule to review the manuscript and for giving us the benefit of his extensive clinical experience. Nathan Levine, M.D., receives our special thanks for sharing medical expertise gained in several different countries. He has added a more global point of view to the final result. We also thank Stuart Garay, M.D., and Paul Ehrlich, M.D., for reviewing the completed manuscript. Our final thanks go to Martin Kahn, M.D., and Robin Persky, Ph.D., for reviewing the manuscript sections appropriate to their work.

Lastly, we thank the asthma patients who encouraged us to write this book and those who acted as our sounding board during the book's development. We single out for special appreciation Carol Bernton, Richard Maizel, Richard Gottlieb, Sandra Samberg, Mary Schuman, and Miki and Paul Jaeger (asthma parents). Added to this group is Sophia Pasierski, a physical therapist who works with asthma patients.

To whatever degree this book helps asthmatics and their families achieve the kind of realistic perspective about asthma that allows them to live calmly and confidently with their disease—and so remove needless limitations from their lives—to this degree our goal will be realized. And whatever thanks we receive and gratification we experience must be shared with those research volunteers who opened our eyes to the need for this book.

FRANCOIS HAAS AND SHEILA SPERBER HAAS

✳✳ 1 ✳✳

An Introduction to Asthma

What Is Asthma?

Asthma is a common lung disease that has been recognized for a very long time. The ancient Greeks clearly described its recurrent symptoms, and their name for it— *asthma* was their verb "to pant," "to breathe hard"—still holds. By 25 B.C., Celsus obviously understood the basis for the asthmatic's classic wheeze, explaining, "On account of the narrow passages by which the air escapes, it comes out a whistle" (Figure 1.1). He also knew that this narrowing of the passages bringing air to and from the lungs is usually of brief duration. In the second century A.D., the famed Cappadocian physician Aretaeus gave this classical description of asthma: "The symptoms of its approach are heaviness of the chest; sluggishness to one's accustomed work, and to every other exertion; difficulty of breathing in running or on a steep road; . . . [patients] are hoarse and troubled with cough. . . . During remissions, although they may walk about erect, they bear the trace of the affection [disease]."

Despite asthma's long medical history, until recently doctors had confusingly applied this term to virtually all

1

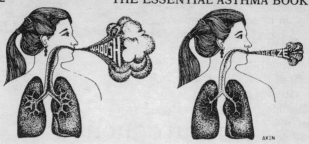

Figure 1.1 The wheeze—asthma's hallmark.

periodically recurring bouts of wheezing and breathing difficulty, even though these symptoms could be due to either lung or heart problems. *Asthma* now refers specifically to a lung-caused difficulty, although the identical constellation of asthmatic symptoms—the recurrent experience of wheezy breathlessness with coughing, plus noticeable difficulty in moving air in and out of the lungs—can be triggered by a variety of apparent causes, or stimuli. After all this time, medicine remains ignorant of the common mechanism that permits these different stimuli to provoke an asthma attack.

Yet for asthma, as for any disease, productive research directed toward an eventual cure cannot adequately proceed without an understanding of the disease's underlying mechanism. This understanding can only develop once a universally accepted definition of the disease has been reached. (*Defining* a disease, in contrast to simply *describing* its symptoms, requires knowledge of the underlying mechanism.) Three concerted attempts by doctors and scientists to arrive at a working definition of asthma (in 1959, 1962, and 1972) failed. The variety of triggering stimuli defied all attempts to ascribe asthma to a single identifiable mechanism. Since none of these medical caucuses could agree on the one mechanism responsible for the range of stimuli causing this similar breathing problem in different people, they finally settled for describing its characteristic symptoms: ''Asthma is a disease characterized by an increased responsiveness of the trachea [windpipe] and bronchi [airways] to various stimuli, and manifested by a widespread narrowing of the airways [bronchoconstriction] that [improves] either spontaneously or as a result of therapy [use of bronchodilators].''

So we know *what* happens—recurrent wheezing and breathing difficulty; we know *why* it happens—the airways narrow because of hypersensitivity to certain stimuli. But we do not yet know *how* it happens. The mechanism that creates this hypersensitivity is still a mystery.

Despite the variety of stimuli or conditions that can provoke asthma, doctors traditionally separate asthmatics into two broad categories based on the general types of stimuli involved (these will be discussed in detail in Chapter 3). *Allergic or extrinsic asthma* episodes are clearly due to the patient's immunological response to an allergen (a substance to which he is hypersensitive), such as dust, mold, pollen, or animal dander. *Nonallergic or intrinsic asthma* episodes cannot be tied to an allergy.

How Common Is Asthma?

Accurately estimating the number of people who have asthma is very difficult. The lack of a generally accepted definition can result in the misdiagnosis of a significant number of asthmatics. The problem is further complicated by the possibility that patients with a classic asthma complaint who appear normal during their medical examination are simply between asthmatic episodes at that time. Even so, asthma constitutes a major health problem in industrialized countries. Estimates indicate that from 2 to 20 percent of the populations of these countries now have, used to have, or will have asthma. In the United States alone, statistics show that a minimum of 9 million people currently have this disease.

Asthma appears to be on the rise. In Birmingham, England, for example, in the 12 years from 1957 to 1969 the proportion of asthmatic children in the group aged five to fifteen years increased by more than 25 percent (from 1.8 percent to 2.3 percent of the group). A study in the United States comparing overall asthma rates in 1969 and 1975 documented a large increase, from 8.1 to 11.7 asthmatics in every group of 1,000 Americans.

Is Asthma Just a Childhood Disease?

Asthma can begin at any age, from childhood through adulthood, although the typical age of onset is not the same around the world. In most of the English-speaking countries (United Kingdom, Australia, and the United States), for example, 30 percent of asthmatic patients say their asthma started before they were 10 years old. Only about 10 percent of the asthmatics in Finland, India, and Nigeria report that their symptoms began during childhood. Patients whose asthma first appeared after the age of 45 represent only 9 percent of all asthmatics in the English-speaking countries, but a whopping 42 percent of the Finnish asthmatics.

There is evidence that whether asthma begins early or later in life bears some relationship to the type of stimulus that triggers an individual's asthmatic episodes. One survey reported that three-fourths of the patients whose asthma began before age 15 had allergic asthma, but in the post-45-onset group only one-third had the allergic variety. So it is possible that the greater incidence of childhood asthma found in some countries may reflect a substantially higher presence of allergens there, or a generally increased susceptibility to allergens in these regions.

Are Men and Women Equally Vulnerable?

Among asthmatic children in countries currently doing such surveys, there are up to three times more boys than girls. The number of asthmatic boys varies from 1.5 to 3.3 for every asthmatic girl. Although no one knows why more boys get asthma, a documented childhood sex difference possibly relevant to the development of asthma—and certainly involved in provoking acute episodes—is that boys are more susceptible to lower respiratory tract infections.

Although this childhood sex difference in asthma prevalence becomes smaller as children get older, whether it fully disappears by adulthood is open to question. In the United States and the United Kingdom, for example, there appears to be no real difference between the number of asthmatic men and women. On the other hand, some Scandinavian studies show many more asthmatic women than men, especially in the older age groups. Their overall adult ratio ranges from an equality of 1 to 1 up to a high of 3.2 women for each man.

Although no one really knows why this childhood predominance of male asthmatics diminishes, or possibly even reverses, any or all of several speculations may be relevant. One is that a larger proportion of boys than girls "outgrow" their childhood asthma. Another is that more women than men develop asthma as adults. Possible support for this theory is the documented association between the menstrual period and a monthly worsening of symptoms, which may indicate that the onset of menstruation during adolescence can precipitate susceptibility to asthma. A further possible factor is that a percentage of asthmatic men may be misdiagnosed. There is some evidence that male smokers complaining of asthma symptoms risk being wrongly diagnosed as suffering from chronic bronchitis (a cigarette-related disease with similar symptoms, but a different process than asthma). Women smokers with identical complaints are more often classified as asthmatic.

Are There Ethnic Differences in Vulnerability?

Different ethnic groups vary widely in the prevalence of asthma. Of those groups studied, it is particularly uncommon among the Papua New Guinea highlanders, villagers in Gambia, and certain tribes of North American Indians and Eskimos. An observer in 1931 discovered Indian reservation hospitals that had never seen a case of asthma. Although the disease is now encountered somewhat more within these groups, it remains impressively uncommon. The estimated rate of asthma among Eskimos in the Mackenzie Delta, for example, is still less than 1 percent.

Without more information, it is impossible to know whether such ethnic differences in susceptibility to asthma are due to genetic variation or to external differences in climate and/or environmental conditions and/or life-styles. So the most promising way to study the basis for these racial differences is to examine sizable groups of immigrants who are now exposed to the environmental influences of a population with a different asthma rate. Do the children of these immigrants show the rate of their ancestral environment, or of their new home?

There is disturbing evidence that when members of low-asthma groups move to urban areas, asthma among them becomes more common. One such study in England found that English-born black children of West Indian descent have an asthma rate similar to white English children, yet those who are born in the West Indies and then move to England have a significantly lower asthma rate. The most detailed report on the relationship of environment and asthma concerns the Tokelau Islanders, many of whom had moved to New Zealand after a hurricane devastated their islands in 1966. (Tokelauns are Polynesians living on three adjacent atolls in the Pacific Ocean about three hundred miles north of Samoa). By the end of the 1970s, 25 percent of the immigrant children had asthma compared with only 11 percent of the Tokelau children residing on the islands.

The general increase in asthma among immigrant children born in urban areas strongly militates against a genetic explanation for initial ethnic differences in asthma susceptibility. Environmental factors implicated when the asthma rate increases among children of immigrants are air pollutants and exposure to such new allergens as dust mites, pollens, and fungi. But why do these environmental irritants eventually trigger asthma episodes only in some people—both immigrants and native—but not others? Environmental factors, although demonstrably of critical importance in the development of asthma, do not deny the specific contribution of genetic factors.

Is Asthma an Inherited Disease?

For any disease, it is vital to know whether people inherit it, or develop it after conception solely because of external factors, or if its presence is the net result of both genetic and environmental influences. The biological blueprint for our inherited characteristics is carried by millions of genes arranged in prescribed order on 23 pairs of microscopic chromosomes, with half of each pair coming from our mother and half from our father. Studying families in which a particular disease occurs, then, helps answer this critical question.

For asthma, there are three ways of approaching such family studies. One is to study the asthma pattern over several generations of a family to see whether it resembles the typical pattern of an inherited trait. The second is comparing identical twins (who share the identical genetic blueprint) and fraternal twins (who may or may not have much genetic material in common) in asthmatic families.

If asthma is an inherited disease, a great majority of the identical twins will either both have it or both be free of it, while often only one of a fraternal pair will be asthmatic. But if asthma is due only to environmental factors, then fraternal as well as identical twins should both have the disease when exposed to the same asthma-producing environment. The third family study approach (if an appropriate group exists) is to uncover the asthma pattern over time in a large intermarried community for which records cover a substantial number of generations. The patterns produced by genetic versus environmental causes are distinctively different.

Maimonides, the famed physician and rabbi in the twelfth-century court of the Sultan Saladin, noticed that asthma tended to run in specific families. But it was not until the middle of the twentieth century that studies were done to confirm this much earlier observation. The immediate relative (such as a sibling or child) of an asthmatic—compared with a person with no family history of asthma—is 13 times more likely to develop asthma by age 49, and 33 times more likely to develop it by age 65! The likelihood that both members in a set of identical twins will have asthma is very high, while the chance of this happening with fraternal twins is much lower.

Members of the large intermarried community on the isolated island of Tristan da Cunha in the South Atlantic—for whom asthma is the most common chronic medical complaint—all descend from the 15 pioneers who settled the island 150 years ago. Three of these settlers suffered from asthma. Medical interviews conducted in London with members of this group, after temporary evacuation from their island in 1961 because of a volcanic eruption, have greatly expanded our understanding of the disease.

The 70 families that formed the island community contained only seven family surnames, indicating the community's highly inbred state. At least half the islanders suffered from asthma at the time of the evacuation. Most of these (almost 90 percent) had asthmatic parents, siblings, and/or children. Since the islanders showed no evidence of being more allergy-prone than the general English population, the hereditary factor responsible for their unusually high asthma rate appears to be increased airway reactivity. That something external is needed to trigger this airway responsiveness is evident from the markedly greater number of asthmatic episodes that would follow each arrival of the island's supply ship. After the boat's arrival, the islanders—who are by and large cold-free—would suffer an epidemic of colds followed by a substantial increase in asthma attacks.

The collected evidence that our genes are an important determinant of who gets asthma is overwhelming. Although a small number of scientists remain unconvinced—noting that the presence of asthma in one spouse increases the likelihood of its developing in the other—most scientists are sure that susceptibility to asthma rests on a group of as-yet-unidentified genes that interact in some unknown and complex way.

The specific role that inheritance plays, however, is not clear. Hereditary factors appear to predispose an individual to asthma, but it seems that external factors are responsible for activating it. Facts to be explained are the number of people who suffer from asthma even though, to their knowledge, no one else in their families does, and the occasional identical twin who remains asthma-free despite an asthmatic sibling. The overall answer lies in some sort of dynamic interplay between genetics and environment.

Is Asthma a Lifelong Problem?

Another baffling aspect of asthma is the pattern of remission seen in some asthmatics (Figure 1.2). Although the good news is that three of four asthmatic children outgrow their symptoms by the time they are 13, we often do not know why this happens. Except for the small number of cases where remission follows a change in environment,

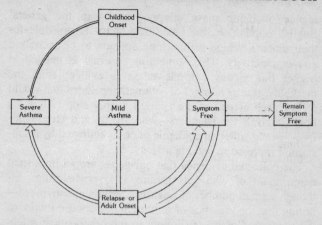

Figure 1.2 Pattern of asthma remission. The width of each subgroup's arrow corresponds to the proportion it represents of its larger group. Of asthmatic children, for example, 80 percent (very wide arrow) become symptom-free. Half of this group (shown by an arrow halved in width) remain symptom-free, and half redevelop asthma as adults. Adults developing asthma for the first time are also represented in this illustration.

the frequent disappearance of childhood asthma cannot be explained by a removal of allergens. A logical possibility is the development of some kind of protective mechanism, such as a natural desensitization to the allergen at fault or the growth of immunity to respiratory viruses.

The bad news is that asthma symptoms can resurface even after many asthma-free years. Although we do not yet know what provokes a recurrence, the majority of asthmatics questioned for this book trace it to one of three situations: a severe respiratory infection, prolonged inhalation of a noxious substance such as an insecticide, or an emotional trauma, such as the death of a loved one. Among adult asthmatics—regardless of the initial age of onset—the chance of permanent remission becomes increasingly smaller with the passage of time.

Is Asthma a Psychiatric Problem?

NO!

It is way past time to bury the two myths that all asthmatics have identical, and highly neurotic, personalities, and that childhood asthma reflects an abnormal child/mother relationship. The turn-of-the-century misconception that "there is, in a majority of cases of bronchial asthma, a strong neurotic element" was energetically disseminated by Sir William Osler, who at the time was probably the most influential physician in the Western world. The two specific myths that evolved from this general view were shaped by the erroneous theories drawn from work done in the late 1940s by the noted psychoanalysts Thomas M. French and Franz Alexander. Many psychologists and psychiatrists still hold to these outdated inaccuracies despite the complete absence of supporting data and the existence of strong evidence to the contrary. We suspect that these *myths* have created an immeasurable—and unnecessary—hardship for asthmatics due to the stigma of psychological abnormality placed on both the patient and his family.

It is obviously difficult to form a clear conception of the actual role of psychological factors in a disease that is so incompletely understood. The view most consistent with existing reliable scientific knowledge is that psychological factors interact with asthma in two very different ways. First, people with severe asthma frequently develop psychological and behavioral problems *as a consequence* of the severe and chronic nature of their handicap. It is important to realize that these psychological and behavioral consequences are the natural reaction to a serious chronic condition, regardless of the particular disease. Second, some asthmatic individuals experience a temporary increase in the frequency and intensity of their attacks during stressful periods of their lives. (Both aspects will be discussed in greater detail in later sections.)

How Serious Is Asthma?

The seriousness of any disease must be gauged from the answers to three separate questions: Is it life-threatening? What is the economic impact on the family and/or society? How does it interfere with an individual's ability to live his life as he would like? A disease can be considered serious in regard to one aspect even though it is negligible as far as the others are concerned.

THREAT TO LIFE

In the United States, asthma is currently estimated to be directly responsible for anywhere from two thousand to six thousand deaths a year. Although this tiny percentage of the approximately half-million severe asthmatics reflects a mortality rate two-thirds lower than it was in 1960, medical authorities believe that this figure should be far lower still. Many of today's asthma deaths appear to be preventable. A key observation concerning these deaths has been the failure of patient and/or doctor to recognize the speed of development and/or the severity of the ultimately fatal attack, and therefore to use the most effective type of medical intervention.

ECONOMIC IMPACT

Asthma is the second most common cause of disability among people under 45 years old. Each year asthmatics lose 5 million days from work and 6 million days from school, and experience approximately 100 million days of significantly restricted activity. In addition to the cumulative effect of this absenteeism on general economic productivity, individual income suffers. The effects of reduced income are compounded by significant medical expenses. A 1968 survey of asthma families in southern California showed that they had spent anywhere from 2 to 30 percent of that year's family income on asthma treatment.

This is a significant sum of money. In 1975, asthmatics

in the United States collectively spent $400 million on hospital and doctors' fees and another $200 million on medicines. In view of the steep increase in medical costs since then, undoubtedly the amounts spent now are considerably higher. It is not uncommon for asthma volunteers in our current research study to need $150 to $300 worth of medicine every month. That amounts to $1,800 to $3,600 for the year in medication alone! Visits to doctors plus occasional hospitalizations dramatically increase this total. So it is not unusual for an asthmatic (or his insurer) to spend thousands of dollars yearly on the management of his condition.

EFFECT ON LIFE-STYLE

Although there are no statistics describing asthma's impact on how asthmatics initially hope to shape their professional and leisure lives, the many anecdotal reports from our patients illustrate the potential seriousness of this disease in even its milder states.

For example, we evaluated a man for exercise-induced asthma who complained of significant difficulty in breathing air out during exertion. We recorded a bronchospasm so mild that most people would be totally unaware of any problem. Why was this man so unusually sensitive? Although his asthma required no medication and did not limit him physically (he had even run several marathons), he was an opera singer who was unable to sing certain operatic passages whenever he had one of his barely existent bronchospasms. The ever-present threat of this unpredictably recurrent singing limitation had prevented him from pursuing the career of his choice.

For most people, experiencing an asthma attack can be very frightening. Although some asthmatics have won Olympic medals in their chosen sport, the physical and emotional consequences of repeated episodes usually impel the asthmatic to cut out of his life everything he fears *might* provoke an attack. Many asthmatics find themselves afraid even to climb a flight of stairs, run for a bus, or walk more than a few blocks at a time. The typical severely asthmatic child is not permitted to enjoy any vigorous activities.

This limiting aspect of asthma turns a serious disease into a crippling one, significantly diminishing the quality of the typical asthmatic's life. But the growing viewpoint in asthma treatment is that these traditional limitations are largely unnecessary, and may in fact worsen the physical symptoms of the disease.

Much of the information in this book is specifically intended to replace disabling misconceptions and fear with the facts that can transform asthma into a far less restrictive disease. We have provided a realistic perspective about asthma so that asthmatics and their families can remove needless limitations from their lives. They will be able to live calmly and confidently—and much more fully—with asthma.

✖✖✖ 2 ✖✖✖

The Respiratory System:
What It Is and
How It Works

The business of the respiratory system is twofold. It supplies the body's tissues with oxygen, the gas needed to burn the food we eat for energy production. (This energy-production process is called *metabolism*.) It rids the body of excess carbon dioxide, the gaseous waste product from energy production. Respiration includes all the processes that contribute to the intake and use of oxygen and to the elimination of carbon dioxide. Breathing is one of the processes that plays a role in this exchange of gases.

Respiration can be examined at two levels, one large and one small. At the organ level is the large machinery that brings about this gas exchange by the activity called breathing. At the level of the individual cell is the microscopic machinery that uses oxygen to transform the food we eat into energy, producing carbon dioxide as the waste product.

The focus here is on the large machinery—airways, lungs, rib cage, respiratory muscles—and those parts of the nervous system that control them. You cannot really understand what asthma is, or why it affects you the way it does, until you have a basic working picture of this part of the respiratory system.

Anatomy

We usually inhale through our nose. But our nose is not just a simple passageway to our airways. The interior of the nose is far more expansive than it appears to the uneducated eye. Within the skull it becomes an extensive labyrinth of passageways that funnels into the throat. The inner walls of the nose are covered with a sticky layer of mucus. They also are richly supplied with heat-radiating blood vessels.

When we breathe in (inspire), three things happen as fresh air is bounced around in this complex array of nasal passages. Virtually all the dust particles this air normally contains are trapped in the mucus (which then travels to the throat to be swallowed), the air is warmed by the blood vessels, and it picks up moisture. This "treated" air passes through the throat, through the voice box (which holds the vocal cords), and into the trachea. (The throat divides into the *trachea*, or windpipe, and the *esophagus*, the tube leading to the stomach.)

The airways form a branching structure that starts with the trachea. The trachea divides into two wide branches, each of these divides in two, then these four branches each divides into two, and so on. In all, the airways divide 23 times—becoming narrower and narrower—from the trachea down to the 350 million tiny air sacs, or *alveoli*, that are the lungs' working units (Figure 2.1).

Healthy lungs are made up of five pink, spongy lobes. Three are on the right side of the chest cavity and two on the left side, with the heart between them (Figure 2.2). Air sacs, airways, and blood vessels are the lungs' primary structural elements (Figure 2.3). These spongy organs are protectively enclosed in a bony, yet flexible, airtight "cage" made up of part of the backbone (called the *thoracic*—meaning chest—vertebrae), the collarbones (clavicles), the breastbone (sternum), and the ribs (Figure 2.2 and 2.4, left). The ribs are attached to the thoracic

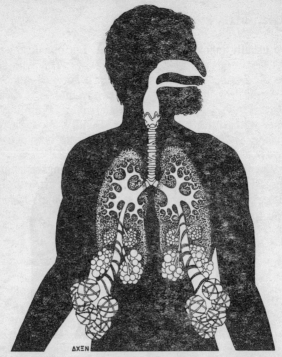

Figure 2.1 Anatomy of the respiratory tract.

vertebrae in a way that allows them to move up and down to change the size of the chest cavity.

The primary muscle of inspiration is the *diaphragm* (Figure 2.4, center), the thin, dome-shaped muscle separating the chest and abdominal cavities. Because the diaphragm lowers as it contracts, it increases the size of the chest cavity by making it longer. The ribs are attached to each other by the two sets of *intercostal muscles*, which also change the size of the chest cavity.

The *external intercostal muscles* contract during inspiration, pulling the ribs outward to help the diaphragm enlarge the chest cavity (Figure 2.4, center). The expanding

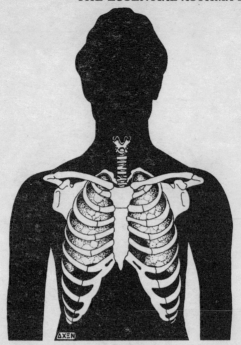

Figure 2.2 Anatomy of the chest cavity. The heart is the shadowed oval structure by the base of the breastbone (*on the reader's right*). Two lobes of the lungs are also on that side. The opposite side contains the other three lobes. These organs are protected by the ribs, breastbone, and collarbones.

chest cavity pulls the lungs along with it. As the lungs' airways and air sacs expand, they cause air to be sucked in through the nose (or mouth) and trachea. What makes this happen is the creation of a vacuum. Your lungs never completely empty when you breathe out. Then, as your lungs begin to expand again, the remaining air suddenly has more room. As it spreads out, its pressure drops. This rapid pressure drop creates a vacuum. And the vacuum sucks air from the outside down into the air sacs. (Think of a vacuum cleaner!)

Figure 2.3 The alveolus—the lungs' functional unit. The long, slender portion is a small airway surrounded by airway muscle cells. It terminates in a group of alveoli. Blood vessels run parallel to the airway and branch into the capillary bed surrounding the alveoli.

The air sacs are where oxygen and carbon dioxide are actually exchanged. The blood circulating around the individual alveoli picks up oxygen while it gives up excess carbon dioxide. (A certain level of carbon dioxide must be maintained in the blood.) This excess leaves the body with the next exhaled breath (expiration).

Return of the chest cavity to its original—or resting—size as the lungs empty of air usually occurs passively, meaning without the help of any muscles. The lungs deflate in much the same way that an inflated balloon or a stretched rubber band springs back to its original size. Then, just as air pressure in the lungs drops when they expand, it increases again as the deflating lungs compress the air back into a smaller space. And this growing air pressure in the air sacs pushes air back out of the lungs and through the nose or mouth. (As the lungs spring back, they pull the chest wall in too.) But expiration must become active during strenuous activity. Then it is helped by contraction both of the *internal intercostals* and of the

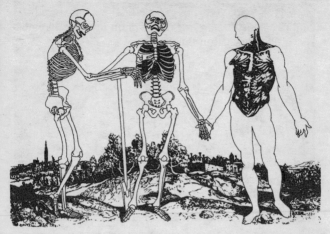

Figure 2.4 Skeletal and muscular anatomy of the respiratory system. *Left*: The rib cage in relation to the skeletal structures around it. *Center*: The major respiratory muscles. The dome-shaped diaphragm (d) is in the lower half of the rib cage. The muscles between the ribs (i) are the two layers of the intercostal muscles. The external layer works during inspiration, and the internal layer works for expiration. *Right*: The accessory respiratory muscles. The neck muscles(s) are the most important inspiratory aids. The large abdominal muscles assist expiration. (Respectfully redrawn from Vesalius.)

large muscles of the *abdominal wall* (Figure 2.4, center and right). It will soon be clear why this is necessary.

In addition to these major respiratory muscles that expand and contract the bony cage surrounding the lungs, a secondary group of muscles—appropriately called the *accessory respiratory muscles*—joins the work during activities that make extremely heavy demands on the respiratory system. These accessory muscles are in the neck, shoulders, and back. They help primarily during inspiration (Figure 2.4, right).

The respiratory muscles are controlled by the respiratory center located in the most primitive part of our brain, know as the brain stem. This control is automatic and continuous. We do not have to be conscious of our breathing for it to work. But this control can be influenced by the more sophisticated parts of the brain involved in emotions, in talking, and in thinking.

Physical Properties of the Respiratory System

When the respiratory muscles work to expand the chest cavity, they must overcome the two characteristics of the respiratory system that oppose any changes in its volume. These are its *elastance* and *resistance*.

Elastance, or elasticity, is an easy concept to grasp because we have experienced it with rubber bands and balloons. After stretching a rubber band or blowing up a balloon, when you let them go they will spring back to their original shape because they are elastic structures. Both the lungs and chest wall are elastic structures. If they were removed from the confines of our chest, the lungs would instantly spring back to a much smaller volume while the chest wall would spring outward to a larger volume. But because the lungs and chest wall are a tightly coupled system, each continuously pulls against the other. The system stops moving at the point where the inward pull of the lungs and the outward pull of the chest wall are equal. This happens when you reach the end of a normal expiration. The lung volume at this equilibrium point is termed the *resting end-expiratory volume*.

Inspiration increases this volume because the inspiratory muscles work against the lungs' inward pull. Then, when these inspiratory muscles relax, the respiratory system springs back to its resting volume (passive expiration). During quiet breathing, and even during mild exercise, this fully describes the respiratory cycle.

But as a person increases the size of his breaths, the inspiratory muscles have to work harder and harder because the lungs' inward pull becomes increasingly stronger. Like a rubber band or balloon, the more the lungs are stretched, the more effort it takes to keep stretching them further. During very strenuous exercise, the still-increasing demands for oxygen and for the elimination of carbon dioxide require the lungs to breathe out more air than usual during expiration and take in even more air than usual during inspiration. Breathing more air out—which also increases the room for inspired air—lessens the volume of air usually remaining in our lungs after exhalation. It is reduced below the resting (or equilibrium) point. The expiratory muscles supply the force needed to overcome the outward pull of the chest wall.

Resistance in the respiratory system is the force opposing the actual flow of air in and out of the lungs' airways. It is like friction. Friction, occurring when two surfaces slide over each other, is the force opposing this movement. Resistance is the friction-like force created when air moves past the airway walls.

The amount of resistance depends on both how wide the airway is and how fast the air is traveling. If an airway's opening becomes twice as narrow, for example, resistance increases 16 times. Then the respiratory muscles have to work much harder to continue breathing the same amount of air at the same speed. To get a feel for what happens, breathe through a drinking straw while it is fully open, and then after you pinch it partially closed. Repeat this experiment, but breathing more quickly.

During inspiration, the inspiratory muscles supply the force that overcomes resistance. During passive expiration, resistance is overcome by the same energy that causes the inflated lungs to return to their normal size. During exercise, however, when breathing is more rapid—or in asthma, when the airways are suddenly narrowed—this may not be sufficient. Because resistance has substantially increased, the expiratory muscles have to work.

Resistance is greatest in the medium-sized bronchi. These are the airways primarily affected in asthma. Asthma causes a large increase in airway resistance—and therefore in the work of breathing.

Several transient factors also affect airway resistance.

Because airway width increases as the lungs expand, resistance lessens during inspiration and rises during expiration. This is one reason asthma interferes with expiration much more than with inspiration. Several other factors will be listed and discussed in the section "What Controls the Airway Opening."

Breathing Is Work

The work of breathing combines the efforts of the inspiratory and expiratory muscles to overcome both elastance and resistance. It is the work needed to move the respiratory system from its resting position, plus the work needed to overcome the friction created by air moving against the airway walls. As just described, taking larger breaths and breathing faster both make the respiratory muscles work harder.

Gas Exchange

At rest, a healthy person moves about 6 liters (close to 6 quarts) of air in and out of his lungs each minute. As the lungs inflate, about 1.5 of these liters fill the larger airways, and 4.5 liters fill the smaller airways and air sacs. Here, in the alveoli, some of the oxygen in these 4.5 liters of fresh air and all the excess carbon dioxide brought to the lungs by the blood are exchanged. (Not all the fresh air participates in this exchange of gases. Air that does not is called "dead space," and includes all the air filling the larger airways and those alveoli that are not, for the moment, receiving any blood, and most of the air entering alveoli that temporarily have relatively little blood circulating around them.)

At rest, the right side of the heart pumps about 5 liters (close to 5 quarts) of blood through the lungs every minute. Then the blood is returned to the left side of the heart, where it is pumped throughout the body. Blood going from the heart to the lungs is called *venous blood*; once it leaves the lungs to return to the heart it is called *arterial blood*. Venous blood is oxygen poor, and rich in carbon dioxide. As venous blood passes through the lungs, oxygen is replaced and carbon dioxide removed. As it flows through the body's tissues the blood loses oxygen and picks up carbon dioxide. Then it returns to the right side of the heart to be pumped through the lungs again (Figure 2.5).

A tiny amount of blood normally does not participate effectively in this gas exchange, because it has gone to inadequately filled air sacs or has somehow bypassed the air sacs completely. Despite this, the amount of blood passing through the lungs each minute so closely matches the amount of air reaching the alveoli each minute that a healthy person's blood—even during exercise—carries close to the maximum amount of oxygen it can, and successfully gets rid of all the excess carbon dioxide that it has picked up.

This gas exchange process is so efficient because of the incredible expanse actually covered by the thin, blood vessel-filled membrane that encloses the lungs' 300 million air sacs. It is this membrane through which the mechanics of gas exchange are achieved. If this membrane could be stretched out flat, it would cover a tennis court!

How Breathing Is Controlled

The brain stem respiratory center tells the respiratory muscles when to contract, how strongly to contract, and what size the chest cavity must expand to. But how does your respiratory center "know" all this?

It "knows" by the amount of carbon dioxide in the freshly oxygenated blood pumped from your heart. Increasing carbon dioxide levels (when, for example, your body burns more fuel to make energy for exercise) excite the respiratory center. Then it strengthens the signal—sent

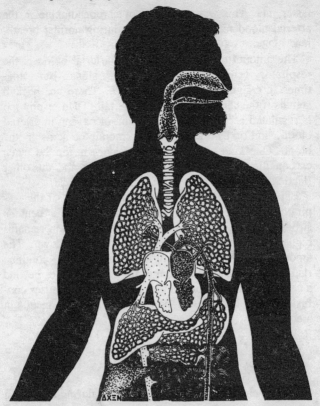

Figure 2.5 The circulatory system. Densely stippled areas indicate a high concentration of oxygen (air, the heart's left side, arterial blood). The lightly stippled areas indicate blood from which oxygen has been removed (in the veins and the heart's right side). Blood gains oxygen as it passes through the lungs, then gives up oxygen as it passes through the tissues.

along the nerves linking it with the respiratory muscles—with which it continuously activates breathing. Responding to this stronger signal, the respiratory muscles increase both the speed and depth of breathing. This increases ventilation, ridding the body of carbon dioxide at a much faster rate. This way, the level of carbon dioxide in the arterial blood returns to what it is during normal breathing.

The amount of carbon dioxide in arterial blood is the respiratory center's primary regulatory signal. But sometimes this signal cannot get through. There are backup signals if the carbon dioxide sensors fail. Then respiration is regulated according to the amount of oxygen in arterial blood, and/or by the increased amount of acids in the blood. One kind of acid (carbonic acid) is formed when carbon dioxide encounters blood plasma, and the other (lactic acid) is a byproduct of exercising muscle.

But whatever the effective regulatory signal, if the respiratory muscles cannot respond to the brain center's stronger message and carbon dioxide production remains higher than normal, the system has broken down. The amount of carbon dioxide in arterial blood will continue rising. Carbon dioxide becomes toxic once it goes beyond a certain level. It disrupts normal metabolism, causes confusion, and—if it goes high enough—eventually results in a coma.

What Controls the Airway Opening

Before discussing what actually happens during an asthma attack, a more detailed knowledge of the structure and function of our airways is important. Figures 2.6 and 2.7, which graphically illustrate this information, will be very helpful to refer to as you read.

The airway walls are made up of cartilage, smooth muscle (one of the three muscle types), mucus-producing glands, connective tissue, and epithelium (the type of tissue that covers all outer and inner body surfaces, including the lining of vessels and other small cavities). Because the relative amounts of these components change as the airway branches become smaller and more numerous, the

Figure 2.6 Low-magnification view of healthy and asthmatic airways and their surrounding tissues. *Left*: Healthy segment. *Right*: Asthmatic segment. *Labels*: gc, goblet cell; c, cartilage; br, bronchi; mg, mucous gland; m, mucus; sm, smooth muscle; alv, alveoli. (Redrawn from Terry Des Jardins, *Clinical Manifestations of Respiratory Disease*. Chicago: Year Book Medical Publishers, Inc., 1984, pp. 2, 158.)

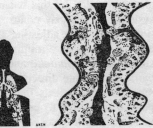

Figure 2.7 Higher-magnification view of the mucus-producing layer of healthy (*left*) and asthmatic (*right*) airways.

large, medium, and small airways are distinctive in composition as well as in size (Figure 2.6).

Connective tissue holds the overall structure together. Mucus—a layer of sticky fluid covering the lining of epithelial cells—is made up of water, large molecules of sugar and protein, and salts. It is produced by goblet cells in the airway lining, and by mucous glands deep in the airway wall. (In a healthy nonsmoker, the proportion of goblet cells greatly decreases as the airways become smaller.) The mucus-producing goblet cells are interspersed among other epithelial cells with moving, hair-like projections called cilia. These two types of cells form a protective alliance. The mucus traps foreign particles that have entered the airways, then the cilia push them up and out (Figure 2.7).

Cartilage—which helps support all but the smallest airways—forms unclosed rings around them. Its presence decreases substantially in each airway generation until it disappears in the smaller airways. A layer of smooth muscle lies between the epithelium and cartilage, forming a continuous muscular ring encircling the airways (Figure 2.6). In healthy lungs, how much it contracts basically determines the size of the airway opening.

How this airway muscle behaves results primarily from the balance between the *autonomic nervous system*'s two opposing parts. (Action of the mucus-producing glands is also controlled by this balance.) The autonomic nervous system continuously controls our automatic bodily functions, constantly adjusting them to maintain our interior environment with a minimum of fluctuation. Its two divisions—the *sympathetic* and the *parasympathetic*—usually work in opposite directions. The nervous system acts via *mediators*, chemicals that it produces and releases. The particular muscle to be affected has specialized areas on its surface called *receptors*. Each receptor is activated only by the chemical mediator for which it was designed. Because a muscle has more than one type of receptor, it can respond to more than one mediator.

When airway muscle receptors sense the presence of the specific chemical mediators they respond to, the machinery that contracts the muscle is either started or turned off, depending on the mediator. Two types of airway muscle receptors cause the muscle to contract. One type is activated by acetylcholine (*cholinergic receptors*) released by the parasympathetic nervous system. The other type recognizes adrenaline (*adrenergic alpha-receptors*) released primarily by the adrenal glands (part of the sympathetic nervous system). Receptors that turn off the contraction machinery, allowing the airway muscle to relax, also recognize adrenaline but are called *adrenergic beta-receptors*. Adrenaline's relaxing (or bronchodilating) effect predominates because there are many more beta-receptors than alpha-receptors. When the healthy respiratory system is at rest—meaning the absence of conditions (such as exercise) temporarily increasing the body's demands on it—the opening size of each airway is the end result of the balance between the cholinergic receptors and adrenergic alpha-receptors on one side, and the adrenergic beta-receptors on the other.

Mast cells, which are found throughout much of the tracheobronchial tree, also contain potent chemical mediators. Their release causes three simultaneous asthma events: the airway muscle contracts, mucus production increases, and specialized white blood cells travel to the immediate area. The first two events narrow airway openings. The white blood cells contain inflammatory chemicals that keep the asthma attack going after it would otherwise stop. But the mast cells also have adrenergic beta-receptors. Stimulating them reduces the amount of mediator release.

As discussed in the chapter on medication, asthma treatment is based largely on substances that stimulate the airway muscle adrenergic beta-receptors to promote muscle relaxation, inhibit the cholinergic receptors and adrenergic alpha-receptors to prevent muscle contraction, and stop the mast cells from discharging their airway-narrowing chemicals.

The Asthma Attack

Although a variety of external stimuli can provoke an asthma attack, at the microscopic level within the body these stimuli all ultimately involve the same mechanisms to produce asthma symptoms. The symptoms vary greatly in severity because the particular segment of the lungs and the total lung area affected can be different with each asthmatic. Obstruction in the bronchial tree can occur just within the medium and larger airways, just within the smaller airways, or at all these levels. It may occur in isolated patches throughout the lungs, or cover a large area. An asthma attack need not include all the events that are about to be described. (These events may be almost simultaneous, or they may take time to develop.)

An attack frequently begins with two sensations: tightness behind the sternum, and being unable to breathe in enough air. Many asthmatics hear themselves wheezing during expiration, and some hear it during inspiration too. Shortness of breath (*dyspnea*) and coughing may occur. Difficulty in breathing is obvious from the asthmatic's flaring nostrils and bulging neck muscles. In fact, the degree to which the neck muscles contract and bulge correlates strongly with the attack's severity.

As the attack progresses, the asthmatic becomes overwhelmed by anxiety and apprehension. Breathing becomes more rapid, shallow, and labored. Blood pressure swings up and down. The heart races from the release of adrenaline. Flushing or perspiration, broken speech, cyanosis (a bluish skin tint from insufficient oxygen in the blood), fatigue, confusion, and agitation all indicate a deteriorating condition.

Anatomy of an Asthma Attack

The common component of all asthma attacks is airway muscle contraction, which narrows the airways. (Figures 2.6 and 2.7 will come in handy again as you read this section.) This may be the only manifestation in mild attacks. In more severe episodes, the obstruction caused by excess mucus narrows the airways still more.

In the most severe attacks, the inner wall of the airways

also swells with fluid (mucosal edema) to narrow the airways even further. When mucosal edema occurs, white blood cells also enter the submucosa, the layer of tissue beneath the cilia and goblet cells. This fluid buildup can become great enough to lift the epithelial cells temporarily away from the underlying tissue. Mucus floods and plugs the airways. If this mucus becomes continuous with the mucus still inside the goblet cells and underlying mucous glands, these mucus plugs become even more difficult to dislodge.

In the most extreme asthma cases, the airways become completely obstructed with mucus plugs, detached epithelial cells, and white blood cells. Unless appropriate intervention is immediate, the patient may suffocate.

Asthma's Immediate Effects

Although asthma is an airway disease, the consequences of these airway changes can change the lungs' efficiency in gas exchange during an attack. This greatly reduces the amount of oxygen reaching the body's cells.

During an asthma attack, the air entering the lungs is distributed very unevenly. Much of it goes to the unaffected—meaning unobstructed—area of the lungs. But the blood coming from the heart to pick up oxygen and shed carbon dioxide is not redistributed to anywhere near the same degree. Too much of it goes to obstructed areas of the lungs, the areas that cannot fully oxygenate it or adequately remove the carbon dioxide it carries (Figure 2.8). This situation is termed a *ventilation-blood flow imbalance*. This imbalance is the major culprit in reducing oxygen and raising carbon dioxide in the blood during an asthma attack.

The asthmatic tries to compensate for his oxygen decrease by breathing faster to increase ventilation. Except in very severe cases, this hyperventilation compensates for poor carbon dioxide removal from obstructed lung areas

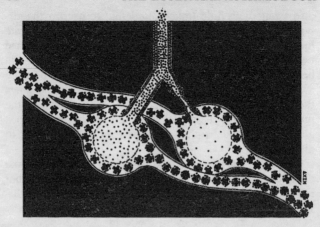

Figure 2.8 How bronchoconstriction affects the amount of oxygen in arterial blood. In this schematic illustration of ventilation–blood flow imbalance, each dot represents an oxygen molecule. Each blood cell is accurately portrayed as able to carry up to four oxygen molecules. Because the obstructed alveolus gets less air than the other one, fewer oxygen molecules are available for the blood circulating around it. The same amount of blood, however, flows around each alveolus. Blood flowing around the obstructed alveolus cannot take in its maximum oxygen load, whereas blood from the open alveolus is fully oxygenated. Hyperventilation—which increases the amount of oxygen in the unobstructed alveolus—cannot compensate for the obstruction-caused inadequate oxygen because these blood cells are already carrying as many oxygen molecules as they can. The net effect of the obstruction depends on how much of the lungs is involved. With only a small obstruction, the lack of oxygen from that area is negligible. In a severe asthma attack, however, the body can become oxygen starved.

by increasing its removal from nonobstructed areas. It does relatively little, however, to offset the low oxygen content of the blood passing through the obstructed areas (Figure 2.8). There is a fixed limit to the amount of oxygen that blood can hold. The blood passing through the hyperventilated areas of the lungs cannot pick up most of the additional oxygen there, because it has already reached this limit.

An asthma attack narrows the airways, so the air entering them meets greater resistance—more than 25 times normal in some asthmatics. If airway obstruction continues to worsen, the increasing resistance to airflow continuously lengthens the time needed for breathing out. Eventually, so much time is needed for each expiration that it cannot be completed before the next inspiration starts. Because this traps air in the lungs, they can no longer fully return to their normal resting position. Although the expiratory muscles initially assist expiration, they become self-defeating. Their effort increases the pressure around the airways, narrowing them further and trapping more air. The lungs are now hyperinflated.

The respiratory system is already stressed from attempting to overcome the high airflow resistance. Now hyperinflation stresses it still more. This additional stress is of two kinds. Because hyperinflation increases the elastic recoil of the lungs and chest wall, the inspiratory muscles have to work much harder. But hyperinflation also impairs the effectiveness of the inspiratory muscles. Because hyperinflated lungs cannot return to their normal resting position, the inspiratory muscles remain partially contracted. Working from this shortened position limits the size of inspirations.

When air is no longer expelled effectively, the cough reflex—which is an important way of keeping the airways clean—can no longer work to clear the lungs of mucus plugs. The cough reflex is activated by irritation of an airway. When the system is working properly, the expiratory muscles contract forcefully while the vocal cords stay tightly shut. This builds up a very high pressure in the lungs. Then the vocal cords fly open and air is blasted out of the lungs, sometimes as fast as 70 mph. But when air is only partially and weakly expired, the cough reflex cannot function.

Working against greater and greater airflow resistance and the stress of hyperinflation can exhaust the respiratory muscles. At this point, respiration fails. The amount of oxygen in the blood starts to plummet, while the carbon dioxide level rises dangerously. The result will be severe metabolic disturbances, increased acid in the blood, mental confusion, and unconsciousness. If this cannot be reversed early enough, the patient may die.

Asthma's Long-Term Consequences

Even asthmatics whose pulmonary function returns to normal between attacks may still show changes in their microscopic pulmonary anatomy. One of the most striking features is an increase in both the size of the mucus-producing glands and the number of goblet cells. The other is an increase in the number and size of the muscle cells surrounding the airways, so that the layer of encircling muscle thickens and extends into the smaller airways, which are normally muscle-free. An additional hallmark of asthma—seen in both mild and severe cases—is thickening of the basement membrane, which is found just underneath the epithelial layer of the airway. (The cause and consequences of this thickening are both unknown.)

Because reversible airway constriction is also common in both chronic bronchitis (a lung disease characterized by constant coughing) and emphysema (a lung disease that destroys many of the air sacs), it was thought that some long-term asthmatics eventually develop one of these permanent lung diseases. But the National Heart, Lung, and Blood Institute in the United States reported in 1981 that there is little evidence suggesting that asthma leads to either of these chronic lung conditions.

3

What Triggers Asthma

Classifying Asthma Triggers

In the twelfth century, Maimonides remarked on asthma's many causes—or triggers—in his treatise on this disease. In the eight centuries since, physicians have tried to classify the many types of asthma according either to the variety of causes (Figure 3.1) or to such constitutional factors as severity of the disease or the patient's response to treatment.

Although no fully satisfying classification has yet been devised, the one used most often was developed soon after the end of World War I. It grew from the observation that people with asthma often suffered, in addition, from allergies that had been documented by an appropriate skin response (reddening and swelling) after injecting the allergic substance under their skin. People whose skin immediately responds this way are described as *atopic*, another word for allergic. The agent causing this allergy is *external*, or *extrinsic*, to the person. So eventually patients with allergy-caused asthma were classified as having *atopic, extrinsic*, or *allergic* asthma. The remainder, patients whose asthma had no such well-defined external cause, were

EMOTIONS **INFECTIONS**

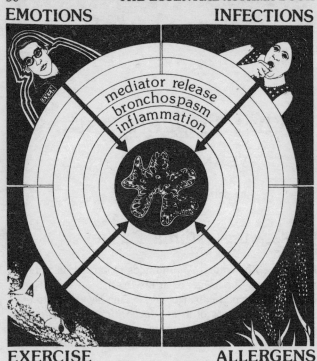

mediator release
bronchospasm
inflammation

EXERCISE **ALLERGENS**

Figure 3.1 The general types of asthma triggers. Different triggers all lead to the same cluster of symptoms recognized as asthma.

noted as having *intrinsic* asthma. Asthmatics are roughly equally divided between these two groups.

Although still useful, this classifying system has become limited. Recently recognized are a subclass of extrinsic asthma (caused by occupational and/or environmental factors) that is not always associated with the classic allergic reaction, and a subclass of intrinsic asthma in which the body's response is similar to that found in the allergic individual. In addition, only a small proportion (5 to 25 percent) of adults who have both asthma and allergies find that their allergies play a significant role in triggering their asthma. There is also a large group of "mixed" asthmatics who have both extrinsic and intrinsic asthma components.

Allergic Asthma and the Immune System

FOREIGN INVADERS AND PROTECTIVE ANTIBODIES

Immunity is the self-protective ability to defend against proteins not produced by one's body. The existence of immunity was noted by the ancients, whose scribes recorded the observation that survivors of the plague were protected from reinfection by their first bout with the deadly disease. Chinese and Arab physicians of the fifteenth century would infect people with pus from smallpox patients in an attempt to prevent them from contracting the disease, but results of this primitive attempt at vaccination were unpredictable. At the end of the eighteenth century, the English physician Edward Jenner inoculated a youngster with fluid from a milkmaid's oozing cowpox sores. (Cowpox is a relatively mild relative of smallpox.) The boy developed cowpox and never contracted the deadly smallpox infecting those around him. Jenner's work established the principle of *vaccination*. Vaccination works because the body's immune system can learn to recognize specific foreign materials—pollens, dust, bacteria, and so forth—and react defensively against them.

Antigens are the foreign substances that provoke an immune reaction. Any antigen entering the body is immediately identified by the immune system, which then mobilizes to destroy it. The immune system has two kinds of defense mechanisms. One directly involves the immune system's various protector cells. The one relevant for asthma is the production of *antibodies*—specialized proteins released into the blood by several kinds of white blood cells.

Such a white blood cell changes permanently when it first encounters an antigen. The cell begins producing large numbers of antibodies *specifically against this antigen* and releases them into the blood. The next time this antigen invades the body, these specific antibodies recognize, attack, and destroy it. (This individual antigen response explains how vaccination—or immunization—works.)

Immunity, however, can be a double-edged sword. Although the immune system's ability to detect and destroy foreign material helps protect us against disease, this same system also produces the harmful reactions called allergies.

Antibodies are technically called *immunoglobins*. There are five kinds: IgA, IgD, IgE, IgG, and IgM. Three are involved in the four types of allergic reactions so far identified. Two of these allergic reactions—and the two immunoglobins associated with them—are implicated in allergic asthma.

IgE is involved in the most common type of allergy, what people always imagine when they hear this word: conditions like hay fever and hives, and asthma reactions to things like cat dander. Because this kind of hypersensitive reaction takes only minutes to happen, medical jargon calls it an *immediate IgE-mediated hypersensitivity reaction* or *type I reaction*.

The second type of allergic reaction occasionally involved in an asthma attack is called an *arthus* or *type III reaction*. This allergic response is both delayed and—once it finally does occur—long-lasting. It does not appear until three to four hours after exposure, and it lasts from 24 to 36 hours. The mechanism of this delayed reaction is obscure. Although there is evidence that IgG is involved, and that a type I reaction to the same antigen must already have occurred at some earlier time, no one understands how a type I reaction can eventually lead to a type III reaction.

The IgE-mediated immune response probably started

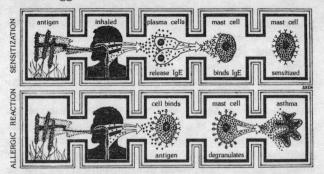

Figure 3.2 Allergic sensitization and an asthma attack. *Top*: The sequence of events leading to allergic sensitization. *Bottom*: How an allergic asthma attack is triggered.

out as a clearly beneficial response, one that speedily prevented microscopic foreign agents from invading the human body. Several types of evidence all point to the possible role of IgE—still—in protecting us against parasitic infections. IgE concentrations are found predominantly at the body's entry points—the skin, digestive system, and airway. Because IgE also mediates allergic reactions, perhaps this suggests that allergic reactions are actually beneficial in a way not yet recognized.

THE MECHANISM OF ALLERGIC ASTHMA

An allergy in susceptible individuals begins—as do all immune responses—with the first exposure to the particular antigen (Figure 3.2). An antigen producing an allergic response is called an *allergen*. This initial exposure to an allergen is termed *sensitization*. Most allergens are proteins small enough to enter mucous membranes. The remaining allergens—including some metals—provoke an allergic reaction after combining with the individual's own proteins. This combination is recognized as foreign by the immune system. (Common respiratory allergens include grass and tree pollens, molds, dusts, animal dander, and foods.)

Normal people are unaffected by allergens. But the immune system of an allergy-susceptible person reacts to the initial allergen contact by producing IgE specifically against that allergen. (No one yet knows why an allergy-prone person develops a response to one particular allergen rather than another. But because IgE is allergen-specific, an antibody to cat dander, for example, will react against it but not against dog dander.) Then these specific antibodies bind to mast cells (many antibodies to each mast cell) in the particular bodily system(s) affected by the allergy. The IgE produced against a respiratory allergen binds to the mast cells abundant in the respiratory system.

At the second encounter, each allergen molecule unites two adjacent antibodies attached to the same mast cell. This allergen-antibody coupling signals the mast cell to release its powerful bronchoconstricting and inflammation-causing biochemicals (Figure 3.2, bottom panel). It is these chemicals that produce, for example, the sneezing and runny eyes of hay fever, the rashes and itching of skin allergies, and the respiratory changes that typify an asthma attack. (The release of these biochemicals by mast cells in the skin causes the redness and swelling in a positive skin test for allergy.)

The mast cells simultaneously release chemicals that attract a particular type of white blood cell to the battle scene. These cells also contribute potent bronchoconstriction and inflammatory chemicals. (One of the most powerful of these—leukotriene C—was finally isolated and synthesized in 1985. It is hoped that this will open up an entirely new area of antiasthma drugs.)

The allergy attack subsides as all the allergen molecules become bound to antibodies, and the mast cell and white blood cell chemicals become inactivated. Afterward, all the cellular debris—including the allergen-antibody complexes—are gradually engulfed and removed by white blood cells (a process called phagocytosis).

PRONENESS TO ALLERGY AND ALLERGIC ASTHMA

Allergen sensitization via antibodies is under strong hereditary control. Allergy-susceptible people have more IgE than normal in their systems, particularly in the skin and the mucous membranes of the respiratory and digestive tracts. And an allergic asthmatic's family members frequently suffer from such allergic problems as hay fever, skin rashes, and hives.

But the genetic predisposition to allergy is not the full answer. It does not guarantee that an allergy will actually materialize, nor that an existing allergy will become an asthma trigger. In fact, in some pairs of identical twins who both have allergic problems, only one develops asthma. The variety of other factors that appear to influence the development of allergies, and of allergic asthma, include age of initial exposure to the allergen, presence of viral infection, general health of the immune system, and anatomical site of exposure.

Age affects overall susceptibility to IgE-based allergies, as well as the type of allergen most likely to produce sensitization. "Wheezy" infants commonly show a high level of IgE in response to foods, but this response disappears by 10 years of age. The production of IgE to inhaled allergens begins later in childhood and is more likely to persist, although the symptoms often become weaker by adulthood. In general, IgE levels in the blood increase from birth to early adulthood. The overall *potential* for IgE-dependent sensitization peaks when people are in their 20s. (In one study, more than half the people in this age group had positive allergy tests, even though most of them had no actual allergic symptoms.) After young adulthood, both overall production of IgE and allergic susceptibility decline.

Two factors—one temporary and one that is sometimes inborn—alter normal immune system behavior in ways that substantially increase the likelihood of sensitization during exposure to an external allergen. These changes make it much easier for such allergens to make contact with IgE-producing white blood cells. A viral infection temporarily alters the microscopic structure of the airway walls. (This might result from injury caused by the virus.) These microscopic changes seem to facilitate an encounter between an allergen and IgE-producing white blood cells circulating through the blood vessels in the airway walls.

The other condition is having too few of the white blood cells that produce IgA. This gives environmental allergens greater access to the IgE-producing white blood cells. Some people are born with a lifelong inability to manufacture a normal amount of IgA-producing white blood cells. They will always be predisposed to allergies. Infants, on the other hand, normally have a low level of these white blood cells, which gradually rises as they mature. But babies are initially protected with immunity gained from their mother (called passive immunity) during the pregnancy. Breast-feeding prolongs this passive immunity. But once passive immunity begins to weaken, and before the baby's own IgA-producing white blood cells reach their highest level, the baby remains more vulnerable to IgE-mediated allergen sensitization.

This early period of immunological imbalance can be critical for the development of allergic asthma. During this vulnerable time, when the infant who is genetically prone to develop an allergic response is exposed to a viral respiratory infection and/or a seasonally high respiratory allergen (such as pollen), asthma will suddenly develop. In a detailed study of identical twins in which only one twin in each pair was asthmatic, in every case the first appearance of asthma was associated with a documented respiratory infection that the nonasthmatic twin had luckily escaped.

Where in the body sensitization to a particular allergen occurs may determine the nature of the allergic reaction. The development of hay fever rather than asthma, for example, may simply mean that sensitization to a particular pollen took place in the nose rather than in the airways.

Allergic Asthma Triggers

All allergens that can cause asthma have two common characteristics. First, the particles must be too small to be filtered out in the nose and pharynx. Then, for sensitization to occur in the airways, the allergen must be in the air in relatively high amounts for relatively long periods of time. Once sensitization has taken place, however, the asthmatic will develop an attack even when the allergen is present briefly and in small amounts.

Three groups of allergens can cause airway sensitization: outdoor, community-wide allergens (like pollens); allergens in the home (such as house dust); and occupational allergens (examples are chemicals and such dust producers as flour and grains). But these categories are designed to facilitate presentation and discussion rather than to set forth rigid principles of separation. For example, some chemicals can be considered occupational allergens inside the factory, but are community-wide allergens when people living outside the factory are affected by emitted fumes. Animal- and food-related allergens can be occupational as well as home problems.

(Occupational triggers are discussed under a separate heading in part because of their increasing importance. The tremendous proliferation of industrial chemicals is thought to be largely responsible for the recent substantial yearly increase in the percentage of asthmatics. In addition, occupational triggers combine both allergenic and nonallergenic substances.)

POLLENS

The problem pollens for the respiratory system are light and are spread easily by the wind. The three major classes come from trees, grasses, and weeds (Figure 3.3). Trees pollinate from late winter through spring, grasses from spring through summer, and weeds from late spring through fall. Detailed information on the range, preva-

Figure 3.3 Some allergy-causing weeds. These are examples of wind-pollinated plants that cause allergic reactions. *Left*: Timothy grass. *Right*: Short ragweed.

lence, and seasonal production of many pollen species is available in standard texts (E. Middleton, Jr., C. E. Reed, and E. F. Ellis, eds., *Allergy: Principles and Practice*, 2d ed., St. Louis: Mosby, 1983; G. Lawlor, Jr., and T. Fischer, eds., *Manual of Allergy and Immunology: Diagnosis and Therapy*, Boston: Little, Brown and Co., 1981).

MOLDS

The major allergenic molds—all in the large group Fungi Imperfecti—include those that grow on plants and decaying vegetation as well as *Penicillium*, the green mold that grows on old bread (Figure 3.4). Molds reproduce themselves by spores, which are spread by the wind. These mold spores are the actual allergen. Unlike pollens, mold spores are not limited to one season. Their airborne concentration, however, varies throughout the year. They are most numerous in the air when a dry, windy period follows a rainy season and reach their lowest concentration during freezing weather.

Both molds and pollens can produce immediate and delayed allergic reactions. One mold is particularly troublesome to the asthmatic because it sets off both type I and type III allergic reactions and can also cause a respiratory infection. When this mold, *Aspergillus fumigatus*, colo-

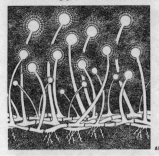

Figure 3.4 Some allergy-causing molds. These are examples of molds that cause allergic reactions. *Left: Aspergillus fumigatus. Right: Penicillium.*

nizes the lower respiratory tract, the resulting infection is called *allergic bronchopulmonary aspergillosis*. Asthma symptoms increase, a great amount of sputum is produced (which sometimes become bloody), and the patient runs a fever. Patients also cough up mucus plugs that contain white blood cells and pieces of the *Aspergillus* mold.

HOUSE DUST

House dust can affect the asthmatic in two ways. In large quantities it is an irritant, causing the airways to narrow via a neurologic reflex mechanism in the airways. In small quantities, dust becomes a typical allergen initiating an IgE-mediated response. This type of asthma can be seasonal in temperate climates, with symptoms worsening during the cold months when houses are closed up and furnaces—which are usually terrible dust collectors—are turned on.

House dust is really a composite of animal dander, indoor molds, vegetable fibers, food particles, algae, dirt, and insect parts and feces. Although each of these individually can be an allergen, recent evidence indicates that feces from mites (minuscule insects in the spider family—Figure 3.5) that live in this dust are by far the most allergenic of them all. Mites tend to favor low-altitude

Figure 3.5 The common house dust mite. Technically known as *Dermatophagoides*. This dust mite is barely visible without magnification.

locations (because of the relatively higher temperature and humidity) and are less of a problem at high altitudes (with their cooler, drier climate). The heaviest mite concentrations tend to be in warm, low-altitude bedrooms, both on baseboards behind the bed and in the bedding itself. In poor, inner-city dwellings, cockroach remnants are also a major house-dust allergen because of their greater presence.

ANIMALS

Asthma triggered by animals is not caused by their hair. Hair cannot trigger an asthmatic reaction unless it is so dense in the air that it is a general irritant (and not an allergen). With some animals—such as cats and dogs—the allergen is their dandruff, a normal skin byproduct called *dander*. The major allergens from domestic and laboratory rats and mice, by contrast, are found in their urine. Cockroach feces are also allergenic. (Socioeconomic status, because it determines living conditions, influences the degree of exposure to cockroach feces and rodent urine.) The feathers used to stuff down pillows and clothing are another important animal allergen.

FOOD: EATEN AND INHALED

The role of ingested food allergens in provoking asthma alone is—*despite* frequent claims to the contrary—exceedingly small. The one exception is with very young allergic children. Ingested food allergens play an important part in their asthma, because young children absorb more undigested allergens than older people do. Older children and adults with positive skin tests to such common food allergens as grains, milk, egg white, nuts, beans, peas, and seafood rarely have asthma symptoms after eating any of them. (The insistence of some that allergenic foods provoke asthma via something other than the type I response does not hold up under properly designed research studies.) But when the response to an eaten food allergen is so severe that it involves all the body's systems, including the respiratory, then asthma is one of these simultaneous allergic reactions. (This body-wide allergic reaction, called *anaphylaxis*, is described more fully at the end of this list of asthma triggers.)

Despite the strong research evidence that allergies to eaten foods play almost no role in adult asthma, physicians we have spoken to describe adult asthma patients who do have asthma attacks after eating certain foods. As any good cook knows, food gives off vapors before, during, and after cooking. Certain odors—as you will see further along in this list of triggers—are important in provoking asthma episodes. To the extent that a particular food gives off vapors, it could act, we believe, as an asthma trigger.

Inhaled food allergens are frequently linked with asthma in the work place. In "baker's asthma," for example, which is relatively common among people who work regularly with flour, asthma symptoms are typically present during the work day but disappear outside the work place. (Eating wheat products, however, does not provoke asthma in flour handlers.) Asthma is also a common problem among susceptible workers who handle coffee beans, soybeans, cottonseed, or other foodstuffs containing an allergen. (Yet eating or drinking any of these products does not produce asthma symptoms.)

"Occupational" Asthma Triggers

The first written awareness that certain occupations can cause respiratory disease is from the second century A.D. Miners of that period covered themselves with sacks and used animal bladders as mouth and nose masks to protect themselves from inhaled dust. Sixteen hundred years later, the eighteenth-century physician Bernardino Ramazzini pointed out in his historic book on occupational diseases, *De Morbis Artificum Diatriba*, that "to the questions recommended by Hippocrates, one more should be added. . . . What is your occupation?"

Asthma is becoming an increasingly greater occupational hazard as the large number of substances that can cause it steadily grows. (Tables 1–3 list occupational agents that can provoke asthma.) These occupational asthma triggers are of three kinds: proteins, small chemical molecules, and nonspecific irritants. The process that triggers the asthma may be allergic (with antibody production) or nonallergic (irritating to airway nerve or muscle). At first, airway constriction is intermittent and reversible, but in some instances—when prolonged exposure leads to chronic respiratory disease—the effects of the occupational asthma trigger extend beyond the factory walls.

People who develop occupational asthma are asthma-free when they start their occupation. The disease first develops anywhere from a few months to a few years later. Although occupational asthma symptoms are the typical combination of cough plus wheezing plus shortness of breath, coughing appears to predominate (because of this, the asthma is sometimes initially misdiagnosed as chronic bronchitis). Symptoms usually improve or disappear on

TABLE 1

Substances of Animal Origin That May Cause Asthma after Frequent Exposure (Usually Occupation-Associated)

Agent	Occupation
Laboratory animals (hair, epidermal squamae, mites, dander, urine, and serum protein)	Laboratory animal (rats, mice, guinea pigs, rabbits) handlers
Domestic animals	Farmers, veterinarians, meat processors and inspectors
Animal organ extracts (ACTH, GTH, pituitary peptone powders)	Pharmaceutical workers
Birds (feathers, serum, droppings)	Bird fanciers, poultry breeders and processors, pluckers
Sea squirt fluid	Oyster and pearl gatherers, oyster shuckers
Prawns	Prawn processors
Culture oysters (marine organisms)	Oyster shuckers
Pearl shell dust	Pearl shell openers
Wool	Wool workers
Amebas and other organisms	Printers using contaminated water
Animal enzymes: hog trypsin, pancreatic extract, bromelin, Flaviastase	Medical and pharmaceutical process laboratory workers, plastic polymer processors, pharmaceutical workers, fibrocystic children and their parents, enzyme processor workers and messengers, pharmacists
Bacillus subtilis	Detergent enzyme workers

TABLE 1

Substances of Animal Origin That May Cause Asthma after Frequent Exposure (Usually Occupation-Associated) (continued)

Agent	Occupation
Esperase	Detergent enzyme workers
Glue (fish)	Bookbinders, postal workers
Human hair	Hairdressers
Insects	
Beetles (Coleoptera)	Zoo curators
Grain weevils	Granary workers, dock workers, mill workers
Grain storage mites	Farmers, dock workers
Locusts	Laboratory workers, schoolchildren and teachers
Mexican bean weevils	Pea and bean sorters
Moths, butterflies	Entomologists
Silkworms (silk hair, silk glue, sericin)	Silkworm cutters, sericulturers
Stick insects	Field workers, laboratory workers, students
Cockroaches	Laboratory workers, students, field workers
Crickets	Outside workers
Housefly maggots	Anglers
River flies	Outside workers
Sewerworm flies	Outside workers
Sewage flies	Outside workers

ACTH = adrenocorticotropic hormone; GTH = gonadotrophic hormone.
(Reprinted with permission from Stuart M. Brooks, "Occupational Asthma," p. 468. In: E. B. Weiss, M. S. Segal, and M. Stein, eds. *Bronchial Asthma*, 2d ed. Boston: Little, Brown and Co., 1985.)

TABLE 2

Substances of Plant Origin That May Cause Asthma after Frequent Contact (Usually Occupation-Associated)

Agent	Occupation
Flour, grain dust	Grain elevator workers, bakers, millers, grain workers, dock workers
Wheat flour	Bakers
Rye flour	Bakers
Buckwheat	Bakers
Hops	Brewery workers, farmers
Soybean flour and dust	Soybean processors
Garlic powder	Spice factory workers
Tamarind seeds	Millers
Tea fluff	Tea makers, sifters, packers
Green leaf tobacco	Tobacco workers and processors
Green leaf tea	Tea workers
Green and roasted coffee beans	Coffee workers
Castor beans	Farmers, millers, chemists, baggers
Maiko	Japanese food workers, millers
Cottonseed	Bakers, fertilizer workers
Linseed	Oil extractors
Flaxseed	Flax workers
Psyllium	Pharmaceutical workers
Lycopodium clavatus	Dentists
Gum acacia	Printers
Gum tragacanth	Printers, candy and gum workers
Strawberry pollen	Strawberry growers

TABLE 2

Substances of Plant Origin That May Cause Asthma after Frequent Contact (Usually Occupation-Associated) (continued)

Agent	Occupation
Wood	
Western red cedar	Woodworkers, carpenters
African zebrawood	Joiners
Cedar of Lebanon	Shuttle makers
South African boxwood	Pattern makers
Oak	Wood finishers
Mahogany	Wood machinists
Mansonia	Sawmill workers, carpenters, wood finishers
Abiruana	Sawmill workers, carpenters, wood finishers
Cocaballa	Sawmill workers, carpenters, wood finishers
Kejaat	Sawmill workers, carpenters, wood finishers
California redwood	Sawmill workers, carpenters, wood finishers
Ramin	Sawmill workers, carpenters, wood finishers
Quillaja bark	Manufacturers of saponin
Iroko	Sawmill workers
Mulberry	Sawmill workers
Plant enzymes	
Papain	Food technologists
Diastase	Food handlers
Pectinase	Pharmaceutical workers
Bromelain	Pharmaceutical workers

TABLE 2

Substances of Plant Origin That May Cause Asthma after Frequent Contact (Usually Occupation-Associated) (continued)

Agent	Occupation
Vegetable gums	
Karaya	Food processors
Arabic	Printers
Acacia	Printers
Tragacanth	Printers
Fungi, molds	
Alternaria and *Aspergillus*	Bakers
Spores of *Cladosporium, Verticillium,* and *Paecilomyces*	Farm workers
Merulius lacrymans	Domestic workers, paprika splitters
Pink rot fungus	Celery pickers
Mushroom molds	Mushroom workers
Molds	Morticians
Fungal amylase	Enzyme processors

(Reprinted with permission from Stuart M. Brooks, "Occupational Asthma," p. 470. In: E. B. Weiss, M. S. Segal, and M. Stein, eds. *Bronchial Asthma*, 2d ed. Boston: Little, Brown and Co., 1985.)

TABLE 3

Substances of Chemical Origin That May Cause Asthma after Frequent Contact (Usually Occupation-Associated)

Agent	Occupation
Metallic salts	
Platinum	Platinum refiners, chemists
Nickel	Platers, chemical engineers
Aluminum (or fumes)	Chemical workers, pot room workers
Vanadium	Boiler and gas turbine cleaners, mineral ore processors
Cobalt	Refinery and alloy workers
Stainless steel	Welders
Chromium	Chrome polishers, chemical workers, cement tanning workers
Tungsten carbide	Hard metal grinders
Chemicals	
Paraphenylenediamine	Fur dyers, chemical workers
Piperazene	Chemical process workers
Formaldehyde	Nurses, pathologists, laboratory workers
Phenol	Chemical workers, laboratory workers
Chloramine	Brewery workers
Sulfathiazole	Manufacturers
Sulfonechloramide	Manufacturers
Tannic acid	Sunburn spray users

TABLE 3

Substances of Chemical Origin That May Cause Asthma after Frequent Contact (Usually Occupation-Associated) (continued)

Agent	Occupation
Orrisroot derivatives	Cosmetic workers, hairdressers
Triethyltetramine	Manufacturing of aircraft filters
Aminoethanolamine	Aluminum soldering
Ethylenediamine	Rubber, shellac manufacturers, photographers
Pyrethrins	Fumigators
Diisocyanates	Chemical workers, polyurethane foam manufacturing
Phthalic anhydrides and other anhydrides	Chemical workers, epoxy resin workers, tool setters, paint manufacturers
Gum arabic, tragacanth	Printers
Ammonium thioglycate	Beauty operators, cosmetic manufacturers
Colophony	Electronic manufacturers
Resin binder systems	Foundry mold makers
Reactive dyes	Dye weighers
Persulfate salts, extract of henna	Hairdressers, chemical workers
Drugs	
Psyllium	Laxative makers
Amprolium hydrochloride	Poultry feed mixers
Antibiotics—penicillin and similar drugs	Pharmaceutical workers
Pesticides, insecticides	Manufacturers, farmers, fumigators

(Reprinted with permission from Stuart M. Brooks, "Occupational Asthma," p. 473. In: E. B. Weiss, M. S. Segal, and M. Stein, eds. *Bronchial Asthma*, 2d ed. Boston: Little, Brown and Co., 1985.)

weekends, but return immediately when the work week is resumed. A major occupational change is usually essential. Even so, asthma symptoms can continue for months or years after making this change.

Any foreign protein—"foreign" meaning not produced by an individual's own body—can sensitize an asthma-susceptible person. A classic example occurred in the soap and detergent industry when powdered enzymes (proteins that speed up chemical reactions) were first added to laundry detergents to make them work better. As many as 25 percent of the workers handling this enzyme powder developed asthma. This result dramatizes the danger that conventional industrial precautions may be sorely inadequate to handle foreign proteins dispersed in the air.

Wood dust can be an asthma problem in two ways. In large amounts it is a nonspecific irritant that can aggravate preexisting asthma. For some individuals, however—such as cedarwood workers, among whom asthma is particularly prevalent—a small concentration of inhaled dust is the specific allergen that first provokes their asthma. This means that they had been previously sensitized to that wood dust immunologically, although the mechanism is not at all clear. The specific antibody has not yet been identified.

The plastics industry is responsible for introducing a large group of asthma-inducing chemicals. Among the best known is *toluene diisocyanate (TDI)*, used in producing polyurethane foams. In high doses TDI is a nonspecific respiratory irritant causing an asthma response. But some workers using TDI for weeks or months without any apparent ill effect suddenly develop recurrent asthma symptoms whenever exposed to even small doses. This suggests specific sensitization to inhaled TDI, although—as with sensitized cedarwood workers—the expected increase in IgE is found in only a small proportion of affected workers. Most likely, another type of antibody remains to be identified.

TABLE 4

Some Commonly Used Aspirin-Containing Drugs

Alka Seltzer	Empirin with codeine*
Anacin	Excedrin
Ascriptin	Fiorinal
BC tablets and powder	Fiorinal with codeine*
Bufferin	Percodan*
Coricidin	Vanquish
Any brands containing the initials ASA, APC, PAC	

*Prescription medicine.

Nonallergenic Triggers

ASPIRIN

Aspirin has been used in the United States since about 1910. In 1911, the first case of an asthmatic reaction to it was reported. At the National Jewish Center for Immunology and Respiratory Medicine (an institution specializing in treating asthma), a recent study found one out of five asthmatic patients sensitive to ingested aspirin. The typical aspirin-sensitive respiratory syndrome is usually restricted to adults, but sometimes children are affected.

The underlying triggering mechanism is still a mystery. Aspirin sensitivity typically begins as a nasal irritation that may lead to the growth of nasal polyps. The eventual hallmark of aspirin sensitivity is the appearance (within one-half to several hours after taking a normal dose of aspirin or an aspirin-like drug) of a flushed face, swollen and tearing eyes, runny nose, and an acute—often severe—asthma attack. A list of drugs containing aspirin, as well as drugs with anti-inflammatory effects similar to aspirin's, and to which aspirin-sensitive people are likely to be sensitive as well, is in Tables 4 and 5. (Although we have tried to make this list as complete as possible, a new aspirin-like drug may have been put on the market after this book was published. You should always check with your physician

TABLE 5

Some Anti-inflammatory Drugs with
High Cross-Sensitivity with Aspirin

Nonaspirin Drugs	
Chemical Name	Brand Name
Fenoprofen	Nalfon*
Ibuprofen	Motrin,* Advil Ibuprofen, Ibuprofen, Nuprin Ibuprofen, Rufen
Indomethacin	Indocin,* Indo-Lemmon, Indomethacin
Mefenamic acid	Ponstel*
Naproxen	Naprosyn*
Phenylbutazone	Butazolidin,* Phenylbutazone*
Piroxicam	Feldene*
Tolmetin	Tolectin*

*Prescription medicine.

or pharmacist before using any over-the-counter medication.)

AZO DYES

A very small number of aspirin-allergic people may also be allergic to azo dyes. This group of coloring agents—derived from coal tar and used to color a variety of foods and drugs—has also been reported to provoke asthma symptoms. The best-known azo dye, technically called *tartrazine* but labeled Yellow No. 5 by the U. S. Food and Drug Administration (FDA), was the focus of an excellent asthma study at the Scripps Clinic in California. This study did not find a single aspirin-sensitive asthmatic patient who was also sensitive to the dye—even when a large concentration was used. Reports of asthma aggravated by other dyes (azo and nonazo) have not been confirmed either. The conclusion is that only a very small number of asthmatics—if any—are sensitive to these dyes.

TABLE 6

Foods and Beverages Commonly Preserved with
Sulfur Dioxide and Sulfites

Canned beverages	Precooked shrimp and other
Canned foods	seafood
(e.g., fruits, vegetables, hash,	Processed avocado
soups)	(e.g., guacamole dip)
Cider and wine vinegars	Processed potatoes
Fermented beverages	(e.g., chips, french fries,
(e.g., wine, beer)	frozen dishes)
Packaged dried fruits	Salads at restaurants and salad
Pickled vegetables	bars

ENVIRONMENTAL RESPIRATORY IRRITANTS

Patients with asthma, no matter what initially kicked it off, are particularly susceptible to a host of environmental respiratory irritants. Their heightened response to these irritants is termed *airway hyper-reactivity*. The list of environmental irritants includes such various general atmospheric pollutants as ozone and sulfur dioxide, dust, smoke, exercise, cold air, and strong odors.

Sulfur Dioxide and Sulfiting Agents

These have been used for centuries to inhibit bacterial growth in food and beverages. The food industry currently uses them as preservatives (see Table 6 for typical items), as sanitizing agents for food containers, as inhibitors of microorganism growth in wine and beer, and to stop fruits and vegetables from discoloring. Because normal (meaning nonasthmatic) people do not experience any ill effects from even large amounts of sulfites, these preservatives are labeled "Generally Recognized as Safe" (GRAS) by the FDA. This classification means that food processing companies can add sulfites to any food and drink (except those containing thiamine—vitamin B_1—because sulfites destroy thiamine) *without having to list them on the product label*. Sulfites are also used as preservatives in over 1,100 pharmaceutical products, including—ironically—

bronchodilators. Yet when sulfites come into contact with saliva or stomach juices, they may generate the gas sulfur dioxide, a common air pollutant that can provoke bronchoconstriction in asthmatics.

The current estimate is that 5 percent to somewhat over 10 percent of all asthmatics are sensitive to sulfites. In 1978, the first reports began appearing in the medical literature describing the acute choking and severe asthmatic distress experienced by these asthmatics within minutes after eating sulfites. Asthmatic reactions have also been observed after inhaling such commonly used bronchodilators as Bronkosol and Isuprel. The two pharmaceutical associations whose members make the great majority of prescription and over-the-counter drugs sold in the United States began requiring their members, as of 1986, to list sulfites in the package insert for oral medications. But the FDA wants a strong warning to be added as well.

Exercise-Induced Asthma and Cold Air

Many asthmatics experience what is called exercise-induced bronchospasm (EIB or EIA). They always wheeze and are short of breath after vigorous exercise. No one really understands why this happens, but there are two basic theories (many doctors and scientists disagree with one or both) that try to explain EIB. One theory points to the fact that exercise—because it makes us breathe a lot harder—cools our airways. Some scientists have conducted studies that they believe suggest that cooling the airways provokes an asthma attack, and that it is mediated neurally via the autonomic nervous system. (This theory also attempts to explain why cold air itself can trigger asthma.) The other theory points to the possibility that exercise may cause mast cells in the airways to release the biochemical mediators that set off allergic reactions.

Strong Odors

Many asthma patients complain that certain odors trigger attacks. Although this relationship between odors and asthma was documented by Sir John Floyer almost three hundred years ago, it is still not recognized by many physicians. A very recent study used odors conclusively to provoke asthma attacks in volunteer patients, and surveyed a large number of additional patients to see how common this reaction is and identify the most frequent odor triggers.

The results: 95 percent of these asthmatics experienced odor-triggered attacks. Almost all of them reacted to insecticide, usually encountered in monthly apartment fumigations and roach sprays. Household cleaners, particularly those containing ammonia, came next. Almost 75 percent of these patients named the smell of perfumes, colognes, and fresh paint. Just over 50 percent reacted to car exhaust or gas fumes, and a little more than 33 percent of these asthmatics reacted to cooking smells.

VIRAL INFECTION

It has been suspected for a long time that viral infections play an important role in provoking acute asthma episodes. (Certain bacterial infections can also trigger asthma, but much less frequently.) The viruses causing the common cold can trigger an asthma attack, and some of the influenza viruses can trigger a severe one. In fact, the initial appearance of asthma is frequently associated with a viral infection.

In one study of childhood asthmatics, the very first episode of wheezing occurred during or shortly after a viral infection. The majority of these children continued to have asthma-like episodes during subsequent viral infections, and some also began to have asthma attacks provoked by noninfective triggers. One large study of asthmatics who developed the disease as adults found that nearly half of them attributed their first episode to a respiratory infection.

There are several proposed explanations for virus-induced asthma. One is that the inflamed airways caused by respiratory viruses stimulate nerve fibers that set off a bronchoconstriction reflex. Another explanation is based on the typical allergy reaction. This view suggests that respiratory viruses are actually allergens that stimulate the production of virus-specific IgE, which then causes the host mast cells to release the biochemicals that stimulate the allergic asthma response whenever this viral allergen is encountered. In addition, virus-infected cells release chemicals that recruit certain white blood cells that also contain inflammatory mediators. A third explanation describes a possible imbalance in the autonomic nervous system that weakens the beta-adrenergic response in airway muscle. (This has been proposed as the mechanism behind asthma itself, as well as possibly explaining the increase in asthma symptoms after viral infections.)

Recent research shows that viral infections can act as asthma triggers once the disease has developed. First, airway reactivity is greater right after a viral respiratory infection. We know this because the lungs are functioning less effectively when they encounter a stimulus that normally causes no problem. In addition, airway damage from an infection takes weeks to heal. One of our nonasthmatic laboratory workers, for example, who was participating in an exercise experiment, found that right after a bout of flu her lung function decreased following exercise much as it normally does with asthmatic volunteers. This problem lasted for several weeks. With an asthmatic, this measurable decrease in lung performance after a viral respiratory infection is added to existing asthma symptoms, and so substantially aggravates them.

Nocturnal Asthma

There is a group of asthmatics who experience acute attacks in the middle of the night. This common phenomenon—first described in the medical literature by Aurelianus Caelius in the fifth century A.D.—has proved to be troublesome and often difficult to treat. But the importance of treating it effectively is underlined by surveys showing a disproportionately high frequency of deaths and nonfatal episodes of respiratory arrest in the early-morning hours. Less severe symptoms still interfere with sleep enough to hurt school or work performance.

For allergic asthmatics, scrupulously avoiding nighttime exposure to allergens dramatically reduces the frequency of nocturnal asthma episodes. In this context, it is particularly important to keep bedding and floor-level wall molding dust-free. These notorious dust collectors would otherwise provide dust mites that are close to the sleeper and very easy to inhale.

But nocturnal allergen exposure does not explain the problem in patients with nonallergic asthma. Most evidence points to the natural daily variation (the "circadian rhythm") of our physiology and biochemistry. Interestingly, both asthmatics and nonasthmatics have circadian changes in lung function that are identical in nature, but milder in degree for people without asthma. So asthmatics may respond much more strongly to the normal rhythm of lung function.

This normal rhythm is accompanied by a regular fluctuation in certain hormones. But it is unclear whether these hormonal changes act on the pulmonary function rhythm, or whether they both respond to something more basic. Epinephrine and cortisol, which are important in controlling asthma attacks, are at their lowest levels during the night. Histamine, which makes asthma worse, is at its highest then.

Two other aspects of circadian rhythm also provide possible triggers, or mechanisms, for nocturnal asthma attacks. One is a sleep-induced lowering of body temperature. Supporting this concept is a recent study showing nocturnal asthma to be preventable by breathing warm, humidified air during sleep. The other mechanism concerns the vagal nerve, which is the parasympathetic nervous system's pathway to the lungs. Vagal nerve activity—which causes bronchoconstriction—increases at night.

The lack of a clear understanding of the mechanism behind nocturnal asthma is a barrier to the effective use of asthma drugs. The two most common bronchodilator medications (the beta-agonists and theophyllines) do not last long enough between doses to prevent nocturnal episodes. So far, a sufficiently high dose of a slow-release aminophylline drug continues to be the most effective—if not perfect—therapy for this potentially serious problem.

Psychological Factors

DAMAGING MYTHS

With a disease as poorly understood as asthma, it is difficult to clarify the role of psychological factors in any depth. Current medical theory and research, however, make it clear that psychological factors can influence asthma in several ways *after* the disease has developed. Unfortunately, in the 1940s the psychiatric theories—that are now known to be erroneous—of French and Alexander spawned the false conclusion that psychological abnormality *causes* asthma. Unhappily, this baseless assumption still holds sway with too many psychiatrists, psychologists, and lay people.

This false conclusion has given rise to several equally false, and highly damaging, myths. One is that all asthmatics share the same disturbed personality pattern. Another is that every asthmatic has, or had, an abnormally overprotective mother. The basic implication is that all asthmatics have a serious psychological abnormality that first caused, and now perpetuates, their illness. Despite substantial contrary evidence, these stigmatizing myths remain widespread and deeply entrenched.

THE REALITIES

A major cause of these errors is that professionals observing asthmatics for psychological characteristics traditionally compared them to medically healthy people. Only recently have they been appropriately compared, instead, with others also suffering from chronic illness. These new studies indicate that personality disturbance in people with any chronic disease results from the severity—rather than the nature—of their illness. Psychological/behavioral problems commonly result from the patient's eternal struggle with the permanent limitations placed on his life by his disease. Because the disability's chronic nature is the critical factor, these psychological problems are similar no matter what the specific disability happens to be.

Another kind of relationship between asthma and psychological factors affects only some asthmatics. For them, periods of stress or intense emotional reactions increase both the frequency and intensity of their attacks. The influence of emotional state was first clearly reported by a nineteenth-century asthmatic, the French physician Armand Trousseau. He wrote of his most severe attack ever, which had occurred while he was in his grain loft after suddenly suspecting his own coachman of stealing his oats: "I had a hundred times been exposed to an atmosphere of dust considerably thicker. . . . [Yet now] my nervous system was shaken from the influence of mental emotion caused by the idea of a theft . . . committed by one of my servants." The attack was obviously triggered by the oat dust, but Trousseau's extreme agitation at that time both dramatically reduced the amount of dust needed to provoke an attack and increased the intensity of his allergic response.

The conclusion is inescapable. Without the initial physiologic susceptibility to asthma, there can be no link with emotional distress. But for some asthma-susceptible people whose asthma has already materialized, these intense emotions can affect how often and how severely their attacks occur.

In a third vein, psychological factors themselves can apparently act as actual triggers—again, only once asthma has already materialized. Most physicians who treat a large number of asthmatics report having some patients whose asthma attacks are occasionally provoked by something clearly psychological. (Yet all the physicians we interviewed emphatically denied that even this subgroup of asthmatics shares a common personality.)

Supporting these clinical observations by chest physicians, numerous studies demonstrate the power of suggestion in starting, as well as worsening, an asthma attack. This large body of research was begun, surprisingly, back in the nineteenth century. John McKenzie, a Baltimore ear, nose, and throat surgeon, wrote in 1885 of a woman whose asthma was tied—as it was traditionally viewed then—to the scent of roses. ''Decidedly skeptical as to the power of pollen to produce paroxysm in her particular case, I practiced the following deception upon her. . . . I obtained an artificial rose of such exquisite workmanship that it presented a perfect counterfeit of the original. I produced [it]. . . . In the course of a minute she said she must sneeze. . . . In a few minutes the feeling of oppression in the chest began, with slight embarrassment of respiration.'' More currently, bronchoconstriction has been provoked in asthmatic children by asking them to imagine something that scares them. In another informative study, an asthmatic group was told that they were going to inhale a bronchoconstrictor. Even though it was actually an innocent solution of salt and water, airway resistance increased in some of them.

WHY DO EMOTIONS INFLUENCE ASTHMA?

In theory, there are at least two mechanisms by which emotions can influence an asthma attack. It is widely believed that one aspect of emotional influence is caused by increased parasympathetic nervous system activity (remember the association between the vagal nerve and bronchoconstriction). In support of this, it has been shown that asthma symptoms reliably provoked by psychological stimuli are prevented when atropine—which inactivates the parasympathetic nervous system—is injected before presenting the psychological stimulus.

Emotions also alter the rate and depth of breathing. Anxiety, for example, tends to make our breathing more rapid and shallow. Breathing this way can cause hyperventilation, which itself can trigger a bronchospasm. The bronchospasm then heightens the anxiety, and a vicious cycle arises.

Anaphylaxis

An asthma attack can be just one component in a complex of simultaneous reactions called *anaphylaxis*. Anaphylaxis is one of the most frightening of medical emergencies. It occurs when the mast cells' chemical mediators, instead of being released locally in the area invaded by an allergen, are released into the bloodstream and circulated throughout the body. This happens when a substance to which a person is sensitive (either via IgE or by some obscure nonimmunological mechanism) enters his bloodstream. This usually happens by injection (as with insect venom) or ingestion (with an allergenic food), and sometimes by absorption through a mucous membrane (e.g., in the nose, mouth, bronchial tree, vagina).

Anaphylaxis—which can be fatal without appropriate intervention—is characterized by a constellation of symptoms that starts with flushing, an increasing heart rate, the throat swelling closed, chest tightness and/or cough, and nausea. It progresses to a dramatic drop in blood pressure, severe wheezing, and abdominal cramps. Anaphylaxis—which can end in cardiac and/or respiratory arrest—is reversible with an injection of adrenaline.

Many agents have caused anaphylaxis in susceptible individuals, but antibiotics, insect venoms, nuts, shellfish, and the intravenous radiopaque dyes used in X-ray techniques seem particularly capable of triggering this life-threatening reaction. Since 1980, a number of cases of exercise-induced anaphylaxis have been reported that were not associated with any ingested or inhaled agents. This suggests that an intrinsic trigger also exists.

One Common Underlying Mechanism?

We have described a variety of different triggers that all lead to the same set of asthma symptoms. At some point in the process before these symptoms are actually produced, this variety of triggering stimuli must all converge on the same physiological pathway. This common pathway must involve regulation of the amount of calcium in our cells.

Calcium—normally present in our cells—is essential in the basic process that causes muscles to contract. Without calcium, no muscle movement can occur. But for appropriate movement, calcium must be present in the right amount. Too much calcium will cause too strong a contraction, resulting in spasm. When airway muscle contracts too strongly, it squeezes—or constricts—the airways (the bronchi). That bronchospasm is the most basic component of asthma. Another major physiologic change occurring during asthma—the mast cells releasing their biochemical mediators—is also caused by an excess of calcium in these cells.

So the last step in this common pathway is known: a

significant increase in intracellular calcium. Obviously, the allergic activation of IgE, the nonspecific effects of exercise, such airway irritants as tobacco smoke, changes in balance between the sympathetic and parasympathetic nervous systems, psychological triggers—these amazingly diverse stimuli all rapidly increase the amount of calcium in our cells. What is not at all apparent—yet—is how each of these seemingly unrelated asthma triggers achieves its effect on the level of intracellular calcium. The answer to this question will pinpoint the mechanism underlying asthma.

❧❧ 4 ❧❧

Seeking Help

Asthma's major symptoms—wheezing, coughing, shortness of breath, and excessive mucus production—are typically transitory. Because they always clear up after each reappearance, the undiagnosed asthmatic often attributes them to a cold or the flu, or ignores them altogether. He finds it reassuring that eventually these symptoms always go away by themselves. Far more important, however, is that these symptoms regularly reappear. Often this persistence is first recognized by a family member or friend rather than the asthmatic.

At what point should a physician be consulted? For infants and the elderly—the high-risk segments of the population—medical help should be sought as soon as the persistence of symptoms, no matter how mild, is noticed. For everyone else, a good time to see a doctor is if and when symptoms become bothersome enough to intrude fairly regularly on their consciousness.

Finding the Right Doctor

WHAT KIND OF DOCTOR?

Four medical specialties overlap for treating asthma: the family physician, the pediatrician, the pulmonary internist, and the allergist. Some asthmatics have only one doctor, and others have several (who may work together or in sequence).

Family Physician

The family doctor (also known as a general practitioner or GP, a primary care physician, or an internist) is usually the first doctor most asthmatics consult. In rural areas, this is often the only doctor an asthmatic ever sees. Starting at this point has a major advantage (unless the asthmatic is new in town or has recently changed doctors). The family doctor knows the asthmatic's history and general state of health. The main disadvantage is that a general practitioner must keep up with changes in so many areas of medicine that—if he does not have a specific interest in asthma—he may not become aware of treatment advances until they eventually filter down throughout the medical community. Despite this, *the family physician can adequately manage most asthma cases*. The occasional complicated case should usually be referred to the appropriate specialist.

Pediatrician

For children, the pediatrician usually plays the major role in asthma treatment. Like the family doctor, the pediatrician tends to be familiar with the child's history and general health. But if the asthma is or becomes complicated, the child should usually be referred to a specialist. (Remember that a child is not simply a small version of an adult. Specialists treating pediatric asthma should be trained in working with children, i.e., a pediatric pulmonologist or pediatric allergist.)

Pulmonary Internist

In areas where a wealth of medical choices exists, people tend to bypass the family doctor and go directly to a specialist. Someone with a respiratory problem would choose a pulmonologist. These physicians first specialize in internal medicine, then spend further years studying pulmonary medicine, and then must pass an examination to become "board certified" in this subspecialty. Because of his focus on pulmonary disease, the pulmonologist is current on the latest treatment advances for asthma.

Allergist

The allergist has gone through a similarly rigorous and time-consuming training program, except that his subspecialty time was spent studying allergic diseases. Consultation with an allergist is recommended for the patient whose asthma is triggered by allergies, or who has coexisting allergic problems (such as hay fever).

WHERE TO LOOK

Unless limited medical resources in your area mean that you have no choice, finding the right doctor can be difficult. A good way to begin is by seeking recommendations, either from friends or acquaintances (particularly someone with a pulmonary problem), or from another physician. Keep in mind that nonmedical people are likely to recommend doctors whose bedside manner is particularly pleasing. Another doctor will recommend a colleague he went to school with, or whose medical competence has particularly impressed him. (A medical student we know has decided to seek friends' recommendations for nonsurgical problems, but would get another doctor's advice if she needed a surgeon.)

Obtaining a personal recommendation is not the only

way. Most large communities have a Lung Association
that can recommend physicians or clinics. The American
Lung Association (headquartered in New York City at 1740
Broadway, New York, NY 10019; 1-212-245-8000) can
also advise you on locating a physician or clinic. (Other
organizations that may be helpful in this regard are listed
in Appendix A.)

Another approach would be to call the appropriate de-
partmental office (pediatric, pulmonary, or allergy) of the
nearest large medical center. This can be particularly helpful if your symptoms become aggravated while you are
traveling and you need nonemergency medical help.

The National Jewish Center for Immunology and Respiratory Medicine (in Denver, Colorado) is one of the
foremost centers for asthma treatment and research. (Denver's National Asthma Center merged with this institution
in 1976. Its name remained part of the institutional title
until 1984.) The Center provides a trained staff of regis-
tered nurses to answer general questions over the telephone about lung diseases. The caller can also request the
names of appropriate hospitals and specialists in his area.
This free "Lung-Line" is manned Monday through Fri-
day from 8:30 A.M. to 5:00 P.M. Messages are taken at
other times, and these calls are returned as soon as the
Lung-Line reopens. The toll-free number if calling from
outside Colorado is 1-800-222-LUNG; from within the
state call 1-303-398-1477.

One source to avoid is a magazine's "Best Doctors"
type of list. These evaluations are subjective and are sometimes little more than a popularity rating.

MAKING THE RIGHT CHOICE

If you have the luxury of choosing among two or more
medically competent physicians, select one whose personality works well with yours. As with other long-term relationships, the effectiveness of the patient-physician duo
depends much on "good chemistry" and the trust and
communication that this helps promote. A physician whose

attitude is "I'm the doctor and you do as I say," for example, will work poorly with patients who find it important to know what is being done, what effects can be expected, and why.

Three complaints were repeated most frequently when we asked a group of asthmatics why they had found it necessary to change physicians. Their former doctor did not explain things sufficiently; was unwilling to try reducing their medication; or was hesitant to try new approaches and treatments. Yet most felt satisfied with their current doctor. The first complaint, as we indicated, is basically a matter of personality. A physician's approach to medication and new treatments depends largely on the attitudes he developed during his medical studies.

The two opposite approaches to medication use are "minimal-to-none" versus "aggressive therapy." There is support for each point of view. The aversion to the newer asthma drugs that many patients and some physicians hold stems from the desire to avoid possible side effects from this drug therapy. Support for this preference comes from the reality that the proportion of deaths attributed to asthma has not decreased radically over the past 80 years despite the introduction of new drug therapies. This suggests that most asthmatics can manage their disease rather well without the new medication. The case for aggressive therapy focuses on the fact that the newer medication enables most asthmatics to lead essentially normal lives, with the risk of side effects quite small compared to this benefit. Most physicians fall somewhere in between these two extreme viewpoints.

As to nontraditional or not-yet-traditional treatments, physicians are trained to be conservative. "Conservative" in this case means not abandoning treatments of proven benefit until something of greater proven benefit comes along. Doctors are rightly skeptical about new treatments that have not yet passed the rigors of modern investigational criteria. Although some physicians we have spoken with adhere only to a traditional treatment plan, the great majority will accept a new form of therapy once they are convinced that it cannot harm the patient and that the patient will continue the traditional treatment along with it.

Although these different philosophies have no effect on a physician's competency in treating asthma, they do affect the doctor-patient relationship. Finding a doctor whose attitudes are in step with your own point of view greatly facilitates good communication. It helps to get an idea of a particular physician's personality and philosophy as early as possible.

When we were looking for a pediatrician for our soon-to-be-born first child, we interviewed several who came highly recommended to us and then chose the one with whom we felt most comfortable. Although we do not know of any medical group other than pediatricians who routinely allow such interviews at no charge, it does not hurt to ask.

Unfortunately, you will probably have to commit yourself to a first appointment in order to gather this important information. Our advice—assuming you can afford the initial fee—is not to settle for the first physician you see unless you feel strongly that he is someone you can work well with. And if a relationship that begins well does not continue to meet your needs as a patient, then it is time to look for another doctor.

If you are a severe asthmatic who must be hospitalized frequently, the hospital affiliations of the doctors you are considering become important. Hospitals vary in their standards of patient care.

Who Is Responsible for What?

You have found a doctor whose personality and attitudes you feel will permit a productive relationship based on mutual respect, confidence, and cooperation. What should you expect from each other as this relationship begins?

YOUR DOCTOR'S RESPONSIBILITIES

You, the patient, are entitled to certain things from your doctor: (1) an accurate diagnosis of your disease and, if possible, identification of the trigger(s); (2) attentiveness to your "story," and honest answers to your questions about symptoms, treatment, and the future; (3) a treatment plan that will permit you to live as normal a life as possible; (4) an education that will teach you both about your disease and about the proper use of medications and other therapeutic techniques; (5) adequately close contact (your doctor should be reachable and return telephone calls in a reasonable amount of time) so that appropriate intervention, when needed, can be done quickly enough to avoid a hospital stay if this is possible; (6) prompt hospitalization when it is needed.

If you become a patient in the clinic of a large city hospital, however, these responsibilities—except for (1), (3), and (6)—usually do not apply. Although the clinical aspects of your asthma will be competently treated, the reduced staff and funds of the typical city hospital leave their physicians without the time needed to pursue the other aspects, even though they are necessary for optimum asthma treatment.

YOUR RESPONSIBILITIES

Your doctor is entitled to expect certain things from you.

1. You are honest in answering all his questions; hiding anything (the recreational use of drugs, for example) diminishes his ability to treat you effectively and seriously weakens the relationship's underpinning of mutual trust.

2. You are committed to getting better and a full partner in whatever treatment plan is developed. (If you do not follow his treatment regimen, you are wasting both his time and yours.)

3. You are gaining insight into your condition. This includes acceptance of your asthma as a chronic disease and

an awareness of what improves or worsens your symptoms.

4. You will call him whenever your symptoms or the effects of your medication change.

5. You will not abuse his responsiveness by calling him for inappropriate reasons. You will gradually learn when it is—and is not—important to talk with your doctor.

For this last point, our pediatrician provided an excellent example. We asked at our interview with him how to decide whether a particular situation required us to call him. He refused to give us any criteria for making that kind of decision because he preferred— *at the beginning*— to be called to the phone about unimportant matters rather than risk missing an emergency. He added that we would learn when it was important to call him as we gained experience in being parents and got to know our particular child. As you gain experience in dealing with your asthma, you will learn when to call your doctor.

Another pediatric story gives an example of abusing the doctor's sense of responsibility. A woman called her pediatrician to discuss what she knew was a minor matter. But because she did not feel like waiting 15 to 20 minutes for his return call, she claimed that her son was in the midst of a medical emergency. She got the doctor on the phone instantly, but once he realized that the "emergency" was the result of her impatience, he told her to find another pediatrician immediately!

6. You will remember that doctors are human beings, and that all human beings have both good and bad days. Do not be offended when your doctor is occasionally somewhat curt or preoccupied during a visit or telephone call. Give him some understanding when he is having an off day, but bring the problem to his attention if it persists.

❋❋ 5 ❋❋

How Do I Know
I Have Asthma?

Asthma is *not* easy to diagnose. Formal discussion of this problem began in 1794, when the distinguished Edinburgh physician William Cullen complained that "the term asthma has been commonly applied by the vulgar, and even by many . . . [specialists], to every case of difficult breathing, that is, to every species of dyspnea. By not distinguishing it with sufficient accuracy from other cases of dyspnea, they have introduced a great deal of confusion into their treatises on this subject."

The three most common chronic obstructive pulmonary diseases—asthma, emphysema, and chronic bronchitis—all present a confusingly similar picture. Wheezing, dyspnea, chest tightness, and difficulty in moving air through the airways are common to all three. Coughing is frequent for all of them. That asthma's characteristic airway hyperreactivity frequently develops when chronic bronchitis temporarily worsens deepens the confusion. (To muddy the waters still further, these symptoms can also appear with heart disease, blood clots in the lung, and cystic fibrosis.)

The principles of treatment for asthma, emphysema, and chronic bronchitis are very similar. Therapy is aimed primarily at decreasing or reversing the airflow obstruction created by airway muscle contraction, abundant mucus secretion, and other inflammatory processes.

If the goal of therapy is the same regardless of the diagnosis, why is there any real need to distinguish between these three respiratory diseases? Current and future plans for coping with the disease's overall impact on your life will be very different if you are asthmatic. There are two important reasons why: for the same degree of obstructed airflow, the asthma patient's prognosis is best; and the same treatment applied to the three diseases is most effective in asthma.

How does a physician distinguish between these diseases? Evaluation of suspected asthma follows a logical, orderly course that combines an accurate patient history, physical findings, and objective measurements from lung function tests and other laboratory studies. Most of this information indicates only whether airway obstruction exists. Once obstruction is proven, a specific laboratory test can identify its cause as asthma.

History-Taking

The history's overall purpose is to establish the nature and time frame of your current symptoms. With asthma, most physicians find that taking a careful medical history is also invaluable in eventually diagnosing it and correctly evaluating its cause and severity. Just from talking, information about agents or events that aggravate your symptoms will come to light. A clear understanding of symptoms can disclose a disability or discomfort that may require therapy, even though the lungs are not substantially impaired. Finally, the conversational give-and-take of the history-taking process provides an excellent opportunity for you and your physician to establish a mutually trusting relationship.

There are five traditional categories of questions that your doctor asks. They concern social history, family history, past medical history, present complaints, and a review of the different organ systems (neurological, digestive, etc.). Each category begins with general questions and proceeds to more specific ones. *Above all, be honest in your answers.* (You will not help yourself by hiding, for example, the recreational use of drugs.) When all questions have been asked, if you think your doctor has missed possibly important information, it is your responsibility to tell him. (Before your appointment, you might consider writing down everything that you see as relevant to your symptoms.)

The Asthmatic's History

Asthma patients usually have some combination of shortness of breath (dyspnea), wheezing, chest tightness, and cough. But some may not wheeze very much, or may cough a lot without having dyspnea, or may simply have chest tightness after exercise. And, as we have emphasized, the symptoms of asthma are seen with other diseases as well. The following kinds of information help your physician attribute your symptoms to asthma rather than to another disease. They also aid in planning your treatment.

Personal/Family History

A personal or family history of allergy, and/or the presence of someone in your family with asthma, make it highly likely that your current complaints stem from asthma. Your medication history is also important, because aspirin and, to a lesser extent, other antiinflammatory drugs and azo dyes (used in a variety of drugs and preserved foods) can produce explosive forms of asthma.

(In contrast, a history of smoking and a long-term cough that always brings up mucus—all predating airflow obstruction by many years—indicates chronic bronchitis. A long-standing cough can also precede emphysema. But these patients relate a history of increasing dyspnea from physical effort, with only minimal mucus production.)

Onset

Allergic asthma typically appears between the ages of 5 and 15. When it begins in adulthood, it is associated with exposure to a new allergen, usually due to a recent change in residence or occupation. Asthma development and recurrence also appear related to the presence of viral respiratory infections.

Current Complaints

Periods of severe symptoms may occur at a specific time of the year, while the rest of the year is symptom-free. Or symptoms may occur after physical activity and worsen with laughter, crying, or drops in temperature. In another typical picture, symptoms occur in the work place but not at home, or occur only in proximity to a particular animal.

Sometimes another disease or condition triggers asthma symptoms. Many asthma patients also have sinusitis and postnasal drip (which, if successfully treated, often improves the asthma). There are recent reports of an association between asthma and gastroesophageal reflux (what is commonly called heartburn—a condition in which stomach acids and partially digested food are pushed back up into the esophagus). Many asthmatic women report a worsening of symptoms just before their menstrual period.

Asthma varies greatly with the individual, so there is no typical description of frequency or severity of attacks. It ranges from an occasional trivial irritation to a chronically disabling and life-threatening disease. You must give your physician an accurate description of the disease's impact on your life. Is some degree of airway obstruction always present, or are there periods completely free from respiratory discomfort? When obstruction is present, can you carry on your usual activities, or are you limited to activities that can be done while sitting, or are you totally occupied with the job of breathing?

Previous Treatment and Results

Diagnosing asthma and planning effective future treatment require knowledge of any past asthma treatment attempts and their results. For example, were you given a steroid drug? Did you change your environment? Did you have immunotherapy? After beginning any previous treatment(s), did your condition improve, worsen, or stay the same?

Life-Threatening Complications

You must let your doctor know if you ever had an attack in which you lost consciousness and/or needed a tube inserted down your trachea (called intubation) to keep you breathing. Although just two out of every one thousand asthmatics have a life-threatening attack in any one year (usually patients who have been asthmatic for many years), once it happens, it is likely to happen again. Of these high-risk asthmatics, 10 percent will experience a life-threatening attack at least once a year. These high-risk patients must be identified by their doctor so that special care can be given immediately whenever their asthma symptoms worsen.

The Physical Examination

When the question-and-answer period is over, your doctor will examine you. First he looks for wheezing—asthma's hallmark—which is incontrovertible evidence of airway obstruction. It is the sound of turbulence caused as air is forced around the obstructions. Although for a long time wheezing was thought to happen only during expiration, recent evidence indicates that it occurs during inspiration too.

Your doctor uses a stethoscope to listen to your wheezing. Wheezes differ in tone and loudness depending on when they are listened to (during inspiration or expiration, during an attack or not), and exactly where. The most severe cases of airway obstruction often have no wheezing at all, because the obstruction is so great that air cannot be pushed through the airways with enough force to produce the amount of turbulence needed to make an audible sound.

A physician once said: "All that wheezes is not asthma." What else will your doctor look for when he examines you? He will look at your inspiratory muscles to see if they show signs of greater than normal use. The asthmatic typically uses his inspiratory muscles to make expiration easier, even during relaxed breathing. He does this by inflating his chest to its maximum capacity during inspiration. (As we learned earlier, the more the chest is inflated during inspiration, the stronger is the elastic recoil force that powers expiration.) The degree of overactivity of two inspiratory muscles in particular (the scalenes and sternocleidomastoids, located in the neck) frequently reflects the severity of airway obstruction. The patient with more severe obstruction gives the appearance of intense inspiratory activity, forcefully inspiring and then expiring slowly against pursed lips.

(Some experts feel that the presence of *pulsus paradoxus* is another useful indicator of severe airway obstruction. The term refers to an abnormal fall in blood pressure during intense inspiratory effort. The degree to which this happens seems to bear some relationship to the severity of airway obstruction, but the overall relationship is far from perfect. Quite a few severe asthmatics do not have pulsus paradoxus, and the condition is sometimes found in people with no lung problems.)

You wheeze, you use your inspiratory muscles excessively, and perhaps you show pulsus paradoxus. All this clearly confirms that your problem involves obstructed airways, but none of it can prove that the obstruction results from asthma. The physical examination's purpose has been to substantiate the existence of airway obstruction that was first suggested by your history. Now that this is confirmed, an array of objective tests should permit your doctor to decide which of the three obstructive respiratory diseases—asthma, chronic bronchitis, or emphysema—is your problem. (Deciding which of the different possibilities is the actual problem is called the "differential diagnosis.")

Laboratory Studies

CHEST X-RAY

An asthmatic's chest X-ray taken during a period of breathing difficulty provides two kinds of information. In the absence of complications, it will simply show changes caused by chronic chest hyperinflation. When a complication exists, the X-ray can also confirm its nature: pneumonia, aspergillosis, local areas of airless lung tissue (called *atelectasis*) due to mucus plugging, and the collapse of large tissue areas from air seeping in between the lung and chest wall (called *pneumothorax*). Because both kinds of abnormalities can occur with all the obstructive respiratory diseases, the X-ray provides additional confirmation of airway obstruction but does not really help identify its cause. But between attacks the asthmatic's chest X-ray is usually normal, so any abnormality appearing between attacks tends to indicate a lung problem other than asthma.

BLOOD TEST

A blood sample is analyzed to assess your general health and to see if you have any as-yet unidentified disease(s) that could complicate the treatment of your respiratory disease. If diabetes is present, for example, certain asthma medications must be used with extreme caution.

One analysis in particular provides information about the possibility of asthma. This is the *blood count*, in which the types of blood cells are identified and the number of each type is counted. Some asthmatics have an abnormally high number of *eosinophils* (so called because they absorb eosin dye when stained for observation under the microscope). These specialized white blood cells engulf invading parasites and release inflammatory chemicals. They are the white blood cells inappropriately recruited—via the release of mast cell chemicals—to the site of an allergic reaction. The eosinophils' chemicals cause much of the airway tissue damage accompanying an asthma attack, and their presence explains why the symptoms of an attack can continue well past removal of the triggering agent. (Once asthma has been confirmed and antiinflammatory treatment begun, some consider that a reduction in the number of eosinophils in the blood signals the treatment's effectiveness.)

SPUTUM ANALYSIS

Examining sputum to aid in diagnosis began in classical times with the physicians of Greece and Rome. Galen (130–201 A.D.), the foremost Roman physician during the reign of Marcus Aurelius, described using sputum analysis specifically to diagnose an asthmatic patient: "An individual with chronic cough, coughing up small quantities of viscous stuff, began to cough up a substance resembling small hailstones. . . . This viscous humor which he had coughed up with great difficulty had taken on, on becoming dry, the consistency of hail. . . . I gave him medicines which are good for asthmatics." The French call these dry balls of sputum—which only some asthmatics produce—asthmatic pearls.

If an asthmatic brings up mucus—dry or wet—when he coughs, analysis of this sputum under the microscope (Figure 5.1) may show eosinophils, plus bits and pieces of a variety of destroyed cells. In some cases, sputum also contains mucus plugs shaped by the small airways in which they formed, and/or pieces of the *Aspergillus* mold.

PULMONARY FUNCTION TESTS

There are two basic types of pulmonary function tests. One group of tests measures the volume of air in your lungs at different points during breathing (lung volume

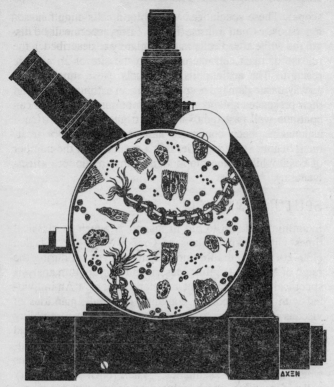

Figure 5.1 Magnified view of sputum from an asthmatic patient.

measurements). The other group of tests is concerned with
the air flowing into and out of your lungs (ventilation measurements). (Although there are many more specific tests
than the ones described below, we discuss only those that
have proved over time to be the most informative.) Most
of these pulmonary function tests provide further evidence
for the presence or absence of airway obstruction, and
document the severity if obstruction exists. One of these
pulmonary function tests also provides the definitive piece
of diagnostic information. It can confirm the speedy reversibility of airway obstruction when a bronchodilator is

used, or the reversibility of relatively normal lung function in response to an asthma trigger. (This aspect will be discussed fully after the tests themselves are described.)

Your performance on each of these tests will be compared to the *predicted values* appropriate for you. These are average measurements from large groups of healthy people, each group combining people of the same race, sex, age, and height. Your measurements will most likely be considered normal if they fall within the range from 80 to 120 percent of the average for your particular group. But predicted values are guidelines, not rigid judgments, and final interpretation of the pulmonary function tests is undertaken in the context of information gained from your history, physical exam, and X-ray.

Lung Volume Measurements

Figure 5.2 illustrates the different portions of the total lung volume usually measured during a pulmonary function test and how they are traced by the spirometer (the test instrument). In all these tests you breathe through a mouthpiece—much like those on snorkels and scuba tanks—attached to the spirometer. You wear a nose clip to make sure all the air moving in and out of your lungs goes through your mouth.

You will be asked to breathe quickly for a few breaths, and then to squeeze as much air out of your lungs as you possibly can. The amount of additional air squeezed out after quiet expiration would have ended is your *expiratory reserve volume*. After this maximum expiration, you will be asked to fill your lungs slowly with as much air as they can hold, and then again squeeze out as much as you can. The amount of air breathed out in going from your maximum inspiration to your maximum expiration is your *vital capacity*. Next you will be told to take another maximum inspiration, then just breathe out quietly. The amount of air breathed out as you go from your maximum inspiration to the end of a quiet expiration is your *inspiratory capacity*.

Some air always remains in the lungs after even a max-

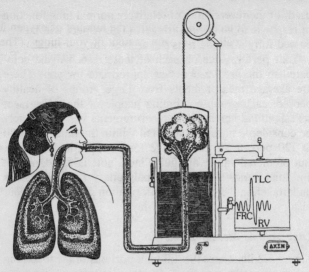

Figure 5.2 Lung function test using classical spirometry. The uppermost point on the chart is *total lung capacity* (TLC), the lowest is *residual volume* (RV), and the difference between the two is the *vital capacity* (VC). When normal expiration ends, the remaining volume is the *functional residual capacity* (FRC). The normal-sized breaths are the *tidal volume*.

imum expiration, an amount called the *residual volume*. Because it can never be breathed out, this residual amount—and therefore the two lung volumes that include it in their total—must be determined indirectly with the spirometer. These other two volumes are the *functional residual capacity* (the amount of air remaining in the lungs at the end of a quiet expiration, i.e., the residual volume plus the expiratory reserve volume) and the *total lung capacity* (the total amount of air contained in the lungs after a maximum inspiration, i.e., summing all the individual volumes).

With one indirect technique, you breathe in a specific amount of helium gas while its concentration in your lungs is measured. Then the amount of air that must be in your lungs to produce that concentration can be calculated. The other indirect technique measures the amount of oxygen it takes to wash all the nitrogen gas out of your lungs. (The air we breathe contains about 80 percent nitrogen.) For either method, all you must do is breathe quietly until the recording equipment indicates either that the helium being breathed in is not being diluted any further or that all your lungs' nitrogen has been expelled.

These static lung volumes document the presence and severity of airway obstruction rather than identifying its cause as asthma. When the airways are obstructed, all the volumes measured directly (expiratory reserve volume, vital capacity, inspiratory capacity) tend to be smaller than normal. How much smaller is usually related to the severity of the obstruction. The volumes that must be determined indirectly (residual volume, functional residual capacity, total lung capacity) are larger than normal. All these changes occur because of hyperinflation and air trapping, as described in Chapter 2.

Because airway obstruction in asthma occurs only during an attack (unless the condition is chronic asthma), these tests will show obstruction in an asthmatic only at such a time. But you need not be in the midst of an unpleasant asthma episode for these tests to be of value. Some measurable attacks are so mild that they do not even penetrate awareness. And when necessary—as we will shortly describe—a brief, controlled asthma episode can be provoked in the testing laboratory.

Ventilation Measurements

These dynamic pulmonary function tests measure two things. One is the *resistance* that inspired and expired air meet in your airways. (Any obstruction in the airways increases resistance. During an asthma attack it often becomes 7 to 10 times normal and can reach 25 times the normal resistance.) The other is *airflow*—the amount of air entering or leaving your lungs in a particular time period—which is partially determined by resistance.

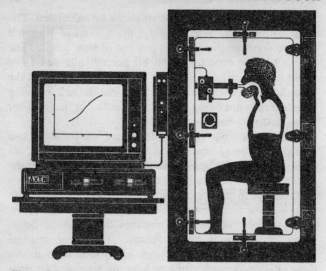

Figure 5.3 Lung function test of airway resistance using plethysmography.

Resistance must be measured in a plethysmograph (which can also be used for the indirect determination of residual volume, functional residual capacity, and total lung capacity). The plethysmograph is a box 5 feet high and 2½ feet wide and deep, with one or more clear sides (Figure 5.3). You sit inside this box, wearing a noseclip and breathing through a mouthpiece. The basic maneuver is repeated several times. First you breathe quietly, then pant gently about once per second. While you are panting, a shutter will close off the mouthpiece for just a few seconds. As soon as it reopens, you breathe quietly again. The information gained from this test is the speed with which air flows out of your lungs and the effort your respiratory system is making (its driving pressure) to push air out at this speed. Airway resistance and various lung volumes are calculated from these initial data.

Airflow is measured with probably one of the most fruitful technological developments for assessing airway

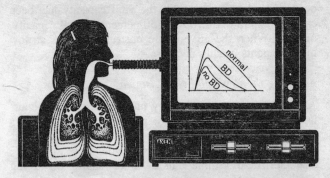

Figure 5.4 Lung function test of expiratory airflow using flow-volume curves. *Bottom curve:* Typical of an airway obstruction. *Middle curve:* Obstruction somewhat reversed by bronchodilator (BD). *Top curve:* Normal pattern, included for comparison.

obstruction. You breathe through a mouthpiece connected to specialized monitoring and recording equipment that gives an instant-by-instant comparison (on a graph) of airflow with the volume of air already in the lungs at that instant. This is recorded on the graph during one maximum expiration (from total lung capacity to residual volume) followed by one maximum inspiration (from residual volume back to total lung capacity). The recording's shape on the graph is curved, and is called a *flow-volume curve*. Because airway obstruction is magnified during expiration, the expiratory portion of this flow-volume curve produces a very characteristic picture when airway obstruction is present (Figure 5.4).

The flow-volume curve contains particularly useful airflow information for determining the degree of airway obstruction: (1) the amount of air that can be pushed out of the lungs in one second (forced expiratory volume in 1 second, or FEV_1); (2) the highest airflow rate achieved during this one second (peak expiratory flow rate, or PEFR); and either (3) the average airflow for the middle 50 percent of the expiratory curve (forced expiratory flow for the mid-50 percent, or $FEF_{25-75\%}$) or (4) the airflow occurring when exactly half the vital capacity has been expired (expiratory airflow at 50 percent of vital capacity, or V_{50}). When the airways are obstructed, these airflow measurements usually decrease.

Assessing the Reversibility of Asthma

Although abnormal pulmonary function tests indicate airflow obstruction, they do not point to the obstruction's cause. And if an asthmatic is in remission, his test results may be perfectly normal. Because the definitive diagnostic characteristic of asthma is its reversible nature, the testing conditions must be adapted to show it.

There are two strategies for doing this. Both involve doing two sets of pulmonary function tests, one right after the other, to show whether an appropriate intervention has reversed the initial condition. For the patient who has been free of asthma symptoms for some time, a controlled asthma attack must be provoked before the pulmonary function tests are redone (more about this shortly). If the second set of tests shows evidence of airway obstruction, the asthma trigger obviously reversed the normal condition of the patient's airways. If an attack is in progress, the pulmonary function tests are redone after the patient uses a bronchodilator. If the second tests show significantly improved airflow, then a diagnosis of asthma can be made. (If airway obstruction has not diminished substantially, then the doctor will have to look elsewhere for the cause.)

Failure of a patient to respond to the bronchodilator on the first try does not automatically exclude the diagnosis of asthma. A retest should be done as long as other factors still suggest asthma, because there are several possible reasons for an initial failure to respond. Unfamiliarity with the proper technique for taking a bronchodilator often prevents enough of the drug from reaching the airways where it is needed. If the primary area of obstruction is in the smaller airways, it cannot be reached by an inhaled bronchodilator. If the obstruction is caused by a neurally mediated bronchospasm, it will be only modestly affected by the bronchodilators usually used in laboratory testing. Finally, a bronchodilator cannot counteract obstruction caused by the mucus plugging and inflammatory changes in very severe attacks.

The only problem with the pulmonary function retest after using the bronchodilator is the lack of firm guidelines for establishing whether adequate airflow improvement has indeed occurred. Because various tentative recommendations are all that currently exist, most physicians use their own personal criteria. The following recommended criteria for true bronchodilation seem logical to us. Post-bronchodilator measurements should be greater than the initial measurements by 15 percent in FEV_1, 20 percent in $FEF_{25-75\%}$, and/or 10 percent in vital capacity even without any improvement in airflow rates.

Provoking an Asthma Attack

For the person with negative clinical tests despite a history of asthmalike symptoms, three types of inhaled stimuli have been used to provoke a controlled asthma attack (a bronchodilator is given when the testing is finished). Pharmacologically induced bronchoconstriction is usually produced using methacholine or histamine (acetylcholine is frequently used in Europe). Allergen inhalation tests and occupational exposure tests (such as with chemicals in the plastics industry) measure the airway response to allergens or specific sensitizers. Exercise and cold air are also used to assess airway hyperreactivity. The first and last types of "challenge" are both safe, do not usually stimulate prolonged responses, and have the greatest clinical value.

At the point of testing, you should be symptom-free. Your spirometer tests—most particularly before a pharmacologic challenge—should all be normal (i.e., not below 80 percent of your predicted values). You will usually be instructed to stop your medication temporarily for at least 12 hours before the provocation test. Cromolyn sodium, antihistamine, and other long-lasting medications should be stopped even earlier. Do not use cigarettes, colas, coffee, tea, or chocolate for at least 6 hours before. Avoid exercise and direct exposure to air pollutants (including tobacco and marijuana smoke) for at least 2 hours before the test. All these factors, plus recent allergen or occupational exposures, viral or bacterial infections, and vaccines, can artificially alter your sensitivity to the challenge.

Pulmonary function is measured using airway resistance, or by flow-volume curves, both before and after the challenge. When a pharmacologic agent is used, the patient first takes 5 breaths of the neutral solution (delivered in spray form) to which the challenging substance will be added. If the patient's airways are hyperreactive to this neutral solution, no further testing can be done. If there is no hyperreactivity, these initial measurements will be used in the comparison. The tests are repeated 10 minutes after the patient takes 5 breaths of a weak solution containing methacholine or histamine. This procedure is repeated—doubling the dose each time—either until a chosen aspect of pulmonary function (FEV_1 is the most popular) has decreased by a predetermined amount, or until the maximum dosage has been reached—whichever comes first. (The dose level at which FEV_1, for example, drops by 20 percent for at least 3 minutes is the *provocation concentration* [PC_{20}] or *provocation dose* [PD_{20}].)

You can expect side effects from inhaling one of these pharmacologic substances. The more common reactions to histamine are flushed face and neck, sweating, blood pressure drop, heart rate increase, and deeper breathing. Throat irritation and coughing are possible. Methacholine's side effects are similar but less intense. At its higher concentrations, the chemical smells and tastes like rotten eggs. The effects of a challenge with these two agents are normally short-lived, although there are some patients whose reactions have lasted for hours.

The provocation tests using allergens or specific irritant triggers are similar in concept to what was just described, but they are not well standardized. They are also potentially dangerous and must be done under a physician's direct supervision. Such tests often produce a prolonged asthma response. The possible side effects are particularly serious. Allergens can trigger a long-lasting or type III reaction, and they can cause severe anaphylaxis with edema and closing of the throat. Because patients can experience increased airway reactivity for years after their last allergen exposure—as with Western red cedarwood—it is recommended that allergen challenges *not* be routinely done in the doctor's office.

Exercise and cold air tests are done in a similar way. With an exercise challenge, the patient either works at a moderate exercise level for about 8 minutes, or works progressively harder until a predetermined level of ventilation is reached. With a cold air challenge, the patient breathes freezing air for 5 minutes at a ventilation level equivalent to moderate exercise. Pulmonary function tests are repeated 6 to 10 minutes after the challenge is over. (An unusual reaction with some patients has been a delayed asthma response to both these challenges. The delayed reaction to cold air lasted for several days.) The big advantage to these two tests is that they can be used for strongly suspected asthmatics whose pulmonary function is currently abnormal, but who did not respond to the bronchodilator. These tests' only disadvantage is that they rely on patient cooperation.

Provocation tests validate the presence of airway hyperreactivity in suspected asthmatics. An asthmatic response to the challenge confirms the presence of asthma. And the degree of response—because it can be quantified—helps in developing an appropriate plan of treatment.

SKIN TESTING

One final laboratory test is prescribed if allergy is indicated by your history and your doctor's physical examination. Skin testing is done to identify the primary offending allergen(s) and to suggest other allergens that may be contributing to symptoms.

Injecting specific allergens under the skin has been the main approach for detecting IgE-mediated responses for the past 60 years. There are two traditional methods for producing the telltale "wheal-and-flare" reaction (a *wheal*, or raised area, is surrounded by a *flare*, or reddened area). In the *intracutaneous test*, a small amount of an allergen extract is injected under the skin. In the *epicutaneous prick test*, the top layers of the skin are pricked by a needle that has just pierced—and so contaminated itself with—a drop of allergen-containing solution placed on the skin. The prick test's drawback is its poor precision, but because it is a thousand times less sensitive than the intracutaneous method, it holds much less risk of inducing anaphylaxis when the patient has a strong response to the allergen. The prick test is used first when a strong response is anticipated.

A newer method directly measures the amount of allergen-specific IgE in the patient's blood. Some physicians request the *radioallergosorbent test*—called *RAST* for short—when one or both of the other skin tests have been negative despite strong clinical suspicion of an allergic sensitivity. It is also used for patients with skin problems and for patients with such intense allergic sensitivities that both skin tests pose a danger.

It is not yet clear whether the newer or more traditional techniques are most desirable overall. For the time being, this issue is controversial.

The Formal Diagnosis

Arriving at the formal diagnosis of asthma takes all the above kinds of information into account to determine that the patient's airway obstruction is both periodic (it comes and goes), and reversible (when the airways are obstructed, a bronchodilator alleviates the obstruction; when they are clear, a challenge provokes obstruction). No matter how strongly your history has suggested this diagnosis, it must be confirmed in the pulmonary function testing laboratory. If you are experiencing symptoms, then after using a bronchodilator you must show at least a 20 percent improvement in your expiratory airflow rate, or a 10 percent increase in your vital capacity. If you are without symptoms, you must show reduced expiratory airflow rates after you are challenged with an appropriate asthma trigger, then a return to normal after using a bronchodilator.

Some asthmatics do not fall neatly into one of these categories. Then the physician must add the fruits of experience and intuition to complete the picture.

Symptom Severity

Once you are diagnosed as having asthma, the severity of your asthma symptoms must also be determined. The need for a standardized system for gauging the severity of an individual patient's asthma has led to a number of classification proposals. In integrating what we consider the most informative of these attempts, we have arrived at four levels.

1. *Mild or minimal.* Annoying, but with no marked discomfort; one or two attacks a month, with only one or two days monthly of restricted activity. Drugs are needed only occasionally for good control over attacks.

2. *Moderate.* Marked discomfort, but not enough to interfere with usual activities. About two attacks a week, during which time activity is restricted. Treatment requires long-term use of nonsteroidal drugs, with occasional periods of steroid use.

3. *Severe.* Daily attacks with some sleep interference, but not incapacitating. Almost daily restriction of activity, with occasional emergency room visits. Good response to long-term use of steroid drugs allows an essentially normal life.

4. *Incapacitating.* Does not respond well to medication. Continuous attacks cause intolerable disruption of daily life. Patient is unable to perform ordinary daily activities and needs frequent hospitalization.

✵✵ 6 ✵✵

Asthma Medication: Bronchodilators

The basic treatment goal for asthma is improving the asthmatic's quality of life. This means reducing as much as possible his discomfort, the degree to which the disease handicaps him, and the anger this handicap has caused. Accomplishing this requires one or more of five therapeutic elements: medication to relieve symptoms and prevent new attacks; education of the patient and his family concerning the disease and its therapy; environmental controls and/or desensitization; respiratory and/or physical therapy to improve physical fitness; and stress and anxiety management and sexual counseling.

The mainstay of asthma therapy is medication to maintain open airways and reduce bronchial reactivity. The variety of appropriate medications are covered in this and the next chapters. This chapter first presents the historical evolution of asthma medication (when and how it started, and where in the world), then discusses the major bronchodilators in current use. The other types of medication are described in the next chapter. The remaining four elements of asthma therapy are included in later chapters.

Note: All discussions of medication purposely avoid any mention of appropriate dosage. This book is designed to help educate you, not treat you. Any questions that your reading of this book may raise concerning your medication must be taken up with your doctor.

History of Asthma Medication

Greek and Roman physicians conceptualized diseases as various imbalances in the body's "humors." They designed treatment to correct the particular imbalance. In this context, Galen pointed out the overproduction of mucus in asthma: "If the breath makes a raucous sound, this indicates obstruction due to an abundance of viscous or thick humors which are stuck to the bronchi of the lung and cannot be easily loosed."

Western medicine's earliest pharmaceutical attempts at treating asthma were directed at ridding the patient of mucus. Paulus Aegineta wrote in the seventh century about "consum[ing] the viscid and thick humor by attenuant and detergent medicines." This approach—which lasted well into the twentieth century—called for expectorants, which increase and liquify mucus so it is easily coughed up, and detergents, which break up mucus plugs.

By the nineteenth century asthma treatment was logically worked out, aerosols had been invented, and a variety of agents were available for physicians to prescribe. Among those with a clear benefit were expectorants such as potassium iodide and the extract from the root of the Brazilian ipecacuanha plant (also the active ingredient in ipecac, used to induce vomiting to treat poisoning), and such bronchodilators as coffee and atropine.

The drug caffeine, coffee's effective ingredient, is closely related to theophylline, which has been basic to asthma management for the last 60 years. Tea (Figure 6.1), also effective against asthma, contains both caffeine and theophylline.

Plants containing atropine were first used in India to relieve asthma, and were certainly used in Europe by the seventeenth century. The leaves were smoked until "the

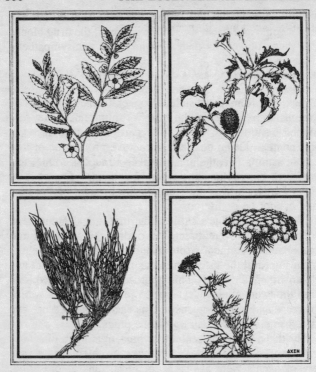

Figure 6.1 Medicinal plant sources of antiasthma drugs. *Clockwise from upper left:* Tea, theophylline source; *Datura stramonium*, atropine source; *Ephedra*, ephedrine source; *Ammi visnana*, cromolyn sodium source.

chest, throat, and head became light, and the cough reduced.'' The most popular atropine-containing plant used for asthma was *Datura stramonium* (Figure 6.1). Its common names are Jamestown weed, jimsonweed, stinkweed, and thorn apple.

In large doses, atropine becomes a deadly poison (a muscle paralytic) that causes death from respiratory muscle paralysis. (The name *atropine* comes from Atropos, one of the three mythological Greek fates. Her job was severing the web of life woven and measured by her sisters, Clotho and Lachesis.) In lower doses, the drug blocks the vagus nerve (the path by which the parasympathetic nervous system activates the airways).

As an antiasthma medicine, atropine has recently come into favor again after a checkered history. Its current use is partly due to the ineffectiveness of other bronchodilators in certain cases. Atropine-like bronchodilators are now successfully used in Europe and Canada and gained FDA approval here in 1987.

In the early twentieth century, ephedrine was rediscovered and epinephrine (adrenaline) was first discovered. The Chinese were already using ephedrine as a bronchodilator four to five thousand years ago. They called it *ma huang*, an herbal remedy for coughs and colds made from the *Ephedra* family of plants (Figure 6.1). These small wild shrubs are still found in much of Asia and southern Europe. A record of ephedrine's use before it disappeared as a tool in Western medicine comes from the Roman historian Pliny the Elder. He noted that asthmatics took it in sweet wine for treatment of their disease. Then its antiasthma properties were forgotten until Japanese investigators rediscovered them at the beginning of this century. From this they created *Asthmatol*, the first "modern" bronchodilator. Ephedrine also became the very first in a new class of drugs called *sympathomimetics*, which mimic the effects produced by the sympathetic nervous system.

Epinephrine—or adrenaline, as it is more usually called—was discovered and isolated only at the turn of the century. At that time it was learned that the adrenal glands on the kidneys released large amounts of adrenaline into the bloodstream during periods of acute stress, and that one of adrenaline's many effects was to open up the bronchi. In the 1920s, adrenaline was developed as a bronchodilator for asthmatics. *Adrenaline is still often used for emergency treatment of acute asthma attacks.*

(Interestingly, the London physician and asthmatic H. H. Salter wrote in the 1860s that intense excitement—which we now know releases adrenaline—can ease asthma attacks. He described a patient who "was suffering severely from asthma . . . , and was in bed" when his sister was "seized with sudden illness that seemed to threaten suffocation. He jumped out of bed in great alarm, and found then that his asthma was perfectly cured. He was sufficiently well to run for a doctor, and continued well throughout the day.")

The commercial production of ephedrine and adrenaline was followed by attempts to synthesize compounds with properties similar to the natural substances. The most successful result—known both as isoprenaline and isoproterenol—was synthesized in 1940 and is still in use.

In 1949, cortisone (one of the steroid group of drugs) became the next breakthrough in asthma treatment. It was first used on a patient with acute rheumatoid arthritis, and results were dramatic. Then it achieved striking success in treating life-threatening asthma attacks. But the high rate of relapse once the cortisone treatment was completed led to cortisone's long-term use. Then it was discovered that maintaining patients on this drug led to serious, progressive side effects. By the 1960s, this unwitting indiscriminate use of cortisone had created a backlash against steroid drugs. Now, with greater understanding of how steroids work plus the development of steroids in aerosol form (aerosols are inhaled, and much smaller doses are needed), the pendulum has returned to a sensible middle position that acknowledges the benefits of steroids in treating asthma.

Lastly, in the 1960s Dr. Roger Altounyan discovered a new drug while he was investigating an ancient Egyptian remedy described as a bronchodilator. This new drug was disodium cromoglycate, also called DSCG, cromolyn sodium, or simply cromolyn. It is extracted from khellin, a compound that relaxes smooth muscle (remember that the airways are surrounded by smooth muscle). Khellin itself comes from the seeds of the Middle Eastern plant *Ammi visnana* (Figure 6.1). This drug is now marketed as *Intal*.

Current pharmaceutical research progresses in two directions. One is synthesizing more effective versions of existing drugs. The other is discovering new types of drugs that act on points in the asthma chain of events as yet unaffected by existing medications.

Modern Medication

The modern drugs used to treat asthma are designed to prevent and/or reverse an attack. This strategy breaks down into five avenues of approach.

1. Induce bronchodilation by stimulating beta-receptors (which bronchodilate) and/or preventing the destruction of cAMP (which in turn reduces intracellular calcium) (Figure 6.2).

2. Stop acetylcholine from stimulating cholinergic receptors (which would otherwise bronchoconstrict).

3. Prevent mast cells from releasing their bronchoconstricting and inflammatory chemical mediators.

4. Prevent or reverse the inflammatory consequences of an asthma attack.

5. Directly reduce both the amount of calcium reaching the airway muscle cell proteins that actually cause contraction, and the amount involved in the release of mast cell mediators.

The three basic types of bronchodilators—that is, the first two categories—are discussed in the rest of this chapter. The other three categories of medication will be treated in Chapter 7.

EMOTIONS   INFECTIONS

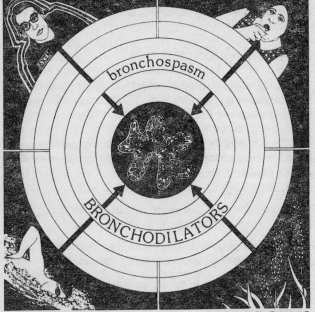

EXERCISE   ALLERGENS

Figure 6.2 How bronchodilator treatment affects asthma. A high
cAMP concentration in airway cells causes *bronchodilation*.
Bronchodilators prevent or reverse an asthma attack by increasing the
cAMP concentration. Beta-2 stimulators increase cAMP production,
whereas theophylline prevents its destruction.

Drugs That Stimulate
Beta-Receptors

THE BIOCHEMISTRY OF
BETA-RECEPTOR STIMULATION

In Chapter 2, we described the two kinds of airway muscle
cell receptors recognized by the chemical mediators de-

signed specifically to stimulate them: cholinergic receptors and adrenergic receptors. Adrenergic receptors are subdivided into alpha-receptors and beta-receptors. Cholinergic receptors and alpha-receptors constrict; beta-receptors relax. The degree to which the airway muscle relaxes or contracts (which is what muscle tone means) depends on the balance between these two actions.

When a mediator is released, it recognizes and binds to its designated type of receptor. This binding sets off a chain of chemical events inside the muscle cell. When the cholinergic receptor or alpha-receptor on an airway muscle cell is bound by its appropriate mediator (acetylcholine or adrenaline, respectively), *cGMP*—cyclic guanosine monophosphate—is eventually formed. Because cGMP raises the amount of calcium (a necessary element in muscle contraction) available to the cell's contractile proteins, muscle contraction increases.

Remember that adrenaline binds to beta-receptors when they are present in equal or greater numbers than the alpha-receptors. When adrenaline binds to beta-receptors, *cAMP*—cyclic adenosine monophosphate—is eventually produced. Because cAMP lowers the amount of calcium available to the contractile proteins, muscle relaxation occurs.

The cGMP and cAMP that are produced to regulate airway muscle tone are eventually broken down by enzymes in the muscle cells. (The production and breakdown of these compounds form a regulatory cycle.) When acetylcholine comes unbound, it is inactivated by the enzyme cholinesterase. Unbound adrenaline is rapidly inactivated by the enzyme monoamine oxidase (MAO).

Mast cells also have beta-receptors that can counter bronchoconstriction. Their activation reduces mast cell degranulation, apparently by preventing calcium from entering the cell. How this is achieved is not understood.

Stimulating beta-receptors also relieves the asthmatic's cough, but the underlying mechanism is not clear. Coughing is one way the pulmonary system tries to rid the lungs and bronchi of excessive mucus produced during an attack. When the mucociliary system—which seems to be controlled by the parasympathetic nervous system—is stimulated, mucus production increases. But mast cells that degranulate during an asthma attack release chemicals that are also potent mucus-stimulating agents. So when activating beta-receptors relieves an asthmatic's cough, it is not yet known whether the mucociliary system is being affected directly (by decreasing mucus production and increasing ciliary activity); or the effect is on the sensory neural pathways carrying information about airway irritation; or perhaps the airway smooth muscle is being directly acted upon.

Although how beta-receptors function is not completely understood, it is clear that maintaining adequate beta-receptor activity is central to managing most asthma patients. Drugs that stimulate the beta-receptors—technically called *beta-agonists*—imitate the action of adrenaline. (Table 7 summarizes the beta-stimulating, or adrenergic, bronchodilators currently available in the United States.)

NONSPECIFIC BETA-RECEPTOR-STIMULATING DRUGS

Adrenaline

Adrenaline—or, more correctly, epinephrine—is a natural catecholamine produced by the adrenal glands, with greater amounts produced during stress. (Catecholamines are mediators whose effects mimic those of the sympathetic nervous system.) Adrenaline is injected under the skin during a severe asthma attack. In aerosol form—for inhaling—it is widely available in both nonprescription (over-the-counter) and prescription formulations. But adrenaline cannot be taken orally because it is inactivated in the digestive tract. In addition, its injected and inhaled effects are relatively short-lived because it is so quickly destroyed by enzymes in the blood.

(A caution about over-the-counter bronchodilators: *DO NOT USE THEM!* The existing prescription formulations are much more effective and have fewer side effects. And

TABLE 7

Commonly Used Prescription Beta-Receptor-Stimulating Drugs

Medication	Brand Name	Injection	Oral	Inhaled
Albuterol/	Proventil	No	TL	MDI
Salbutamol	Ventolin	No	TL	MDI
Bitolterol	Tornalate	No	No	MDI
Ephedrine	Generic	Yes	TL	MDI
Epinephrine/	Adrenalin chloride	Yes	No	Neb
adrenaline	EpiPen	Yes	No	No
Isoetharine	Bronkometer	No	No	MDI
	Bronkosol	No	No	Neb
Isoproterenol	Isuprel HCl	Yes	No	Neb
	Isuprel HCl Glossets	No	Yes	No
	Isuprel Mistometer	No	No	MDI
	Medihaler-Iso	No	No	MDI
Metaproterenol	Alupent	No	TL	MDI, Neb
	Metaprel	No	TL	MDI, Neb
Terbutaline	Brethaire	No	No	MDI
	Brethine	No	T	No
	Bricanyl	Yes	T	No

Abbreviations used: L, liquid; MDI, metered-dose inhaler; Neb, nebulizer; T, tablets.

if you already know enough to use an aerosol bronchodilator, then you should be seeing a physician.)

Ephedrine

Ephedrine—unlike adrenaline—is taken orally. The effects are similar to an adrenaline injection, although achieved somewhat differently. Adrenaline stimulates the beta-receptors directly, but ephedrine initiates the release of catecholamines—including adrenaline—that are already stored in the body. This is its biggest drawback. Its effects depend on the availability of catecholamine in the body at the time it is given, and these concentrations vary. This makes ephedrine an unreliable bronchodilator, and so a poor choice for the asthmatic now that better agents are available.

Ephedrine has sometimes been mixed with other drugs in one preparation, most commonly with *theophylline* and a tranquilizer. (Examples are *Marax* and *Tedral*.) Because the proportion of each drug is always the same, this kind of formulation is termed fixed-ratio combination drug therapy. It is usually a poor idea, because the side effects of one of the medicines often make it impossible to include enough of the others. For the few patients who are doing well on this type of therapy, however, there is usually no good reason for stopping it—especially since these combined preparations are generally cheaper than taking each of the medicines separately.

Undesirable Effects

Adrenaline and ephedrine also have adverse effects. The beta stimulation that they achieve is not always completely desirable. It can sometimes disturb the heart's normal rhythm. But the biggest problem with adrenaline and ephedrine is that they are nonspecific sympathomimetic drugs. Their effects are not limited to the beta-receptors. These drugs also have strong alpha-receptor effects that can constrict artery and vein smooth muscles (increasing blood pressure) and constrict the bladder opening (causing urine retention). Other possible adverse effects are headaches and overstimulation of the brain. This major problem led to the search for drugs that specifically stimulate beta-receptors and ignore alpha-receptors.

SPECIFIC BETA-RECEPTOR-STIMULATING DRUGS

The prototype beta-receptor stimulator is *isoproterenol*. It replaced adrenaline in popularity because of its potent beta-stimulant properties plus the virtual absence of alpha effects. But this adrenaline derivative retains other disadvantages of its parent compound: ineffectiveness when taken orally, relatively short duration of action, and undesirable cardiac effects. This last limitation is the most troublesome.

BETA-2-SPECIFIC-STIMULATING DRUGS

Happily, there is more than one type of beta-receptor. Beta-1-receptors are abundant in the heart, and activating them causes the heart to beat more quickly and forcefully. Beta-2-receptors are the primary ones in the airways, and their activation causes bronchodilation. Pharmaceutical research is now looking for cardiac medication that blocks beta-1-receptors—to prevent the heart from beating too fast—and has no effect on beta-2-receptors. The goal for antiasthma drugs is potent beta-2 stimulation with minimal beta-1 action.

Currently, there are five major beta-2-selective bronchodilators available. Although they vary in potency and duration of action, they all last longer than isporoterenol, and their cardiac effects are less pronounced. They are *isoetharine, metaproterenol, terbutaline, albuterol* (known as *salbutamol* everywhere except in the United States), and *bitolterol*. A sixth, *fenoterol*, is not yet available in the United States but should be approved in the near future. Preliminary studies comparing it to the others indicate that it is even more beta-2-selective, more potent, and longer acting.

It has been observed that beta-2-receptors in airway muscle lose sensitivity after a patient begins using a beta-stimulator drug. This explains the noticeably decreased effectiveness of these drugs over the first several weeks of use. After this initial change, however, response to the drug becomes relatively stable. This sensitivity loss is the body's attempt to reduce what it perceives as overstimulation of the beta-receptors. It reacts by actually decreasing their number. We are not aware of any studies that suggest increasing the dosage of beta-2-stimulating drugs to counter this loss of sensitivity. (The long-term implications of this phenomenon for the patient are not yet clear.)

Administration

The effectiveness of these drugs is partly determined by how they are taken: orally, by injection, or by inhalation. Inhalation—which is the most common—has two big advantages: because the drug is deposited directly in the airways, less of the drug is needed for a given result than when it must be distributed throughout the body to reach the airways; and because less of the drug travels throughout the body, the side effects are less. But inhalation also has two disadvantages: because the drug lands primarily in the large airways, the dilation benefit is concentrated in the central airways; and a severe respiratory obstruction prevents inhaled drugs from reaching obstructed airways (but oral and injected medication will, because they travel in the blood).

Side Effects

The degree of side effects is determined by the amount of a drug that reaches organs other than the lungs. With the typical inhaled doses, side effects—aside from a rare case of local irritation from the propellant in the spray—are minimal. With oral and injected medication, and with higher doses of inhaled drugs, side effects become more common.

Because selective beta-2-stimulators are only *relatively* selective, heart rate increases from activated beta-1-receptors in the heart. Because of the relaxing effect on the smooth muscle encircling the blood vessels, blood pressure may fall slightly, and nasal congestion is sometimes aggravated (from relaxed blood vessels in the nose). Because these drugs do not reach the brain, effects on the central nervous system are slight. These effects—if they occur—include occasional restlessness, sense of apprehension, headache, and neurally induced muscle tremor.

Skeletal muscle tremors are a much more common side effect. Activation of the beta-2-receptors in these muscles causes tremors. This occurs with lower drug doses than the other side effects do, but it does not warrant concern from patient or physician. In fact, this tremor can be useful. Its occurrence is often a concrete indicator that an effective dose has been achieved. And the degree of tremor usually diminishes within a few weeks because the beta-2-receptors in these muscles lose sensitivity.

INTERACTION OF BETA-2-STIMULATORS WITH OTHER DRUGS

Theophylline

Beta-2-stimulators and theophylline (an asthma drug discussed in a following section) are often used together. In combination they act synergistically, meaning that the presence of each one makes the other more effective. Because of this synergistic action, the dose of each can be reduced when they are combined. The combination often achieves greater bronchodilation than the higher dose of either drug alone, and the lower doses make side effects less severe.

Corticosteroids

These asthma drugs, which are covered in the next chapter, are often used to treat asthmatics. This group of drugs intensifies beta-2 effects by raising beta-2-receptor sensitivity, possibly by increasing their numbers.

Monoamine Oxidase (MAO) Inhibitors

These drugs are used in the medical treatment of severe emotional depression. Because they inhibit the enzyme that would otherwise destroy excess adrenaline, the concentration in the body of this natural beta-receptor stimulator becomes much greater than usual. Caution is advised in considering the use of oral beta-stimulators for asthmatics already taking MAO inhibitors because of possible intensification of cardiovascular effects from adding a synthetic beta-stimulator to an already high concentration of adrenaline.

Beta-blocking Drugs

Beta-blockers (designed to inactivate beta-1-receptors) are increasingly popular for treating cardiovascular disorders. In sufficient doses, however, they block the effects of beta-2-stimulators. In asthmatics, the results are devastating. This strongly applies to the nonspecific beta-1-blockers (e.g., *propranolol, nadolol, pindolol, timolol*), and somewhat less to the specific beta-1-blockers (e.g., *metoprolol, atenolol*). Even when used as a topical eye medication (*Timoptic*) for the treatment of glaucoma (a potentially blinding eye disease), enough of the beta-blocking agent can be absorbed into the blood to cause clinically significant bronchospasm. When at all possible, every attempt should be made to exclude use of beta-blocking medication with asthma patients.

Note: Make it a rule to clear any nonasthma medication—including over-the-counter drugs—with the physician treating your asthma before you use them. This becomes especially important if you are seeing more than one doctor, because then the chances increase of being on conflicting medications.

Use and Care of Metered Dose Inhalers

Beta-stimulators (as well as anticholinergic and steroid drugs) can be inhaled as an aerosol using a *metered-dose inhaler (MDI)*. This is a hand-held, pressurized cartridge device in which the drug is either carried in a propellant gas (such as freon), or turned into a spray by passing a stream of air over a solution containing the drug. The MDI's advantages are its easy portability and its ability to deliver a fixed dose of medicine. Its disadvantage is the degree of coordination needed to get the most effective amount of medicine into the lungs. This means that young children, and others who have difficulty coordinating complex maneuvers, cannot use this technique effectively. (These individuals should use a home nebulizer. This larger unit does not require any dexterity. The asthmatic simply breathes medicine from it for several minutes.)

Another frequent barrier to using an MDI effectively is not knowing the proper technique. *This is the proper way to use a hand-held MDI* (Figure 6.3): Hold the device right in front of your *open* mouth. Do not close your lips tightly around the mouthpiece, no matter what the written instructions say! Blow out all the air you can, and depress the MDI—which automatically releases the right amount of medicine—as you start breathing in. Slowly keep the inhalation going (think of slowly sipping hot soup from a big spoon). Hold your breath for 10 seconds. Then slowly breathe out.

No matter how good you are at using an MDI, however, most of the medicine ends up on the back of your throat— perhaps as much as 90 percent. It is absorbed through the surface of the mouth and throat instead of reaching the lungs directly. One reason for this is that the medicine jets out too fast. An *ineffective* solution to this problem is to hold the MDI 1 or 2 inches away from your mouth. This just makes coordination harder.

What we find really helps is to use a *spacer* between the MDI and your mouth. A spacer is simply a tube about 3 inches long and about 2 inches wide. Because it slows the speed at which the medicine travels before it enters your mouth, evaporation makes the aerosol droplets smaller and so able to penetrate deeper into the lungs. This kind of aid has been shown to deposit more of the medicine in the lungs more effectively.

At least one company, Rorer (in Fort Washington, Pa.), builds a spacer into its steroid MDI (*Azmacort*). Key Pharmaceuticals (in Miami, Fla.) makes *InspirEase*, an add-on device that can be used with any MDI. The InspirEase (Figure 6.3) is an inflatable plastic bag with a reed-containing mouthpiece that whistles if you inhale too quickly. The medicine is released into the inflated bag, and you inhale from the bag slowly enough to keep the

ΔΧΞΝ

Figure 6.3 How to use a metered-dose inhaler. *Top:* Without a spacer. *Bottom:* With a spacer. (Adapted from T. J. H. Clark, *Steroids in Asthma.* Sydney, Australia: ADIS Press, 1984, p. 214.)

whistle from blowing. After holding your breath for 10 seconds, you exhale back into the bag. (Repeat the procedure if more than one puff is needed.)

Unfortunately, the patients we have spoken to complain that these commercial aids break too easily. They may be

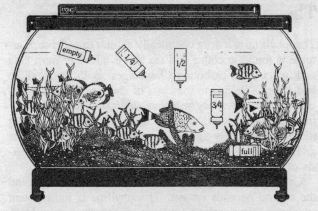

Figure 6.4 Checking how much medicine remains in a metered-dose inhaler. Drop the *canister only* into a *glass of clean water*. Empty: It floats on top. Partially full: It floats submerged. Full: It sinks to the bottom. (Note: Use a glass, *not* a fish tank. The fish tank was used in this illustration strictly to add a touch of humor.)

most appropriate, then, for those who need an easily portable inhaler but have difficulty mastering the use of an MDI without such an aid.

A practical problem in using an MDI is not knowing when it is almost empty and your prescription needs renewing. There is a way! Place your MDI cartridge—the part containing the medicine—in a glass of water (Figure 6.4). If the MDI sinks, it is full; if it floats fully submerged, it is three-quarters full; if the bottom breaks the top of the water, it is half full; if more shows, it is one-quarter full; and if it floats horizontally, it is empty.

The dispenser in which the MDI cartridge fits should be cleaned periodically. One technique involves an initial cleaning with liquid detergent and hot water, then soaking the dispenser for 30 minutes in a solution of half water and half white vinegar. Dry with a towel afterward. The tip of the MDI cartridge should be rinsed in hot running water after each day of use.

Theophylline

Theophylline is a drug chemically similar to caffeine. Caffeine is found in coffee and tea and is added to most cola and many other carbonated beverages. Both theophylline and caffeine belong to the class of chemicals called *methylated xanthines*. They stimulate skeletal muscles, the central nervous system, and the heart. They relax smooth muscles, especially the airway muscles. Both theophylline and caffeine are effective diuretics, but the relative emphasis of their effects is different.

Caffeine is primarily a stimulant of skeletal muscles and the central nervous system. Theophylline is most potent as a heart stimulant and a relaxer of smooth muscle. More recently, theophylline's ability to strengthen the diaphragm and reduce its fatigue has come to be appreciated. Most recently, it has been learned that theophylline stimulates mucociliary clearance of the airways, inhibits the release of mediators causing anaphylaxis, and suppresses the edema that often accompanies asthma.

HOW THEOPHYLLINE WORKS

For a long time, researchers thought they understood how theophylline worked. They were confident that it simply maintained a high level of cAMP in the body by blocking the enzyme that would otherwise destroy it. This in turn would lower the amount of calcium available for smooth muscle cell contraction.

More recent investigations have thrown serious doubt on this enzyme-blocking explanation, and have also raised other possibilities. Some researchers believe theophylline changes the way calcium enters and leaves smooth muscle cells. Some think it may inhibit certain compounds—called prostaglandins—that have been tentatively implicated in some forms of asthma. Other suggestions have been raised as well. Now nothing is certain beyond acknowledging the complexity with which theophylline produces bronchodilation.

EFFECTIVE DOSE RANGE

The beta-2 bronchodilators are effective over a relatively broad range of concentrations in the blood. For theophylline, however, the range between effective and toxic doses is extremely narrow. With a concentration of less than 10 milligrams of the drug for each liter of blood plasma, there may be little or no therapeutic value even though some side effects may occur. Above 20 milligrams per liter of plasma, the drug is toxic. It can be life-threatening if the blood concentration is allowed to rise high enough beyond this.

A drug's concentration in your blood depends on how much of it is taken, how fast it is absorbed, which organs it enters, and how fast it is then removed (metabolized) from your blood. Several factors can dramatically alter this removal rate. Smokers—of both tobacco and marijuana—remove theophylline twice as fast, on the average, as nonsmokers do. So smokers need a higher standard dosage to compensate for this rapid elimination. What you eat is also important. A high-protein, low-carbohydrate diet means that theophylline will be eliminated 25 percent faster than otherwise. And a low-protein, high-carbohydrate diet slows its removal by 25 percent. Although it is not yet known why, eating a charcoal-broiled steak also speeds up theophylline's removal!

Viral illness and certain medications also affect the rate at which theophylline is removed. These circumstances all require an appropriate dosage change. Theophylline's removal rate is slowed by fever from viral infections, drugs used for heart disease (such as *Inderal*), some antibiotics (e.g., *erythromycin, troleandomycin*), high doses of gout medicine (e.g., *allopurinol*), and drugs used for some digestive tract problems (such as *Tagamet*). The removal rate is slightly increased by intravenous use of isoproterenol (during severe asthma attacks), and high doses of *pheno-*

barbital (a barbiturate) for convulsions. A slight increase in removal rate becomes important only if the blood concentration is already at the low end of the effective range.

Despite the intricacies of using theophylline, it has been highly popular in the past 15 years. A precise technique for accurately determining the drug's concentration in a patient's blood (this concentration is called *serum theophylline*) minimizes the chances of ineffective or toxic doses. But this means that—if you are using a theophylline preparation—the level of the drug in your blood must be monitored periodically, and additionally whenever your asthma symptoms become inexplicably worse or symptoms of toxicity appear. *THE ONLY RELIABLE INFORMATION FOR WARNING YOUR DOCTOR OF IMPENDING TOXICITY IS THE LEVEL OF THEOPHYLLINE ACTUALLY IN YOUR BLOOD.*

A second word of warning concerns commercial laboratories that determine serum theophylline. They do not all do the test carefully. In one observation of 28 commercial laboratories, an amount of theophylline equal to a concentration of 15 milligrams per liter of plasma—right in the middle of the 10 to 20 milligram effective range—was added directly to the blood sample given to each laboratory. The serum theophylline measurements returned by these laboratories ranged from less than 10 milligrams to more than 20! Once you are sure that your doctor is using a reliable laboratory, he and you can rely on its services to guide your dosage adjustments.

Wherever there is a medical problem, you can usually be sure that there is someone, somewhere, trying to solve it. A new method for determining serum theophylline has very recently been introduced. Results are available in less than 20 minutes, the test can be done in your doctor's office, and it is also somewhat less expensive than the traditional test.

SIDE EFFECTS

Theophylline can produce a wide range of negative effects on a variety of organ systems. When an asthmatic first starts using this drug, central nervous system stimulation and slight nausea or queasiness are common. These effects usually disappear as tolerance for the drug develops. At higher therapeutic doses (and beyond), a racing heartbeat—called tachycardia—and heart palpitations are frequent.

THEOPHYLLINE OVERDOSE

When the dose level goes beyond 40 milligrams of theophylline per liter of blood plasma, the heart can lose its normal rhythm or stop altogether. The initial central nervous system effects are restlessness, irritability, and increased nausea. They can progress to severe insomnia, agitation, and vomiting, and culminate in convulsions and coma. Intestinal pain and diarrhea occur, and the kidneys increase urine production.

Prompt emergency treatment is essential after overdosing with theophylline. First, syrup of ipecac is given to induce profuse vomiting. Then the patient is given at least 30 grams of charcoal (an absorbtive poison antidote) and 10 grams of sodium sulfate (a laxative).

Even low effective doses of theophylline can have grave consequences if an asthmatic patient also suffers from heart failure or liver dysfunction. These conditions slow the rate of theophylline removal to such a degree that low doses automatically become high ones. Then the intense side effects also seriously exacerbate the other medical condition.

USING THEOPHYLLINE EFFECTIVELY

Initially, theophylline was regularly combined with several agents, including ephedrine. This is rarely done now, in part because of a better understanding of theophylline's effects. The development of specific beta-stimulators has also played a part, as has the disenchantment with fixed-ratio combination drugs.

Theophylline products now exist in numerous forms (Table 8). A recent listing of all FDA-approved prescription drugs lists 126 different preparations that contain theophylline. This gives your doctor great flexibility if he needs to prescribe theophylline for you.

Selecting a theophylline product, and determining the best dose and time between doses, must take into account the patient's clinical needs, the absorption characteristics of different formulations, and the drug's removal rate in the particular patient. The dose and dose interval decided on, plus the rates of theophylline's absorption and removal, each affect the fluctuation of its concentration in the blood. For maximum benefit from the drug, the blood concentration must be maintained within the narrow therapeutic range around the clock. This means that the above four factors must be coordinated to keep fluctuations at a minimum.

Confusion has been created by the rapid proliferation of sustained-release formulations and by manufacturers providing inconsistent dosage guidelines and inappropriate dose-interval recommendations. The rate and extent of absorption differ between different slow-release formulations, and sometimes even between different doses of the same brand. (The absence of meaningful FDA regulation and the promotion of generic drug substitution have only increased the difficulty.) The optimal theophylline formulation, dose, and dosage interval can be determined only via the patient's blood concentration measurements. Once a patient has invested the time and money that this requires, he should continue using the brand that was finally decided upon. The generic equivalent is *not* equivalent when it comes to theophylline. Your doctor's prescriptions should always include the instruction *Do not substitute*.

Understanding the relative strengths of different types of theophylline preparations is very important for the patient. A preparation's strength is determined by the actual amount of theophylline in it (called *anhydrous theophyl-*

TABLE 8

Commonly Used Theophylline Preparations

Medication	Brand Name	Comment
Aminophylline (100mg* is equivalent to between 78 and 86mg pure theophylline)	Generic (tablets) Aminophylline (tablets) Somophyllin-DF Oral Liquid	
Oxtriphylline (100mg* is equivalent to 64mg pure theophylline)	Choledyl (tablets) Choledyl SA Tablets Choledyl Elixir	Sustained release Contains 20% alcohol
	Choledyl Syrup	Vanilla-mint flavor
Theophylline Short-acting (requires frequent dosing)	Bronkodyl (capsules) Elixophyllin Capsules Quibron-T Divitabs	Can be divided accurately into smaller doses
Sustained release (requires less-frequent dosing)	Slo-phyllin Tablets Aerolate Capsules Constant-T Tablets Elixophyllin-SR Capsules	
	Quibron-T/SR Divitabs	Can be divided accurately into smaller doses
	Slo-bid Gyrocaps	Long-acting dye-free beads
	Slo-phyllin Gyrocaps Sustaire (tablets) Theo-Dur Tablets	
	Theo-Dur Sprinkles	Can be mixed into foods
	Theo-24	One dose per day for certain patients

*mg = milligram, the usual unit that medication is prescribed in.

TABLE 8

Commonly Used Theophylline Preparations (continued)

Medication	Brand Name	Comment
Liquids	Accurbron (liquid)	7.5% alcohol
	Aerolate Liquid	No alcohol, sugar, or saccharine
	Aquaphyllin Syrup	No alcohol, dye-free
	Elixophyllin Elixir	20% alcohol
	Slo-phyllin 80 Syrup	No alcohol, no sugar
	Theoclear-80 Syrup	No alcohol, dye, sugar, artificial sweeteners, or corn products

line). The amount of medicine that you take each time refers to the amount of your preparation, not the amount of anhydrous theophylline. So the identical dose of different preparations will not each give you the same amount of anhydrous theophylline. If your doctor changes your theophylline medication, do not be alarmed if he also changes your dose and/or dosage interval.

For example, if you have been taking 200-milligram doses of a pure theophylline preparation and then switch to 200-milligram doses of theophylline sodium salicylate (a theophylline salt), you would suddenly get only 100 milligrams of anhydrous theophylline per dose—half the previous amount. To obtain the same therapeutic benefits that you did with the stronger preparation, you would have to take either 400 milligrams on the same schedule, or 200 milligrams twice as often.

ADMINISTRATION

Theophylline preparations basically fall into two groups: rapidly absorbed and slowly absorbed. The rapid-absorption products—which are usually used during an acute asthma attack—are normally given intravenously. An alternative to intravenous theophylline is a rectal solution. A rectal solution can be particularly useful with young children who tend to vomit oral medication. But a theophylline rectal solution should not be used for more than

24 to 36 hours because it is very caustic and can cause severe local irritation. (Rectal administration via suppository used to be a very popular way to give theophylline—it is still a preferred way to give many medicines in France—but it has fallen into disfavor because it tends to be erratically absorbed.)

The sustained-release theophylline preparations are used for maintenance therapy because they can be scheduled for longer intervals. These sustained-release or slow-release products are given by mouth in either a tablet or a bead-filled capsule. Liquid syrups are generally more easily accepted by children, although the taste of theophylline is extremely bitter. (A prescription for a liquid preparation should state the dose in milligrams. Ask your pharmacist to give you a measuring device to use that will ensure accurate dosing.)

The slow release rate reduces fluctuation in blood concentration, which in turn improves symptom control. The longer dosage intervals result in better patient compliance. The patient's drug removal rate must be accounted for in determining this interval. For asthmatics with particularly rapid rates, even the sustained-release preparations may have to be taken every 8 hours instead of every 12 to prevent symptoms from breaking through before the next dose. Asthmatics with particularly slow rates can control their symptoms adequately with one dose every 24 hours.

INTERACTIONS WITH OTHER DRUGS

Beta-2-Stimulator

The first type of interaction to consider is the synergistic reaction when theophylline is teamed with a beta-2-stimulator. For the mild asthmatic with only occasional brief wheezing attacks, an inhaled beta-2 bronchodilator may be all that is needed. For almost all other asthma patients, the preference in the United States is for theophylline, instead, as the controlling drug. But if it cannot satisfactorily control the symptoms, a beta-2-stimulator is added. In Europe the philosophy is reversed, with a beta-2-stimulator being the initial drug of choice and theophylline playing the supportive role.

Although there is little hard evidence as to which is the more effective philosophy, it is known—as already indicated—that giving these two asthma drugs together means the effective dose of each can be lowered, which then reduces the risk of side effects. This is particularly helpful when the optimum theophylline dose otherwise needed for maximum bronchodilation is above the nontoxic range.

Drugs Affecting Theophylline's Removal

A different type of drug interaction involving theophylline occurs when another medication that the patient is taking changes theophylline's removal rate. See the earlier section, "Effective Dose Range," for a listing of the kinds of drugs that slow this rate down or speed it up.

Theophylline's Effects on Other Drugs

In two cases, theophylline alters the effect of another drug. *Phenytoin*—an anticonvulsant—seems weakened when it is taken with theophylline. *Lithium*—taken to control manic-depressive psychosis—is eliminated from the patient's system much more quickly. Because researchers are not yet sure whether it is only the initial simultaneous dose(s) or each individual dose that acts so dramatically, lithium blood levels should be monitored regularly whenever a patient is also using a theophylline preparation.

Anticholinergic Drugs

The vagus nerve is the parasympathetic nervous system's pathway to the lungs. It affects airway muscle tone and mucus secretion. When the vagus nerve is stimulated, it releases *acetylcholine*, the cholinergic mediator. This mediator contracts the airway muscle and increases mucus production. Because this whole mechanism involves nerves, its direct effects are termed "neurally" mediated. (Acetylcholine may also act indirectly, causing the mast cells to release their airway-narrowing mediators.)

These cholinergic mediator effects can be stopped by a drug that blocks the action of acetylcholine. *Atropine*, described in the historical survey of asthma treatment, does just that. Atropine inhalation was a standard asthma treatment until the 1930s, when the sudden popularity of the newly available epinephrine pushed it off center stage.

Ipratropium bromide, an atropine derivative, is available as an MDI under the brand name *Atrovent*.

Clinical studies with ipratropium bromide show convincingly that many asthmatics gain significant bronchodilation. Anticholinergic therapy is most effective for asthma triggered by inhaled irritants (such as cold air and cigarette smoke), for asthma that becomes worse during stress, and for asthmatics whose major symptom is coughing. Ipratropium bromide works well with any age patient but is at its best with very young children and with adults over 40. This therapy is least effective in treating the symptoms of allergic asthma.

Side effects are almost nonexistent because very little of the inhaled ipratropium bromide crosses into the blood. The one possible adverse reaction is that this drug can cause bronchoconstriction in a very small number of asthmatics. Unfortunately, anticholinergic therapy has been plagued with the baseless warning that it makes mucus thicker and so more difficult for the patient to clear from his airways. If ipratropium bromide has any effect on mucus, it is to improve clearance.

Ipratropium bromide has been studied in comparison to various beta-stimulators. For many asthmatics, it often provides the same degree of bronchodilation as isoproterenol, terbutaline, albuterol, metaproterenol, and fenoterol. For very young children and older adults, it can be even more effective than the beta-stimulator.

The time span is different, however. One dose of a beta-stimulator takes less than 30 minutes to achieve the maximum amount of bronchodilation, but it only lasts for three to four hours. One dose of the anticholinergic drug takes from 30 minutes to three hours to achieve maximum bronchodilation, but the effects last for four to eight hours.

For some asthmatic patients, combining these two kinds of bronchodilators is more effective than using either one alone. There is slightly more bronchodilation, and one dose lasts far longer. Theophylline and steroids also increase the potency of an anticholinergic drug.

For asthmatics who respond best to anticholinergic therapy, or equally to anticholinergic and beta-stimulating drugs, anticholinergic treatment or a combination of the two could be beneficial for maintenance therapy. When they are used together, the beta-stimulator dosage can be reduced. Combining ipratropium bromide with other commonly used asthma medications may permit those dosages to be lowered also.

Beyond Bronchodilators

The beta-stimulators and theophylline are the mainstays of asthma therapy. These bronchodilators are used almost universally to control mild to moderate cases. Although the anticholinergic bronchodilator ipratropium bromide cannot be used with as many patients, when it is appropriate it equals or surpasses the beta-stimulators and theophylline. But bronchodilators—however basic they are to asthma therapy—are only part of what the pharmaceutic world has to offer.

The effectiveness of sodium cromoglycate—like that of the anticholinergic agents—often equals or surpasses the two common bronchodilators for the smaller patient group in which it is appropriate. Severe asthmatics need corticosteroids. There is also a group of medications (e.g., expectorants and mucolytic agents) that play an auxiliary role rather than directly affecting the course of an asthma attack. All these drugs are discussed in the next chapter.

❧❧ 7 ❧❧

The Rest of the Antiasthma Drugs

This chapter covers the variety of drugs other than bronchodilators that are used in treating asthma. First we examine two kinds of drugs that are often prescribed—the corticosteroids and cromolyn sodium. Then we discuss those drugs that either have not yet been widely accepted in the United States or are still in an experimental stage.

The chapter ends with two peripheral groups of medications. One plays only a minor supportive role, and the other is composed of outdated treatments that should no longer have a place in modern therapy.

Corticosteroids

NATURAL AND SYNTHETIC STEROIDS

Natural corticosteroids—usually simply called steroids—are hormones produced in the body by the outer layers (the cortex) of the adrenal glands, which are located on the kidneys. These hormones are essential to life. They play a critical role in such diverse bodily processes as energy metabolism, kidney function, and the immune system.

The corticosteroids fall into two groups. One of them—called the *glucocorticoids* for their effect on glucose (a kind of sugar) metabolism—has strong antiinflammatory properties. When the word *steroids* is used in relation to asthma, it refers to this particular group of steroids.

Steroid production is controlled by the body's master gland, the pituitary, via its secretion of *ACTH* (adrenocorticotrophic hormone). The pituitary releases ACTH into the bloodstream, which brings it to the adrenal glands. The arrival of ACTH at the adrenal cortex is its signal immediately to manufacture and release steroids. (Their release temporarily stops any further release of ACTH.)

Steroids are produced in their greatest amounts shortly after a person wakes up. They are lowest during sleep, with the lowest production of all usually between 2:00 A.M. and 4:00 A.M. (As we shall see, this diurnal variation must be kept in mind when steroid drugs are prescribed.) The amount of steroids normally produced at any given time of the day or night can be increased by stress.

Soon after the glucocorticoid hormones were synthesized in the laboratory and their dramatic antiinflammatory characteristics identified, they were brought into the treatment of asthma. In the early 1950s, steroids revolutionized life for many asthmatics whose symptoms responded poorly to the other drugs then available. Instead of being incapacitated by their disease, these patients found their symptoms suddenly disappearing and their dependence on other forms of treatment lessening.

But the unexpectedly high price paid for this miracle soon became obvious. The catalogue of far-ranging side effects included many that were extremely serious: poor wound healing, loss of calcium from the bones, severe stomach bleeding, psychosis, and stunted growth in children. The use of steroids in asthma was rejected about 10 years after they were first introduced.

Now the situation has changed again. A deeper and more objective understanding of steroids' therapeutic effects has clearly established them as the most potent antiasthma agents available. They are often capable of preventing or reversing asthma attacks in patients unresponsive to all other medications. New synthetic steroid compounds have been discovered that can be administered by aerosol, which greatly lessens side effects. And advances in our understanding of the body's response to steroids has led to auxiliary techniques that also help minimize side effects.

HOW STEROIDS WORK

Steroids work along two different avenues simultaneously. Their action is rapid by one route and slower by the other. The net effect is that steroids inhibit the release and further formation of the body's inflammatory chemicals (Figure 7.1). The eosinophil white blood cells involved in allergic reactions disappear from the circulation.

Steroids also prevent the initial decrease in beta-receptor sensitivity that otherwise happens when beta-stimulating bronchodilators are used. In addition, some investigators believe that steroids directly relax airway muscle, inhibit bronchoconstricting cholinergic mechanisms, increase mucociliary activity, and decrease mucus production.

USING STEROIDS

Steroids dramatically relieve symptoms for almost all asthmatics. Because of the side effects that must be dealt with, however, steroids should be added to your drug regimen only if the highest tolerable doses of all other available medications cannot control your symptoms adequately. This holds true whether the context is reversing an acute attack or one of preventive maintenance. Even then, they should be discontinued—or at least reduced—as soon as it is appropriate to do so.

When in the day you take your steroid preparation, and how much you take, are extremely important in minimizing an otherwise critical side effect. The natural production of steroids temporarily cuts off the pituitary gland's production of ACTH. Until ACTH starts up again, no further steroids are produced.

EMOTIONS   INFECTIONS

inflammation

STEROIDS

EXERCISE   ALLERGENS

Figure 7.1 How steroids affect an asthma attack. They prevent or reverse an attack by reversing (and preventing more) accompanying inflammation and by restoring beta-2 receptor sensitivity.

Steroid drugs participate in this negative feedback cycle because the pituitary gland does not distinguish between natural and synthetic steroids. When you start taking a steroid drug, the pituitary gland immediately decreases or stops its production of ACTH. This means that the adrenal glands decrease or stop producing steroids. Your body's own source of steroids temporarily dries up, so to speak. But this effect is minimized if your dose schedule is properly dovetailed with your body's natural steroid production rhythm. Taking steroids in the morning—which is the high point of ACTH production—interferes the least with the adrenal glands' natural activity.

Only minor interference occurs when steroid therapy lasts for just a few days, and this disappears rapidly as soon as the drug is stopped. Natural steroid suppression is greater, and lasts longer, as both dose level and length of therapy increase. (No one is sure, however, at exactly what drug dose such suppression begins.) After a relatively short course of steroid medication, it takes about three days for the adrenal glands to resume their normal steroid activity. If steroid treatment lasts for months or years, it may take six months or more before the adrenal glands are functioning normally again.

Because there is always a time gap between ending steroid treatment and the body's resumption of its own steroid production, the drug should never be ended abruptly. It should be tapered off gradually as the adrenal glands slowly regain their capacity to produce the amount of steroids normally needed.

Short-term steroid therapy consists of one dose each morning for 4 to 10 days. If longer treatment is needed, one dose is taken only every other morning. If symptoms start to break through, then a daily morning dose must be tried. If symptoms still reappear between doses, the only other alternative is taking several doses spread over the day. This should be changed to one of the less-frequent schedules as soon as symptom control improves.

Only several days are needed to taper off after a relatively short, low-dose treatment. But as dose and/or duration increase, the tapering-off time becomes proportionately longer.

ADMINISTRATION

Steroids can be taken orally or by injection, or by using an MDI to deliver them directly to the airways. (A method rarely used today involves taking ACTH to stimulate the adrenal glands to produce more steroids. Although this keeps the adrenal glands functioning, the lack of selectiv-

TABLE 9

Corticosteroids Commonly Used in the Treatment of Asthma

Medication	Brand Name
Beclomethasone	Beclovent Inhaler Vanceril Inhaler
Betamethasone	Celestone Tablets Celestone Syrup
Cortisone acetate	Generic (tablets)
Dexamethasone	Decadron Tablets Decadron Elixir Decadron Phosphate Respihaler SK-Dexamethasone Tablets
Flunisolide	AeroBid Inhaler
Hydrocortisone	Generic (tablets) Cortef Tablets Hydrocortone Tablets
Methylprednisolone	Medrol Tablets
Prednisolone	Generic (tablets)
Prednisone	Generic (tablets) Liquid Pred Syrup
Triamcinolone	Aristocort Tablets Aristocort Syrup Kenacort Diacetate Syrup Azmacort Inhaler

ity is a major problem. All the adrenal steroid hormones are increased, not just the glucocorticoids.)

Oral preparations are used far more often than injected steroids (see Table 9). The most common oral steroids are *prednisone, prednisolone,* and *methylprednisolone.* Because prednisone is changed to prednisolone once the body metabolizes it, some experts think that using prednisolone or methylprednisolone to start with makes it easier to predict the blood concentration of this drug that a particular dose will achieve. Methylprednisolone may also have better anti-inflammatory properties than the other two, and it definitely causes less sodium (a salt) retention. A salt increase in the body can raise blood pressure.

Using inhaled steroids dramatically reduces the frequency and severity of side effects. This is in part the nature of the inhaled drug, and in part because inhaled steroids help reduce the need for oral forms of the drug. A full dose of inhaled steroid can be substituted for a low oral dose. This means that asthmatics who need only a low oral dose can often avoid oral steroids completely. Asthmatics who would otherwise need a high dose of oral steroids can take a lower one when they use it along with an inhaled steroid. The only time an inhaled steroid cannot be used is during an acute asthma attack. The airway obstruction existing then prevents the drug from reaching the deeper airways where it needed.

The available inhaled steroid preparations are *beclomethasone dipropionate* (*Vanceril* and *Beclovent*), *triamcinolone acetonide* (*Azmacort*), and *flunisolide* (*AeroBid*). Since an inhaled steroid penetrates into the lungs most effectively if the airways are dilated, it should be used 5 to 15 minutes after an inhaled bronchodilator.

INTERACTIONS WITH OTHER DRUGS

Drugs That Affect Steroids

Certain drugs change the rate at which steroid drugs are removed from the body. Steroids are metabolized more quickly when they are taken together with *barbiturates*, *ephedrine*, and *rifampin* (a type of antibiotic). Steroids are metabolized more slowly when they are used at the same time as *estrogen*, certain other *antibiotics*, and *cromolyn sodium* (although its effect is slight). In another type of effect, *indomethacin* (used in treating arthritis) increases steroids' potential for causing stomach ulcers.

One antibiotic in particular, *troleandomycin*, belongs to a family of antibiotics that increases the effects of a given steroid dose. This was first known in 1970, but troleandomycin received little clinical attention until the early 1980s. There are two groups of asthmatics who benefit from troleandomycin. One is made up of those who—when they use it—can control their disease with significantly lower oral steroid doses than would otherwise be possible for them. Troleandomycin also helps steroid-resistant asthmatics gain therapeutic benefit from steroids. Although troleandomycin's effect on steroid activity is not related to its antibiotic properties, how it does achieve this effect remains a mystery.

Drugs Affected by Steroids

Steroids also affect other drugs. As pointed out earlier, they enhance the action of *beta-stimulating bronchodilators* by preventing the beta-receptors from becoming less sensitive. Diabetic asthmatics should use steroids with caution, because steroids can dangerously reduce the action of the *oral hypoglycemic* medication many diabetics depend on. Taking steroids along with *potassium-depleting diuretics* increases the risk of dangerously lowering the body's potassium level. This in turn also increases the likelihood of toxicity for heart patients taking any of the *cardiac glycosides* (a group of heart medications that includes *digitalis*).

SIDE EFFECTS WITH LONG-TERM USE

The exact nature and degree of these problems are determined by a variety of factors, including each asthmatic's individual biological reaction to steroids, the particular steroid preparation used, dose size and schedule, and the use—or lack—of measures to counter specific effects.

The single most important side effect of inhaled steroids is thrush, which is a yeast infection in the mouth. It has occurred in up to 77 percent of oral steroid users. Large doses, diabetes, poor dental hygiene, and the simultaneous use of antibiotics all increase this risk. It is extremely important to gargle and rinse your mouth carefully with water after each inhaled dose.

The milder negative effects from all systemic steroids (referring to oral or injected preparations, because they travel throughout the body system) include increased appetite, some facial bloating, and acne. Moderate effects include leg cramps, insomnia, headaches, and unexplained mood changes.

The group of serious side effects includes such hazards as juvenile growth retardation (minimized by alternate-day doses); skeletal muscle weakness (which responds to exercise); poor wound healing (countered by meticulous wound care plus vitamin A supplements); poor control of diabetes (countered by increasing the insulin or oral hypoglycemic agent); suppressed adrenal glands (countered by increasing steroid doses during stress); weakened immune response (countered by meticulous surveillance for infection); potassium loss (countered with potassium supplements); and calcium loss from bones (minimized with calcium-plus-vitamin D supplements and exercise). People who are susceptible to diabetes are at increased risk of developing this disease.

The most serious side effects—stomach ulcers, gastric hemorrhage, intestinal tears, pancreatitis, cataracts, high blood pressure, and psychosis—all require more sophisticated medical attention. Asthmatics who already suffer from any of these conditions should completely avoid steroid drugs if at all possible. If steroids must be used, an inhaled preparation is preferable when possible.

Some experts believe that asthmatics who have had tuberculosis run a further risk when they are on long-term steroid therapy. Because their immune system has been weakened by the steroids, the tuberculosis may recur. Rather than take this chance, these experts suggest, such patients should use antituberculosis medication along with steroids.

Cromolyn Sodium

Cromolyn sodium's action is unique among the antiasthma drugs. It is not a bronchodilator. It does not block the production of mast cell mediators, nor does it counter their inflammatory effects. Cromolyn sodium specifically pre-

EMOTIONS   **INFECTIONS**

EXERCISE   **ALLERGENS**

Figure 7.2 How cromolyn sodium works. This drug prevents asthma attacks in part by preventing mast cell degranulation, which means that the mast cells cannot release any chemical mediators.

vents the release of mast cell mediators that have already been formed (Figure 7.2). And it works in other ways to control neurally mediated asthma and nonspecific bronchial hyperreactivity.

Cromolyn sodium—in contrast to steroids—is meant for long-term prophylactic (i.e., preventive) use. Its success has been solidly documented in several areas. Actual physiological improvement has been measured in all age groups of allergic asthma and nonallergic asthma patients. Cromolyn sodium is also effective with many types of asthma

mediated by neural reflex (including occupational asthma
due to toluene diisocyanate and to Western red cedar);
nonspecific bronchial hyperreactivity (e.g., bronchospasm
due to exercise); and day-night swings in airway reactivity.

(Cromolyn sodium also effectively treats rhinitis, an inflammation of the mucous lining of the nose that frequently coexists with asthma. Asthmatics whose rhinitis
has been relieved find their asthma easier to deal with.)

No other asthma drug to date reduces bronchial reactivity to such a broad range of asthma triggers. And reducing
nonspecific bronchial reactivity—another unique aspect of
cromolyn sodium's usefulness—is one of its most important pluses. The degree of an asthmatic's general bronchial
hyperreactivity is strongly correlated to the clinical severity of his disease. In fact, it may even determine the severity. As bronchial hyperreactivity diminishes, the asthma
becomes less severe. Once this happens, the disease may
become more easily managed with other drugs.

Cromolyn sodium's clinical advantages would seem to
make it the obvious first choice for treating moderate and
severe asthma. Its acceptance by physicians as a first-
choice antiasthma drug, however, has been slow. Cromolyn sodium has been available in the United States since
1975. Yet theophylline therapy is still commonly tried first,
with cromolyn sodium held in the wings as an alternative
if theophylline proves unsatisfactory. But in the United
Kingdom and elsewhere, cromolyn sodium is regarded as
a first-choice treatment.

Several myths arising in the United States have sparked
much of this reluctance to use cromolyn sodium: cromolyn sodium works only with allergic asthma; cromolyn sodium works only in young asthmatics; cromolyn sodium
is less effective than theophylline and should be used only
for asthmatics with severe symptoms that no longer respond to anything else. But sufficient data are available to
refute all these myths.

Well-designed and -conducted studies prove cromolyn
sodium's long-term effectiveness in at least 65 percent of
adult and juvenile patients. There is no evidence of this

drug being more effective against allergic asthma than against the other kinds. At least five excellent studies comparing cromolyn sodium and theophylline show similar profiles of clinical effectiveness, and both American and British investigations of steroid-dependent asthmatics find that almost half of them are able to give up steroids completely or reduce the dose to a minimum after they begin taking cromolyn sodium!

Awareness of such data should, we hope, grow and help cromolyn sodium attain full acceptance as a first-choice asthma drug. Then more of the asthmatics in this country will be able to enjoy its better benefit-to-risk ratio compared to theophylline, its fewer side effects compared to theophylline and steroids, and the long-term advantages of lessened overall airway hyperreactivity.

HOW CROMOLYN SODIUM WORKS

Intensive effort is being devoted to figuring out how cromolyn sodium prevents mast cells from releasing the mediators that cause allergic and nonallergic inflammatory reactions. There is no answer yet, just hypotheses that attempt a logical explanation for what scientist have so far observed. The most promising of these hypotheses involves calcium "gating": cromolyn sodium seems to affect the way calcium enters and leaves the mast cells.

Cromolyn sodium's ability to control asthma symptoms due to the variety of nonallergic triggers is known to be independent of its mast cell action. But again, explanations for how this happens are just educated speculation. By preventing neurally mediated airway muscle spasm—as occurs in occupational asthma—it may stop airway irritant receptors from becoming excited. By controlling nonspecific bronchial hyperreactivity—particularly striking in its clear-cut prevention of the asthma response to exercise—it may directly affect the airway muscle.

The overall clinical improvement after therapy with cromolyn sodium may be due to the cumulative, combined effects of the long-term prevention of mast cell mediator release, the blocking of airway irritant receptors, and the effects on airway muscle.

SIDE EFFECTS

Cromolyn sodium appears to be one of the safest drugs available. One study reported side effects in only 2 percent of the asthmatics taking this drug; most were minor, including throat irritation, hoarseness, dry mouth, acute cough, and a sensation of chest tightness or an actual bronchospasm. These last two side effects can usually be prevented by inhaling a beta-stimulating bronchodilator before taking cromolyn sodium. Nausea, vomiting, and facial and skin rashes have also occurred, as has nasal congestion appearing several weeks after starting cromolyn sodium therapy. A few rare cases of pneumonia-like complications have been reported.

Cromolyn sodium is eventually inactivated by the liver and then removed from the system by the kidneys for excretion in the urine. The drug manufacturer suggests that asthmatics with a liver or kidney problem should not use this medication because it would not be metabolized and removed quickly enough, and the additional work could further harm the already weakened liver or kidneys. Other than this, there are no limitations as to asthmatics who can safely use cromolyn sodium.

ADMINISTRATION

Cromolyn sodium is not absorbed well from the gastrointestinal tract because it dissolves poorly in fats, so oral preparations are useless. The drug is available primarily as an inhalable white powder. In the United States it is sold under the brand name *Intal* (manufactured by Fisons), and in Europe it is called *Lomudal*. Although the effective duration of one drug dose was initially thought to be only four to six hours, recent evidence indicates that it is much longer lasting.

The powder was designed to be inhaled through a special apparatus called the Spinhaler. The manufacturers claim that 50 percent of the powder will reach the airways if the user's inspiration is adequately forceful. Studies by others show that a patient's breath must also be held for 10 seconds immediately after this forceful inspiration. A less-than-forceful inspiration, or not following the breath-holding instructions, lowers the amount of drug inhaled. Incomplete or incorrect usage instructions appear to be the primary cause of patients' difficulty in using this powder.

A nebulized liquid solution of cromolyn sodium was recently approved by the FDA. This was followed first by an MDI that aerosolized this solution for nasal use, then—in spring 1986—by an MDI for oral use. All three liquid preparations are marketed as *Intal* in the United States, and as *Lomudal* in Europe. The nebulized solution is especially useful for very young children, and for adult asthmatics who cannot coordinate use of the MDI and cannot tolerate the inhaled powder because of an unusually sensitive cough reflex.

Optimal effects from cromolyn sodium can be expected if some simple guidelines are followed.

- Learn to use the Spinhaler or MDI properly.

- Do not skip a dose, especially during the first few weeks.

- Do not stop taking the medicine if you feel no difference after 1 or 2 weeks, but call your doctor about increasing your dose. Give it an honest try for 8 to 12 weeks before you and your doctor decide if this drug is worth your while (and expense).

- If you are going to exercise, take the drug 15 minutes beforehand. If you are going to visit a friend who has an animal you are allergic to, take the drug 30 minutes before you expect to arrive.

DRUG INTERACTIONS

We have found no evidence in the literature of negative drug interactions involving cromolyn sodium.

THE FUTURE

It was inevitable that the pharmaceutical industry would try to synthesize oral drugs combining cromolyn sodium's basic characteristics with greater potency. There have been a number of experimental attempts to date, such as cinnamoyl, anthranilic acid, M&B compound 22948, and ketotifen. But with the possible exception of ketotifen, these new synthetic drugs appear to be more active in the test tube than in humans!

Ketotifen

Ketotifen's one advantage over cromolyn sodium is that it can be taken orally. It is the first oral antiasthma agent intended for preventive use that is not primarily a bronchodilator. Unfortunately, this drug is not currently available in the United States. It is still in the midst of clinical testing.

Ketotifen has proved to be an adequate preventive drug in about 75 percent of the asthmatics tested, regardless of the asthma trigger. It is most effective, however, in reducing the frequency and intensity of allergic asthma attacks. Although this drug is more effective for children than for adults, a child needs an adult dose level to experience the maximum effect. All asthmatics who start on ketotifen must wait 4 to 12 weeks before it attains full effectiveness.

Since the first long-term clinical studies on ketotifen's effectiveness were done abroad, similar work has been carried out in many additional countries (except the United States). They all confirm this new drug's prophylactic capacity, plus its ability to block the allergic response (probably by reducing the amount of calcium in mast cells). As with cromolyn sodium, both bronchodilator and steroid therapy can gradually be reduced.

The only side effect to mention is sleepiness, which wears off after the first two weeks on this drug. It occurs with only 10 to 15 percent of the adults using ketotifen, and far less often with children. If sleepiness appears, it can be lessened substantially by first reducing the dose, then increasing it slowly over two weeks.

Calcium Antagonists

Calcium ions are important regulators of a diverse variety of physiological functions. Some of these are involved in producing asthma symptoms: airway muscle contraction; mast cell mediator release; mediator release from the white blood cells collecting in the airways during an attack; mucous gland secretion; and vagus nerve activity (providing the neural pathway for bronchoconstriction).

None of these can happen unless free calcium ions increase in number inside the particular cells. Normally, there are about ten thousand times more calcium ions outside the cells than inside. When the cell is stimulated to do its job of contraction or secretion, the amount of inside calcium increases about one hundred times. Some of this extra calcium enters from the outside through special calcium channels, and some of it is internally freed from the cell's own membrane.

A new direction in asthma treatment research has focused on directly preventing this buildup of calcium ions within the relevant cells, which would then prevent the asthma attack. Success in developing medication to do this would result in the most effective antiasthma drugs possible.

The older existing drugs—the beta-2-stimulators and theophylline—work inside the cell to prevent its membrane from freeing calcium ions. Cromolyn sodium is different.

It stops outside calcium ions from entering the cell after an asthmatic is exposed to an allergic trigger (although no one knows how this happens).

The new drugs now being created and tested directly block the cells' calcium entry channels. The first successes were actually achieved in another medical area, when calcium blockers dilated the heart's arteries to stop the pain (called angina) caused by inadequate blood flow to the heart. Using calcium blockers for asthma is so recent that the *Physicians' Desk Reference* (PDR)—for which drug manufacturers provide detailed information on all prescription drugs approved for use in the United States—has not yet included this use in its descriptions of *verapamil* and *nifedipine*, currently the two most popular calcium blockers.

Clinical testing of calcium blockers' ability to prevent asthma attacks shows significant action against bronchospasm caused by exercise, cold air, and allergic triggers, but not every study has had the same degree of success. Some studies also show calcium blockers to have a direct bronchodilating effect, but others do not.

Although this approach is obviously promising, the current calcium blockers will not be the dreamed-of breakthrough in asthma treatment. Most likely, selective calcium blockers will be synthesized for airway muscle cells and possibly also for the other kinds of cells that participate in producing the multiplicity of asthma symptoms.

The current calcium blockers, however, are proving invaluable in treating the asthmatic who also has heart disease that ideally requires a beta-blocking drug. A beta-blocker can be disastrous for the asthma, and a beta-stimulator can be disastrous for the heart condition. The calcium blocker is good for both.

Antihistaminic Drugs

Histamine is a mediator found in all body tissues, but especially in mast cells. The lungs hold the greatest concentration of histamine, which stimulates H_1 receptors there. (There are two species of histamine receptors, H_1 and H_2.)

Several pieces of evidence emphatically suggest that histamine has a prominent role in asthmatic bronchospasm: histamine is a potent bronchoconstrictor; the mast cells release histamine during an allergic challenge; asthmatics are abnormally sensitive to inhaled histamine; and drugs that block the H_1 receptors also prevent bronchospasm when histamine is inhaled. Based on this, scientists expected these same drugs to be highly successful in controlling asthma symptoms and preventing further attacks.

But that has not been the case. The several theoretical explanations for antihistamines' ineffectiveness in asthma all point to the same problem—getting the drug to the right place in high enough doses to block (or antagonize) the H_1 receptors sufficiently. And high doses of the older antihistamines have unacceptable side effects. New, more potent compounds have milder side effects but are also disappointing in preventing bronchoconstriction.

So, except for the asthmatic with rhinitis (which responds very well to the H_1-selective antihistamines), the role of these drugs in antiasthma maintenance or preventive therapy appears very limited.

Nonsteroidal Anti-inflammatory Drugs

The same kind of thinking that suggested antihistamines for asthma treatment also focused on nonsteroidal anti-inflammatory drugs because they inhibit prostaglandin formation. Among this group of drugs are aspirin, indomethacin, ibuprofen, and ketoprofen. (A more complete list is in Tables 4 and 5.) But clinical evidence indicates that most asthmatic patients are unaffected by them, up to 25 percent find their asthma seriously aggravated by these anti-inflammatory drugs, and less than 1 percent seem to improve.

Coping with Mucus: An Auxiliary Role

A heavy flow of thick bronchial mucus often accompanies bronchospasm. Not only are the narrowed bronchi more easily blocked by this mucus, but the less forceful expiratory airflow makes coughing less effective in bringing mucus up. Drugs that make this mucus easier to bring up are a big help during an asthma attack. Over the years, a large number of pharmacologic agents have been used to cope with this outpouring of thick mucus. They are *mucokinetic drugs*. The entire process of easing the mucus-clearing difficulty is called *mucokinesis*.

Several kinds of antiasthma drugs that have already been discussed are also somewhat mucokinetic: the beta-2-stimulators, theophylline, the glucocorticoid steroids, and the anticholinergic drugs. Seven other kinds of drugs are devoted exclusively—with greater and lesser success—to mucokinesis.

1. *Antibiotics*. Mucus becomes thicker and stickier (more viscous) during an infection. Because antibiotics fight infection, they ensure a mucus that is less viscous and therefore more easily cleared from the airways.

2. *Diluents*. Diluents work on the theory that increasing the water content of mucus—hydrating it—makes it less viscous. Hydration is a wise precaution for the asthmatic. Some diluents, such as water or a salt solution, can be administered directly into the airways with a nebulizer.

3. *Surfactants*. Surfactants act as a detergent or wetting

agent, somewhat like dishwashing soap. Soap weakens the sticky hold of fats and food adhering to dirty dishes. Surfactants weaken the sticky hold of mucus adhering to the airway walls. *Sodium bicarbonate*, a popular surfactant, is delivered directly to the airways via aerosol.

4. *Bronchomucotropics*. Bronchomucotropics increase both the amount of mucus and the amount of respiratory tract fluid that is secreted. Familiar examples are eucalyptus and menthol, the aromatic inhalants found in Vicks VapoRub. Although these products have an amazingly large following, there is no proof of their effectiveness. But since they have not been disproven either, we should not automatically equate lack of proof with lack of value. Any asthmatic who finds bronchomucotropics useful should not be dissuaded from using them.

5. *Mucolytics*. These agents make mucus less viscous by breaking down the mucus molecules. The most effective mucolytics are the amino acid *L-cysteine* and its derivative, *acetylcysteine*. This derivative is marketed in the United States as *Mucomyst*, and elsewhere as *Airbron*, *Mucolyticum*, and *Nac*. Because the solution smells like a cross between rotting eggs and burning hair, the aerosol may be so irritating that it actually causes a bronchospasm.

In the United States, enzymes—particularly *dornase*—have also been used to break down mucus molecules. Enzymes once had many proponents, but their value in treating asthma has never been satisfactorily demonstrated.

6. *Expectorants*. Expectorants are taken by mouth to produce a greater amount of mucus of a consistency that can be coughed up more easily. Although expectorants were the mainstay of the nineteenth-century version of asthma therapy, there has been little hard evidence—until recently—that these drugs actually do increase an easily cleared mucus. The most effective expectorants may combine the characteristics of the bronchomucotropics and the mucolytics. This list of expectorants includes *iodide, ter-*

pin hydrate, and various salts, herbs, and plant derivatives.

7. *Mucoregulators*. Mucoregulators alter the action of the mucous glands so that they produce less viscous mucus. (These drugs may also affect the airways directly to reduce bronchospasm.) Many of the herbs and plants used in folk medicine have been studied in this context.

One derivative makes mucus less viscous by apparently causing the glands to produce mucus with smaller molecules. Although this drug—*bromhexine*, sold in Europe as *Bisolvon*—has not yet been studied extensively in relation to asthma, its potential value is doubtful. Variations of this derivative may prove more potent. S-carboxymethylcysteine—a derivative of L-cysteine—has been intensely studied as a mucoregulator. Results so far are contradictory as to its effectiveness.

MISCELLANEOUS MUCOKINETIC AGENTS

Many items have been tried over the years in the search for a good mucokinetic agent. Some continue in use although there is little, if any, proof of their effectiveness. Some run more risks than benefits, and many others have long ago fallen by the wayside.

Two items from Grandma's pharmacopoeia are still successful after hundreds of years. One is *garlic*. Folk tradition considers this potent herb of great value in treating asthma and bronchitis. Many formal pharmacopoeias throughout the world list garlic among the expectorants.

The primary component of garlic is the nonodoriferous compound alliin (S-allyl-L-cysteine sulfoxide). When garlic is crushed, an enzyme breaks down the alliin into allicin, the aroma we all know. Interestingly, the alliin molecule bears a remarkable resemblance to S-carboxymethylcysteine. Similar molecules exist in horseradish, radishes, onions, hot peppers, and mustard, all edibles that stimulate respiratory mucus production. Garlic, and other pungent herbs and spices, may act by stimulating mucus-producing vagus nerve reflexes. The odoriferous component of garlic obviously leaves the body via the lungs, where it may have a local bronchomucoregulatory effect.

The second item—*hot chicken soup*—was first prescribed in writing centuries ago by Maimonides. His twelfth-century *Treatise on Asthma* contained his humble apology for not being able to cure the disease, plus his suggestion that "the soup of fat hens is [an] effective remedy." Chicken soup (also known as "Jewish penicillin" and "Bohbemycetin") is a potent mucociliary stimulant. It is reasonable to regard a pungent, peppery, garlic-laden chicken broth to be the ultimate in mucokinesis. This is obviously the standard to which all potential candidates for the honor must be compared.

Outdated Treatments

GOLD

Gold has been assigned magical healing powers for many centuries. Modern-day gold therapy began in the late nineteenth century after Robert Koch, who had discovered the bacterium that causes tuberculosis, learned that gold cyanide stopped this bacterium's growth. Then gold was used to treat tuberculosis plus other ailments—including asthma—that were believed to result from infection. Arthritis, although mistakenly considered an infectious disease, was one of the few conditions that responded well to gold treatments.

In the 1930s, gold was found to be useless in treating tuberculosis. It was also dropped then as an asthma treatment, even though there were isolated reports of benefits. Gold therapy for asthma has been largely forgotten except in Japan, where it has remained part of the standard treatment for the last 50 years.

Gold has many physiological actions. Those relevant to asthma treatment are its ability to suppress the immune response and its anti-inflammatory action. But even more important than the lack of good clincial studies assessing possible asthma benefits is the long list of serious side effects. These include bone marrow toxicity, blood loss through the urine, and "gold lung," characterized by dyspnea, cough, and diminished lung function. Gold therapy should never be considered for asthma.

ALCOHOL

Alcohol has also been around for quite a while as an asthma treatment. In 1863, Dr. Henry Hyde Salter published the cases of three asthmatic patients whose bronchospasms could be relieved only by drinking large amounts of hot "spirits" (i.e., Scotch whiskey, gin, and brandy). Yet Salter also carefully warned of the dangers of depending on alcohol for asthma therapy.

Despite the poorly done studies of alcohol as an antiasthma agent, there is some evidence suggesting that it can produce short-lived bronchodilation in some patients. But the problems of chronic alcohol use far outweigh any possible benefit, and these patients would find equal or greater symptom relief from the less risky therapies available.

Afterthought

In writing this chapter, we frequently found ourselves noting that a particular antiasthma drug was "not available in the United States." You may have been wondering why the rest of the world has so many more effective drugs for treating asthma than we do. There are two reasons.

One is the aftermath of the frightening discovery in the late 1950s that a sudden—and large—number of severely deformed infants were all born of mothers who had used the new sedative thalidomide early in their pregnancies. The FDA responded to the loud public and congressional outcry by clamping down on the testing requirements new drugs have to meet. These rules—now the world's most

rigorous—translate into at least five years of clinical testing before a new drug can be marketed. Although this
stringency minimizes the public's risk of using a drug with
serious side effects, it also means that needy patients will,
for a fairly lengthy time, be denied a drug that is both
effective and safe. A prime example for the asthmatic is
albuterol, which was available in both Europe and Canada
for 10 years before it was approved here.

The second factor is the physician's natural conserva-
tism. It takes most doctors a relatively long time to switch
from a known drug that they are comfortable prescribing
to one with whose dosages and side effects they are unfa-
miliar. Cromolyn sodium is a star example. This excellent
medication is still not prescribed with anywhere near the
frequency one would expect, even though it has been
available in the United States since 1975.

✴✴ 8 ✴✴

Asthma and . . .

When cardiovascular disease and/or diabetes coexist with asthma, asthma treatment becomes much more complex. It is essential that all the doctors treating such a patient be especially knowledgeable about how antiasthma drugs affect the other disease(s), and how diabetic and/or cardiovascular medications affect asthma.

When more than one chronic condition requires treatment, the rule of thumb is that the most threatening one receives priority in terms of medication chosen. Beyond this, the drugs selected to control the other problem(s) must not aggravate this most critical one. Fortunately for the asthmatic, there are various points along the symptom-producing pathway that respond to existing antiasthma drugs. This range provides a variety of drug combination choices for the safe and effective pharmacologic treatment of these complex situations.

We repeat that it is not our intention to dictate the "right" drug combinations, but rather to explain the basic principles that a knowledgeable physician uses in making such a treatment decision.

Cardiovascular Disease

The term *cardiovascular disease* actually refers to several different problems involving the heart and circulatory system.

- In *congestive heart failure*, the heart—which is a highly specialized muscle—has become too weak to pump blood adequately.

- In *ischemic heart disease* (also called *coronary insufficiency*), the arteries providing oxygen-rich blood to this specialized muscle have become so narrowed by deposits (called plaque) that the heart cannot get as much oxygen as it needs. *Arteriosclerosis* and *atherosclerosis* are common terms for this condition.

- *Hypertension* is high blood pressure, which refers to the force with which the blood pushes through the arteries as it is pumped through the circulatory system. Several different problems can cause hypertension, and sometimes the cause cannot be identified.

- *Cardiac arrhythmia* is malfunction of the heart's electrical activity, with disruption of the electrical signal that coordinates and paces its pumping action. This can make the pumping action of the heart less effective.

When asthma coexists with one of the cardiovascular diseases, asthma drug therapy must meet two additional goals beyond providing effective asthma control. Most important is that the process of establishing this control must not aggravate the heart condition. This means no anti-asthma medication is used that would make the heart work harder or disturb its electrical activity. The second goal is to choose drugs, when possible, with a direct or side effect that actually helps the heart. An example follows.

An asthmatic patient with chronic congestive heart failure suddenly becomes wheezy and much shorter of breath than usual. The medication problem is that both symptoms can result from either of these diseases. (In fact, cardiac symptoms can mimic asthma to such a degree that the term *cardiac asthma* was popular in medical literature until fairly recently.) Before prescribing treatment, the patient's doctor first must determine whether the asthma or the heart failure is the cause. Sometimes the only recourse is trial and error. The doctor might temporarily prescribe a diuretic, which—because it removes water from the body—reduces the heart's work. If the wheezing and dyspnea immediately improve, the patient's heart problem was probably causing them. In this case a theophylline preparation would be appropriate. In addition to its main effect of bronchodilation, its side effects include diuretic action (making the body get rid of fluid) and making the heart beat more strongly.

HOW CARDIOVASCULAR DRUGS AFFECT ASTHMA

Negative Effects

One treatment of choice for cardiovascular disease is a *beta-adrenergic blocking agent* (e.g., *propranolol, nadolol, timolol*). Although drugs that block the beta-1-receptors in the heart are good for cardiac problems, they can affect asthma adversely, particularly those that also block airway beta-2-receptors. Ideally, beta-blockers should not be given to asthmatics. If a beta-blocker must be used, it should be one of those more selective for beta-1-receptors (e.g., *metoprolol, atenolol*).

Drugs that mimic the effect of *acetylcholine*—the mediator causing bronchoconstriction when the vagus nerve is stimulated—are sometimes given to stop the heart from racing. The problem for asthma is that these drugs sometimes cause bronchospasms. But drugs with the opposite (that is, anticholinergic) effects, such as *disopyramide*—which are given to prevent arrhythmias—can cause bronchial secretions to dry and accumulate. They are best avoided as well.

Aspirin, which acts to reduce blood clotting, can trigger an attack in the susceptible asthmatic.

Positive Effects

Some drugs used to treat cardiovascular disease can also be used to treat asthma, because they cause bronchodilation. *Calcium channel blockers*, which effectively prevent bronchospasm, are also useful in treating both angina pectoris (the chest pain occurring when insufficient oxygen reaches the heart) and high blood pressure.

Nitrates (e.g., *nitroglycerine*), which are potent blood vessel dilators, are also used to alleviate angina pain. In the early 1800s their general dilation effects brought them into use for asthma treatment. Asthma patients would burn nitrite paper and inhale the smoke for bronchospasm relief. (Nitrates and nitrites both derive from nitrogen-containing salts.) Although the nitroglycerine doses used in angina do not cause bronchodilation, at least this drug cannot worsen asthma.

HOW ASTHMA AFFECTS THE HEART

Asthma attacks stress the cardiovascular system, increasing the heart's work load. Heart rate goes up from two different effects of asthma attacks: anxiety, and the respiratory muscles' greater oxygen demands. Asthma attacks are also associated with more frequent *premature ventricular contractions*, in which the heart's ventricles—the two large chambers that propel blood to the lungs and to the rest of the body—are contracting out of their normal sequence. Severe asthma often changes the heart's normal electrical pattern even in people with no signs of heart disease. And we have previously mentioned pulsus paradoxus, the rapid blood pressure swings that can occur with a severe attack.

These cardiovascular stresses can become proportionately more dangerous when the heart's oxygen supply has been reduced by a combination of asthma and ischemic heart disease. It can be hazardous, therefore, to withhold asthma medication, or to use ineffective doses, through the misplaced fear of harmful cardiac side effects.

HOW ANTIASTHMA DRUGS AFFECT THE HEART

Adrenergic Stimulators

Both *epinephrine* and *ephedrine* have been used to treat bronchial asthma. Because these drugs nonselectively stimulate alpha- and beta-receptors, they constrict blood vessels. This in turn increases blood pressure, heart rate, and the force of the heart's contractions. Because of this substantial increase in the heart's work load, these drugs are contraindicated—meaning they should not be used— for patients with any kind of cardiovascular problem.

A slightly better choice would be *isoproterenol*, which stimulates beta-receptors only (although nonselectively). Better still are the beta-2-selective drugs: *terbutaline, salbutamol (albuterol), fenoterol,* and *metaproterenol.* Not only do they have relatively fewer beta-1 effects, but their vasodilation side effect lowers blood pressure. This makes them a particularly effective and appropriate choice for the asthmatic with high blood pressure.

Theophyllines

Theophylline and its derivatives are well known both for their potent cardiovascular and central nervous system side effects, and for their narrow therapeutic range (there is little ground between the minimally effective and toxic levels). Both these characteristics require particular caution if a theophylline preparation must be used to treat an asthmatic who has a cardiovascular problem.

Considerable care must be taken to ensure the lowest dose that is still effective for the asthma so that cardiovascular side effects are avoided as much as possible. Because some heart conditions—such as congestive heart failure—can dramatically slow the rate at which theophylline is metabolized, blood theophylline levels must be monitored even more frequently than in uncomplicated asthmatics. Toxic levels of theophylline are associated with—among other things—rapid heart rate and arrhythmias.

Anticholinergic Agents

Western physicians have used anticholinergic drugs (*atropine* is the best known) to treat asthma for about two hundred years, although they are not currently among the more common medical choices. Recent advances, however, in understanding the effects of acetylcholine in the lungs have rekindled interest in the drugs that control these effects. This is to the immense benefit of those asthmatics who also suffer from cardiovascular problems.

Ipratropium Bromide

This derivative of the parent drug *atropine* is a relatively specific bronchodilator. And it is remarkably free of side effects because it is poorly absorbed across the airways. Beyond this, when ipratropium bromide is combined with beta-2-agonists or theophyllines, the effects of the two different antiasthma drugs are either additive (the total effect equals the effect of one plus the effect of the other) or synergistic (the total is even greater, because each intensifies the effects of the other). So adding ipratropium bromide usually permits reducing the other drug dosage.

Cromolyn Sodium

The many virtues of this drug were described in Chapter 7. Its benefits plus its lack of side effects make it a drug of choice in treating asthmatics with cardiovascular disease. Remember, however, that cromolyn sodium is a prophylactic drug only. It has no role in treating an asthmatic attack once it develops.

Steroids

Steroids, as discussed in Chapter 7, can be lifesaving for the patient with severe asthma. There is an unavoidable side effect, however, that is potentially dangerous in the presence of cardiovascular disease. Steroids increase the amount of salt retained in the body, which causes water retention, which then raises blood pressure. Of the oral steroids, methylprednisolone causes the least salt retention. When possible, inhaled steroids should be substituted for the oral drug to reduce these side effects still further. In either case blood pressure must be regularly monitored, with careful adjustment of both diuretic and blood pressure-reducing medication.

For some patients, an aerosolized bronchodilator plus a steroid can be a reasonable alternative to a theophylline-plus-beta-stimulator combination, as long as blood pressure increases can be prevented.

SUMMARY

When a patient has both asthma and a complicating cardiovascular problem, cromolyn sodium is a reasonable first-choice medication. If more active bronchodilation is needed, ipratropium bromide is helpful and has no negative cardiovascular side effects. Either drug can be augmented by an aerosolized beta-2-selective drug such as salbutamol. For the asthmatic whose cardiac problem—such as high blood pressure—does not involve arrhythmias, theophylline can be added to the menu. If theophylline is contraindicated, but the other nonsteroid medications cannot control the asthma adequately, then an inhaled steroid should be considered. When oral steroids cannot be avoided, special monitoring and therapeutic attention must be given to water retention and resulting blood pressure changes.

Diabetes

When an asthmatic has diabetes as well, his doctor must consider a few essential issues when choosing an appropriate antiasthma medicine. For all such patients, the physician must know which antiasthma drugs affect the body's release of stored sugar and its metabolism of sugar in general. For diabetics whose disease has affected their autonomic nervous system, the doctor must know what the implications of this are for asthma, and which antiasthma drugs may worsen this impairment.

Also, diabetics are much more susceptible to all sorts of infections. The diabetic asthmatic, then, needs aggressive surveillance by clinical examination, laboratory tests, and X-rays. Intervention should start immediately when a beginning infection is indicated.

HOW ASTHMA DRUGS CAN AFFECT SUGAR METABOLISM

Creating a *glucose* (sugar) imbalance in the diabetic asthmatic is a particular worry when *steroids* must be used to treat the asthma. Glucose is the body's primary energy source. The presence of insulin allows cells to take in the glucose they need. Then the cells use oxygen to burn—or metabolize—this sugar to produce their energy. Because diabetics do not produce the amount of insulin needed to allow their cells to take in enough glucose, they must take supplemental insulin (or a related drug).

One effect of *gluco*corticoids—the group of antiasthma steroids—is to increase the amount of glucose in the blood while also disrupting the cells' ability to take in sugar. In addition, steroids promote the breakdown of proteins within each cell as a substitute energy fuel. So the blood is flooded with excess sugar, while the cells are burning protein for energy because so little of this sugar is available to them.

When a diabetic asthmatic must take steroids for his

asthma, these side effects can be somewhat reduced by using large doses of aerosolized steroids instead of smaller oral doses. This, however, produces its own set of problems. Oral yeast infections and loss of voice are frequently troublesome with high inhaled doses. The use of a spacer between canister and mouth can reduce the amount of steroid deposited in the mouth, which may diminish these difficulties. Also helpful are the prophylactic use of antifungal medication (such as oral *nystatin*), plus fastidious oral hygiene (brushing teeth and, especially rinsing the mouth) after each use of an inhaled steroid. Although inhaled steroids reduce the diabetes-promoting problem somewhat, they by no means make it disappear. So the primary countermeasure must be an increase in the diabetic asthmatic's antidiabetic medication.

Adrenergic drugs of the beta-2-selective group also increase the amount of glucose in the blood, especially when they are given orally. Even when these drugs are used in aerosolized form, the diabetic asthmatic must pay greater attention to monitoring his glucose level.

ANTIASTHMA DRUGS AND AUTONOMIC DYSFUNCTION

The autonomic nervous system in diabetics can develop problems related to heart rate, blood pressure regulation, urination, and male sexual function. In theory, vagal nerve (part of the autonomic nervous system, and an asthma pathway) dysfunction could improve asthma by removing this pathway. In reality, asthmatics with this loss of autonomic control appear to have a greater chance of respiratory failure. Laboratory studies of asthmatics with this problem have shown that when their oxygen level falls, they fail to increase their rate and/or depth of breathing to compensate. This becomes a critical concern during an acute asthma episode. That is why diabetic asthmatics with autonomic nervous system impairment are more likely to be given supplemental oxygen and have their blood gases monitored.

Both the beta-2-stimulators and the theophyllines improve the ventilatory response to falling oxygen and increasing carbon dioxide. In theory, these drugs would appear to be especially appropriate for this subgroup of diabetic asthmatics. We are unaware, however, of any scientific work indicating whether they actually are particularly helpful. It is known that beta-2-stimulators must be given cautiously with these patients to prevent a rapid, uncontrolled drop in blood pressure.

CONCLUSION

The order of medication preference for the diabetic asthmatic is the same as that followed for the asthmatic with cardiovascular disease. First choice is typically cromolyn sodium, then ipratropium bromide (if available), then inhaled beta-2-stimulators. Next in line are the theophyllines (with careful monitoring), then aerosol steroids and—only if they cannot be avoided—oral steroids.

Asthma Emergencies

An asthma emergency is an asthma attack that is severe enough to need emergency room (ER in hospital lingo) help. Only a small fraction of the estimated 10 million asthmatics in the United States ever have such a severe attack, but we advise *every* asthmatic—and the person who would most likely accompany him to the emergency room in such an event—to read this chapter. Do not skip over this information because you think you will probably never need it. Remember that asthma can be unpredictable. Spare yourself the highly unpleasant possibility of needing it in the future—and not having it.

First, Try to Avoid the Emergency Room

Although emergency care is invaluable, it is even better not to need it in the first place. That means doing your best to prevent a severe asthma attack. Central to this is avoiding any laziness in keeping to your medication schedule.

In addition, you, your family, and your physician should

TABLE 10

Some Commonly Used Asthma Medicines in the United States and
Their European Equivalents

U.S. Name	Brand	Equivalent Name	Brand
Beta-2-Stimulators			
Albuterol	Ventolin Proventil	Salbutamol	Ventolin
Isoproterenol	Isuprel	Isoprenalin	Medihaler-Iso
Metaproterenol	Alupent	Orciprenalin	Alupent
Terbutaline	Bricanyl	Terbutaline	Bricalin
Theophylline			
Aminophylline	Aminodur	Aminophyllinum	Theodrox
Oxtriphylline	Choledyl	Choline theophylline	Choledyl
Theophylline	Theo-Dur	Theophyllinum	Theograd
Corticosteroids			
Beclomethasone	Beclovent	Beclomethasone	Becotide
Betamethasone	Celestone	Betamethasonum	Betnesol
Cortisone	Cortone	Cortisone	Cortistab
Dexamethasone	Decadron	Dexamethesonum	Decadron
Hydrocortisone	Cortef	Hydrocortosone	Cortef
Methylprednisolone	Medrol	Methylprednisolone	Medrol
Prednisone/ prednisolone	Predoxine	Prednisonum/ Prednisolonum	Codelsol
Cromolyn Sodium			
Cromolyn sodium	Intal	Cromolyn sodium	Lomudal

work out a "crisis plan" to handle potential asthma emergencies. A crisis plan involves knowing in advance how to modify your medication if asthma symptoms unexpectedly break through, or you will not be able to avoid one of your asthma triggers (your brother is getting married and many of the guests will be smoking), or you will be far from medical help (a camping trip in the Rocky Mountains). Modifying your medications involves knowing when, and how, to increase them, particularly steroids. (Some doctors prescribe a reserve dose of steroids to keep in the medicine cabinet until needed.) If you expect to travel outside the United States, know what your medications are called in other countries. (Table 10 lists the different names of common antiasthma drugs.) Your doctor may also want to teach you and/or a family member how to inject adrenaline. (This is particularly important for asthmatics who are likely to have an anaphylactic allergic reaction, and for those who are not near medical help.)

Part of every asthmatic's crisis plan must cover how to recognize when—despite all precautions—your asthma attack is becoming severe. Last of all, you must know which ER to go to if this happens. In your home area, this should be at the hospital with which your doctor is affiliated. When you are going to be away from home, first check with your doctor or your local Lung Association for a hospital in your destination city that provides the kind of pulmonary care you might need.

Knowing a Severe Attack Is Coming

The speed with which a severe asthma attack develops is not predictable. It can take a few hours or many days. But no matter how long it takes, one thing is always the same. The attack is accompanied by a steady, remorseless worsening of symptoms.

The earlier you can recognize what is happening, the easier it will be for the ER staff to stop your respiratory deterioration and then reverse it. Your recognition skills will be substantially increased once you understand the purpose of each medication that you take, know when they are no longer working effectively, and are aware of the circumstances likely to make them less effective for you (a respiratory infection, start of the pollen season, work deadlines, etc.).

Below are some specific signs that indicate a severe attack is developing.

A frequent warning bell for the onset of a severe asthma attack is the sudden absence of expected relief from your regular dose of bronchodilator aerosol. If this happens, you may find yourself using your bronchodilator more and more frequently without realizing it.

One possible reason for this sudden lack of bronchodilator effectiveness is that edema and mucus plugs can develop before you become aware of a bronchospasm. This obstruction, combined with the effects of rapid, shallow breathing, would prevent the aerosolized drug from reaching the deeper parts of your lungs. A second possibility is that your prescribed dosage is no longer adequate. Perhaps it is suddenly being cleared more quickly from your body, or perhaps there is an unexpected drug interaction.

Another sign is greater change in your lung function from the time you wake up to later in the day. An asthmatic normally finds that his breathing and respiratory comfort are at their worst first thing in the morning, improving as the day goes on. A number of studies show that these breathing difficulties upon awakening get worse and worse as an asthma attack develops. And the most severe attacks are heralded by the sudden absence of any improvement at all in daytime lung function.

A growing number of doctors believe it is important for their severely asthmatic patients to identify this kind of trend as soon as it begins. The patients record their peak expiratory flow rate first thing every morning and then later in the day. They do this with a *peak flow meter*, a small plastic device for measuring the flow of air out of the lungs.

To use the peak flow meter, you simply breathe in as much air as you can, then blow it out as fast as you can. A daily decrease in peak expiratory air flow, as well as an increasing difference from morning to afternoon, both reflect a deteriorating condition.

- You are wheezing more frequently, particularly at night.

- You are more short of breath than usual, and it begins happening with less exertion than usual.

- You are coughing more often, but it is harder to bring up sputum. Whatever you do bring up is extremely sticky. It may be yellow, gray, or green, indicating some type of respiratory infection.

- There are subtle and not-so-subtle mood changes partly due to heightened anxiety, insomnia, and irritability.

This outline should be your alarm system. Call your doctor if you notice any of these signs. Your conversation will resolve whether you can continue caring for your condition at home, or need to visit his office, or need emergency care.

But you may not be able to reach your doctor in time for him to make this decision. It might take awhile before he can answer your phone call, yet your condition is obviously deteriorating. Or you may be away on vacation or business. Then the decision must be yours alone.

If you are in any doubt about what to do, going to the ER is the right choice. If your attack turns out not to be as serious as you had feared, at the worst you will have wasted a few hours of your time. But if you really need the ER, not going can be deadly! If you are in your home town, remember to choose the hospital with which your doctor is affiliated. If you need to be hospitalized, he can admit you and then treat you once you are in. (A description of what hospitalization involves comes later in this chapter.)

How Many Asthmatics Need Emergency Care?

Only a tiny proportion of asthmatic patients ever need emergency care, but they need it fairly often. Four percent to 6 of all ER visits are from asthmatics. One-third of the asthmatics needing emergency care in any given year have already been to an ER during an attack at least once before.

A disturbing fact is that, in inner-city hospitals, 15 to 19 percent of all ER visits are from asthma patients. This is four times the overall proportion, even though asthma is not more prevalent in the inner city. Why is this so? Evidence indicates that socioeconomic factors influence the severity of asthma for inner-city residents and the treatment they receive for it.

Because most inner-city residents cannot afford a private physician, asthmatics in this group do not have access to the close patient-physician relationship that is so critical in controlling asthma. These asthmatics may also not be able to afford essential daily medication. Beyond this, the poor condition of much inner-city housing exposes many allergic asthmatics to allergens—roach parts and feces, rodent urine, mold spores—that seriously aggravate their disease. In addition, inner-city hospitals do not have the staff or time for educating the asthmatics who come to their clinics for treatment. So changes in asthma symptoms that might otherwise be easily controlled result, instead, in ER visits.

An interesting fact is that the overall pace of asthma visits to the ER is not constant. There are clear daily, weekly, and yearly peaks. Some are easily explainable, and some are not. Asthmatics need emergency help most frequently during weekdays between 7:00 A.M. and 12:00 noon. This probably reflects the asthmatic's normally poorer lung function in the early morning, exacerbated by the tensions of the work environment. Sudden changes in humidity and/or temperature in either direction are also associated with a rise in asthma attacks.

ER visits also increase dramatically every fall, usually from late September through the end of November. In some parts of the United States this is the time of year for hay fever, decreased humidity, the onset of cold weather, and a jump in viral infections. The slight increase in severe asthma episodes during the spring probably results from the change in weather and pollens suddenly in the air.

The very occasional acute asthma epidemic is usually associated with a period of unusually high air pollution with particulate matter, ozone, sulfur oxide, carbon monoxide, metals, or photochemicals. Two notable incidents involved American servicemen in Yokohama, Japan, in 1954, and residents of New Orleans, also in the mid-1950s. In fact, this kind of acute attack has since been dubbed "Yokohama asthma" and "New Orleans asthma."

ER visits of all kinds—including those for asthma—increase substantially around the Christmas and New Year holidays. So do suicides. These holidays involve a great deal of stress for many people.

Your First Time in the Emergency Room

For the first time in your life you have decided—with or without your doctor's help—that you need emergency care for your asthma. What will happen once you step through the ER door?

In a relatively busy ER, the first person to greet you is the *triage nurse*. (The term *triage* is a French word meaning selection.) The triage nurse must decide which emergency needs the most immediate attention, which is next most in need, and so on. If, for example, you are not on the verge of fainting from lack of oxygen when you arrive at the ER, and someone with chest pains and another person with a possible broken arm come in about when you do, the available medical staff will see the person with chest pains first, you second, and then the possible broken arm.

Tell the triage nurse *exactly* how you are feeling. If you have not yet called your doctor, have the nurse call him. (ER staff must do this if you request it.) You will reap two benefits from this. First, your doctor can give helpful treatment information to the ER staff. Second, a sad but true fact is that nurses and house staff (interns and residents) often give more considerate care to patients whose doctor is affiliated with their hospital.

But be forewarned that the majority of ER staff—however competent their medical care—are not usually known for their bedside manners. In fact, we heard a typical experience while we were writing this section. Our baby-sitter called us, fresh from an ER visit in a Greenwich Village hospital. She had gone with a friend suffering her first allergy attack. Her friend was the only patient present, yet she waited half an hour to be called. Then she waited at least that long again before receiving treatment. Her treatment was appropriate—an antihistamine and adrenaline—but the staff told her nothing about the usual side effects (like the shakes, heavy perspiration, and a sense of panic) other than "You may feel your heart beat a little faster, honey." When our baby-sitter complained to them, they were uncompassionate and rude.

So after you have spoken with the triage nurse, relax, do not take any rude behavior personally, and do not get excited if you have to wait awhile for treatment. You can expect your treatment to be correct, but do not look for much compassion or TLC. If you do find it, it is a nice bonus.

But if you are having any difficulty breathing, or if you feel your condition worsening quickly, you should not have to wait at all for treatment. If this starts to happen while you are waiting, you should not have to wait any longer. Make sure that the triage nurse knows how you are feeling, and *stand up for your rights*.

A final piece of advice is to fight the urge to breathe rapidly. Keep your breathing as relaxed as you possibly can. In a later chapter we will describe some tricks that may help you control your breathing when you feel panicky.

What Does Emergency Care Involve?

Once you are called from the waiting room bench, what will happen to you?

GETTING TO KNOW YOU

First you will be asked very specific questions, usually by a nurse, about your medical and asthma history. The ER doctor will probably ask them again when he sees you. They are looking for the facts that will determine the kind of medication you will be given, and whether any added precautions will be needed.

They especially must find out what initiated your current attack (allergen, irritant, viral infection, emotional stress, abrupt steroid withdrawal, etc.); what medications you use, on what schedule and dosage, and when you last took them; and if you have any diseases complicating your asthma treatment such as heart disease, high blood pressure, or diabetes.

The ER staff must also find out if you are a high-risk asthmatic. They will ask you about the usual frequency of your attacks, if your asthma has ever required emergency or hospital care in the past, if you have ever used a respirator during an attack, if you are currently taking high steroid doses, and how much time passed between the start of this attack and your arrival at the ER.

You might consider carrying a card in your wallet containing the important points in your history, your current medications (with schedule and dosage), and any drugs you might be allergic to. High-risk asthmatics would be well advised to wear a customized *Medi-Alert bracelet* (made by Medi-Alert, P.O. Box 1009, Turlock, CA 95381-1009). It would indicate that you have asthma and the antiasthma drugs that you take, and note whatever drug allergies you might have. It also states that a more complete medical history is stored in the company's central computer, which means that all this information will be available to the ER staff if you are brought in unconscious.

Physical Examination

After you answer the questions, the doctor in charge of your case will examine you. First he will look for signs of anxiety, fatigue, cyanosis (a blue tinge to the lips and fingernail area), sweating, and flushing. He will listen to your breathing for wheezing sounds (telling him that obstruction is only partial) or silence (meaning extremely severe obstruction). The doctor will also determine your heart rate and blood pressure. (Heart rate, normally between 60 and 80 beats per minute, can go over 120 beats per minute during a severe attack. Blood pressure during an attack can swing up and down as you breathe in and out [pulsus paradoxus].)

The ER doctor will check your lungs for hyperinflation by seeing if your chest moves only slightly as you breathe, then by tapping your back—called percussion—to hear if your lungs sound hollow through the stethoscope. Percussion may also reveal the presence of bronchopneumonia. How much you are using your neck muscles to help you breathe will tell the doctor how much respiratory distress you are experiencing. Finally, some simple pulmonary function tests will be done, either forced expiratory volumes or peak expiratory flows.

Possible Tests

If the ER doctor finds evidence of complicating factors, he will order appropriate tests. If you are cyanotic, blood will be taken from your artery so that the amount of oxygen and carbon dioxide in it can be measured. (If you hear anyone use the term *blood gases*, this is what is being referred to.) Knowing your blood gases tells the doctor to what degree you are being deprived of oxygen and whether carbon dioxide has built up to a dangerous level. An X-ray will be taken to make sure you do not have pneumonia or air in your chest (called pneumothorax). If you have a history of heart disease, or are showing any sign of such problems, the doctor will order an electrocardiogram (ECG or EKG) for you.

Treatment

What follows is a composite of several different asthma treatment plans described in the professional literature. Keep in mind that each ER has its own variation of a standard plan. And in each individual ER, this standard plan must be tailored to fit the individual asthmatic. Remember, too, that ERs do their job well.

You will most likely be given oxygen. This is usually done via a tube with two prongs at one end that fit into your nose, with the other end attached to the oxygen tank. Sometimes an oxygen mask is used instead.

The initial group of drugs that you will be given are beta-stimulators. The first one will be given by injection. Epinephrine (adrenaline) continues to be popular for this (except for patients with heart disease, high blood pressure, a hyperactive thyroid gland, or a disturbingly fast heart rate). Terbutaline is another common choice. After the injection, you will be given a beta-2-stimulating bronchodilator via a nebulizer.

Then you will be started on theophylline intravenously. It is particularly important for the ER staff to know the amount of your last theophylline dose and how long ago you took it so they can keep your serum theophylline below toxic levels.

Finally, you will probably be given a steroid injection (e.g., hydrocortisone). Some doctors prefer to wait awhile before ordering the steroid to see if you are responding well to the other drugs. If you are, then they omit the steroid.

If your respiratory condition has not improved after 15 to 30 minutes, the beta-stimulating drugs are repeated (except for the intravenous theophylline, which has not stopped). Then the injected and inhaled drugs are alternated, with one given each hour. The theophylline continues. If you have a prominent cough, you may be given atropine by nebulizer.

This course of medication continues until your ER doctor decides that you can be discharged, or that you must be hospitalized. *Do not pressure the doctor to send you home.* One of the chief causes of a relapse—which will land you right back in the ER—is ending emergency treatment too soon.

Discharge

Even when the proper amount of time has been spent in the ER, the airways remain very vulnerable to another attack in the days right after a severe asthma episode. So if you are discharged, make sure that you see your own doctor in his office the very next day. He will review the treatment that you received and make any necessary modifications. This might even mean a new treatment plan designed specifically to prevent a relapse.

Who Is Hospitalized?

The patient who does not respond satisfactorily to ER treatment is diagnosed as *status asthmaticus*. This is the most serious form that asthma can take. Although there is no hard definition as to when a severe attack becomes status asthmaticus, this term evokes the patient who is not responding to ordinary treatment and whose condition is deteriorating to the point of respiratory failure. "Failure" means that the respiratory muscles are exhausted, or the lungs so obstructed that the system is no longer able to provide enough oxygen or remove enough carbon dioxide from the body.

The diagnosis of status asthmaticus automatically carries several presumptions with it: The asthma has become life-threatening; a medical emergency exists, requiring an intensification of all medical efforts; and immediate hospitalization is needed for diagnostic workup, intensive treatment, proper nursing care, and—if appropriate—elimination of the causative agent (such as an infection).

Although only 3 percent of the asthmatics who visit the ER have to be hospitalized, they represent a larger proportion of hospitalizations that come from the ER. Of all patients admitted from the ER in one New York City municipal hospital, 8 percent of the adults and 25 percent of the children were there for asthma. The typical hospitalized adult is a woman between 20 and 29 years old. A hospitalized child—at least those under the age of 6—is twice as likely to be a boy.

Of adult asthmatics overall, there are only slightly more women than men. Yet three adult women are hospitalized for every man. The proportion of asthma deaths in the hospital—two women for each man—is still unbalanced, but less extreme. This difference seems to disappear entirely for asthma deaths occurring outside the hospital.

These curious patterns make us wonder if women are really much more likely to have severe asthma attacks, since three women are admitted for each man, and there are two female deaths in-hospital for each male death. Does the even greater overrepresentation of hospitalized female asthmatics (compared to deaths) also reflect society's acceptance of women seeking help, while men are expected to "tough it out"?

What Does Hospital Treatment Consist Of?

The goal of hospital treatment is to support your breathing by any means necessary—including a mechanical respirator—while reversing your asthma attack with the medication begun in the ER. The kind of breathing support you need depends on how much your asthma attack is impairing the effectiveness of your respiratory system. This can be known only after an extremely thorough clinical and laboratory evaluation.

Evaluation

Chest X-rays are needed if they were not already taken in the ER. You will also be given an electrocardiogram. Blood will be taken to see how much the eosinophil count has increased, to see if your attack has caused damage to nonrespiratory systems, and to check for bacterial infection. Your sputum will also be analyzed for evidence of bacterial infection and of damage to the lungs.

The most important test measures the amount of oxygen and carbon dioxide in your arterial blood (called blood gases). The blood sampling technique we are most familiar with takes venous blood (which is returning to the heart) from the large vein in the inner elbow. It is not painful. But drawing arterial blood from the artery in your wrist—which is needed for accurate blood gas measurements—can be painful, so local anesthetic is sometimes used. Patients who need frequent arterial blood tests will have a narrow plastic tube inserted into this artery, where it safely and comfortably stays until the asthma crisis is over.

Knowing how much carbon dioxide is in your blood is even more important than knowing the amount of oxygen. The carbon dioxide level tells the doctor how well or poorly your respiratory muscles are coping with the intense demands the asthma attack has placed on them.

When a severe asthma attack starts, the airway obstructions reduce the amount of fresh air reaching the air sacs, which in turn begins to lower the oxygen in your blood. The asthmatic instinctively tries to make up for this by breathing deeper and more quickly. But the airway obstructions allow very little extra oxygen to reach the air sacs (not even breathing from an oxygen tank would entirely provide the needed oxygen), while this new breathing pattern causes too much carbon dioxide to be exhaled.

The respiratory muscles are eventually exhausted by the hopeless task of trying to get more oxygen into the body. Then they fail. (The muscles have not stopped working, but they are no longer able to maintain adequate oxygen and carbon dioxide levels.) Oxygen falls even more, and carbon dioxide in the blood begins to rise past acceptable levels. When oxygen falls while muscles work very hard, they produce lactic acid. Lactic acid is dumped into the blood, where it combines with the increasing amount of acid produced by the rising carbon dioxide. The consequences of this great amount of acid in the blood are life-threatening. Much of the treatment you receive in the hospital will be devoted to avoiding this grave situation.

Breathing Support

Bronchial suctioning involves insertion of a fine suction tube into your airways to suck out mucus and mucus plugs. Because even the narrowest tube can only reach into the medium-sized airways, however, the deeper airways will not be cleared. Even so, the large plugs that can be removed will substantially aid your breathing. A recent method to improve suction is called *bronchial lavage*. A salt solution is washed into the airways first to make the mucus plugs less tenacious. Then the solution and mucus plugs are sucked out.

If your blood gases show excessively low oxygen and excessively high carbon dioxide, you will temporarily need a machine (a respirator) to take over from your exhausted respiratory muscles. (Although respiratory muscle exhaustion is usually why an asthmatic needs a respirator, occasionally there are other causes.) To attach you to the machine, a tube is passed through your nose or mouth and into your windpipe (trachea). The tube is then attached to a pump by your bedside that will inflate your lungs at a preset rate and depth. The air pumped into your lungs is properly humidified and warmed.

The respirator increases your oxygen level and lowers the carbon dioxide in your blood while whatever caused your blood gas problems is being dealt with. (If it was due to respiratory muscle exhaustion, your time on the respirator gives the muscles the rest they need.) As carbon dioxide is lowered, the excess acid in your blood begins to decrease. If this does not happen quickly enough, a solution of sodium bicarbonate—baking soda—will be added directly to your blood to buffer the remaining acids.

You will remain on the respirator from 12 to 48 hours. The amount of time obviously depends on how quickly your blood gases improve. After 48 hours, it is important that you start to breathe on your own again.

Sometimes the use of a respirator causes complications. Injury to the throat or airways can occur when the tube is being inserted or removed. If the tube is placed so deep that it goes beyond the point where the bronchus first divides, the lobes on the bypassed side are not ventilated and tissue damage occurs. Tissue can also be damaged if a patient pulls or coughs the tube out, or if an inserted tube is too wide. Complications due to the equipment itself can occur when the respirator and/or alarm malfunction, or when the inspired air is overheated or not properly humidified. Medical complications include under- or overventilation, a collapsed section of lung (termed *atelectasis* or *pneumothorax* depending on the cause), pneumonia, and low blood pressure.

Other Care

Because fear, restlessness, and agitation often accompany a severe asthma attack, it would seem comforting to be given a tranquilizer or sedative. You should not have one, however, unless you are on a respirator. Because a sedated patient's breathing appears to have eased even when his condition is actually getting worse, the hospital staff is likely to gain a false sense of improvement. These drugs also depress the brain's response to the chemical signals that keep breathing going, and they suppress coughing. Some also speed up the metabolism of steroids, which reduces their effectiveness. All these effects are the last thing you need in the midst of an asthma attack.

Care will be taken that you get plenty of fluids, either by mouth or intravenously. This makes your mucus less thick and tenacious.

Prognosis

What happens once the acute attack has been controlled? Your prognosis is good, as long as all contributing causes are thoroughly investigated and a new program is set up for controlling your symptoms.

As with other life-threatening events, this experience provokes a variety of reactions from patients that range from great anxiety and negative life-style changes to denial and complacency. Neither extreme is helpful in coping productively with asthma. When such reactions occur, the patient should be counseled and educated concerning the realities of his situation.

Mortality

Asthma has been known as a disease for more than 30 centuries. Widespread appreciation of its potential for causing death, however, has existed for only 50 years, despite early observations. (In 1698, for example, the physician Sir John Floyer reported an 18-month-old infant's sudden death from asthma.) The leading medical texts of the nineteenth and early twentieth centuries all stated that asthma was rarely, if ever, fatal.

It is now known that a small but significant number of asthmatics die every year, but interpreting patterns in asthma deaths is not easy. For one thing, the changing understanding of asthma over the years means that who is diagnosed as asthmatic has also changed. For another, fewer asthmatics were correctly diagnosed before today's greater awareness of asthma and improved diagnostic techniques.

Asthma deaths can be very sudden. They often occur outside the hospital, frequently at night or in the early morning. The recovery phase from an acute attack appears to be a very vulnerable period, but whether death occurs has no relation to the attack's length or intensity.

What characteristics identify the asthma patient who risks a fatal asthma incident? It is any single element, or combination, of the following: having asthma for more than 20 years; poorly controlled symptoms requiring frequent office or ER visits; previous hospitalization for status asthmaticus, especially if complicated by respiratory failure; current need for large steroid doses; and excessively low morning peak expiratory flows with a pattern of worsening airway obstruction.

The introduction of new asthma drugs in the 1940s steadily reduced the U.S. death rate from its high of 4.5 per 100,000 people to a low of 0.8 per 100,000 people by 1977. But a look at U.S. health data after that year shows a rising death rate again. By 1982 it was up to 1.2 per 100,000, and estimated at 1.6 per 100,000 for 1984. The cause for this increase is only guessed at.

Other countries report a similar unexplained jump in their asthma death rates. In England and Wales the death rate had begun to climb about 20 years earlier, from 0.7 per 100,000 people in 1959 to 2.2 per 100,000 people in 1966. Asthmatics from 5 to 34 years old were the most affected. (But by 1969, the death rate had returned to the lower figure.) Increases during the 1960s were also published for Australia, Ireland, New Zealand, and Norway, but not the other industrialized European and North African countries. New Zealand experienced another alarming increase in asthma deaths about 10 years later, when the mortality rate rose steeply from 1.4 per 100,000 in 1975 to 4.1 per 100,000 in 1979.

Part of the explanation for this disturbing rise in mortality rates may actually be today's greater accuracy in diagnosing asthma. It is not solely that more asthmatics are dying, but that—because more asthmatics are now correctly diagnosed—an asthmatic dying from the disease is more likely to have his cause of death accurately judged. But today's improved asthma medications should cancel out this apparent increase in deaths.

This still leaves much of the rising death rate unaccounted for. Investigators in both the United States and New Zealand have suggested that many of these deaths were preventable. In fact, death was considered unavoidable in only 11 percent of the cases. This means that, for every 10 asthma deaths, 9 of these patients should not have died!

Five factors contributing to these avoidable deaths have been pinpointed: (1) initial failure to diagnose asthma; (2) lack of patient education concerning asthma and when to seek medical help; (3) failure of the physician to use the objective measurements (such as peak flow, pulsus paradoxus, arterial blood gases) that make an attack's severity apparent, thereby failing to intensify bronchodilator and steroid treatment and, when necessary, advise hospitalization; (4) failure to monitor a hospitalized patient closely with repeated objective and clinical evaluations; and (5) inappropriate prescription of sedatives and other drugs.

Certain segments of the asthma population in the United States have always experienced a large proportion of preventable deaths. A look at variation in both the per capita expenditure for health and the doctor-patient ratio makes it clear that appropriate asthma treatment is still denied to many. The higher asthma mortality among American blacks, for example, reflects differences in the availability and quality of medical care that are directly tied to differing socioeconomic status.

Another group of asthmatics at a particularly great disadvantage is those who are psychotic. A study of 23 asthma deaths over a 12-year period showed that one-third involved psychotics or extremely disturbed psychoneurotic people. These patients—particularly paranoid schizophrenics—are especially difficult to manage, because many asthma drugs tend to worsen their psychiatric problems. When doctors and nurses caring for these patients believe that asthma is psychogenic, they may not prescribe adequate antiasthma medication. They do use sedatives and tranquilizers—strongly contraindicated for asthmatics—to treat these patients' psychiatric problems. Their pleas for help during asthma attacks tend to be ignored, too often with fatal results.

✦✦ 10 ✦✦

Controlling Asthma Triggers

Asthma management covers three distinct areas. Two have already been discussed: the regular use of asthma drugs to prevent bronchospasm, and the temporary use of drugs to prevent a severe attack by bringing an episode under control as quickly as possible. The third area—the topic of the next several chapters—concerns the variety of techniques designed to reduce the effect of asthma triggers (Figure 10.1).

Techniques for controlling asthma triggers take several directions: specific medical treatment, environmental changes (which include identifying, then avoiding, eliminating, or neutralizing allergens and/or irritants), and possible life-style changes. Aggressive measures for minimizing asthma triggers are important for every asthmatic. Although some benefit more than others, every asthmatic eventually finds his life significantly improved.

There is no one best plan. Because asthma can be affected by such a variety of factors, because there are so many individual variations, and because asthma is always unpredictable over the long run, each asthmatic has to find his own best combination of preventive measures. And he must be prepared for this to change from time to time.

EMOTIONS **INFECTIONS**

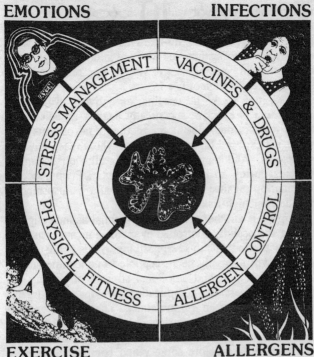

EXERCISE **ALLERGENS**

Figure 10.1 Nonmedical management of asthma.

Medical Safeguards

Since respiratory infections are a common asthma trigger, it makes good sense for certain asthmatics to get a flu vaccination as the flu season approaches—those at high risk for catching infections (health workers and school staff) and those for whom infections could be dangerous (children and the elderly). Serious reactions to the flu vaccine are rare, and the benefits to these asthmatics far outweigh this unlikely hazard.

It is highly unfortunate that adverse reactions to the flu

vaccine have received wide media exposure. The worst that can be expected after a flu shot are a few days of mild fever, malaise, and other flu-like symptoms. The only word of warning is for asthmatics who are allergic to eggs. Because the flu vaccine is grown on egg proteins, egg-sensitive people cannot use it.

In addition to the flu vaccine, an antiviral drug called *amantidine* is effective specifically against influenza A2. Some doctors prescribe it for their asthma patients who were just exposed to influenza A, or who already have flu symptoms. And they prescribe it for all their asthmatic patients during an influenza A epidemic. Pneumococcal vaccination (against a form of pneumonia) is also recommended for high-risk asthmatics.

Surgery is another area where potential asthma triggers can be successfully controlled by medical means. An asthmatic with moderate to severe asthma who is going to have surgery will normally be susceptible to an asthma attack. The physiological and emotional stresses of surgery are potential triggers. If a complication develops after surgery, it can also trigger an asthma attack. The doctor can neutralize the effect of these triggers by temporarily increasing the asthmatic's steroid medication. This should start one to two days before surgery and continue through at least the first day after surgery.

Environmental Safeguards

Completely avoiding an allergen or irritant trigger is the surest way to prevent an asthma attack, but it is often impractical or impossible to do. When complete avoidance is not possible, partial avoidance is still helpful. It does not eliminate symptoms, but it does diminish their severity. (If even partial avoidance is impossible, then allergy shots—for the appropriate person—may neutralize the trigger's effect.)

Environmental allergens and irritants that trigger your

asthma are most easily identified from your history. Suspected allergens can be confirmed by skin testing and/or bronchial provocation testing.

INDOOR AVOIDANCE/ELIMINATION OF TRIGGERS

Although many of the same asthma triggers are found both at home and in the work place, avoidance and elimination techniques are usually easiest to implement at home. So your house is where asthma-proofing efforts should start. If you write down a step-by-step asthma-proofing plan for each room, you will minimize the chance of missing something important. Start your efforts in the bedroom, since this is where people spend the large majority of their household time.

The most common indoor inhaled allergens are house dust, dust mites, feathers, animal dander, mold spores, and odors. Although the extent of your asthma-proofing against these allergens should correspond to the severity of your asthma, do not buy expensive electrical devices or make major changes in your life-style until you have tried the simpler measures. If you live with other people, asthma-proofing must be a cooperative effort. Everyone in the household must share in eliminating offending asthma triggers from your home.

House Dust

House dust is made up of natural and synthetic fibers, plant materials, fungi and bacteria, dried flakes of human skin, pulverized food remnants, inorganic debris, dust mites (the most troublesome component for asthmatics), and sometimes animal dander and/or cockroach and other insect parts and feces. House dust is everywhere, but it causes the greatest difficulty at night for the asthmatic who sleeps with his head buried in dust-laden pillows, mattresses, and blankets.

Scientific studies have not found a strong relationship between the amount of dust mites and how often a house

*is cleaned, how thoroughly it is cleaned, how old the fur-
niture is, or how old the house is.* How you clean is more
important than how vigorously you do it. It is best done
with a damp cloth rather than by vacuuming. Vacuuming
should be kept to a minimum because it stirs up dust. A
particular focus for dust-cleaning efforts are the baseboard
and molding behind the bed and the floor underneath it.

Fabric-covered mattresses collect dust, which accumu-
lates in the nooks and crannies of the weave no matter
how carefully it is cleaned. To eliminate this, either use a
vinyl mattress cover that fully encases your mattress, or
buy a water bed. Feather pillow-stuffing decomposes into
dust, so sleep on pillows stuffed with a synthetic material
and wash them every month. If you prefer foam pillows,
you must replace them yearly. Nightly perspiration makes
them a wonderful breeding ground for molds, and foam,
in addition, eventually deteriorates into dust. Blankets must
also be cleaned or laundered monthly because perspiration
makes them a breeding ground for molds.

Asthmatics must usually give up sleeping with a quilt. A
feather quilt produces its own dust just as feather-stuffed pillows do. And other types of quilts collect dust. This was
discovered from a study of Hong Kong's substantial annual
peak in asthma attacks coinciding with colder weather. The
culprit turned out to be their traditional cotton-filled quilt,
which was put on the bed as soon as the nights grew chilly.
Dust mites are abundant in these quilts, and Hong Kong
asthmatics who change to Western-style blankets find their
attacks less frequent and less severe.

An asthmatic's bedroom should be decorated with items
that do not provide hiding places for dust and are easily
washable. Rugs should be synthetic or cotton. Curtains
should be synthetic (fiberglass is ideal). All flat fabrics
should be tightly woven; the looser the weave, the more it
traps dust. Because *molds* can grow on plants and in soil,
the bedroom should not have many houseplants. An asthmatic child's toys must not be dust collectors; smooth
wood or plastic surfaces are ideal. Every child needs
something soft, but make sure it is not fuzzy in texture.

This approach to furnishing the bedroom should extend to the rest of the house. Avoid upholstered furniture and feather-containing cushions. Use leather or one of the synthetic leather look-alikes. If current upholstered furniture cannot be replaced, all pieces should be thoroughly steam cleaned and then permanently covered with plastic slipcovers. Caned furniture is another alternative, as long as any cushions used with it are filled with a synthetic material and washed regularly. Rugs—preferably synthetic—should be washable, with rubberized pads used under them. Because *molds* can grow on plants and in soil, at best only a few houseplants should be around. They may eventually have to be abandoned completely, including even the annual Christmas tree.

Animals

In general, no furry pet should be allowed inside the house, even when an asthmatic is not sensitive to its *dander*. Particles of dust and *pollens* from outside cling to its fur, and *hair* shed indoors can be an irritant. Sometimes an asthmatic and/or his family must make the heartbreaking decision to find another home for a much-loved pet.

Household Rules

Certain general rules should be adopted for the house. No smoking. No fires in the fireplace. No strong *odors*, such as perfume. Use a kitchen exhaust fan whenever anyone cooks. Do not use aerosol or spray cans. Do not vacuum while an asthmatic is in the house and do not let him return until the vacuuming dust settles. Keep the temperature between 65° and 70°F.

Miscellaneous

Charcoal filters for odors may be helpful. Air conditioners with effective filters can reduce the indoor level of pollens and other outdoor airborne particulate matter. Baseboard electrical heating is much better than forced air, oil, gas, or coal furnaces. It attracts and spreads much less dust than a furnace does and is much cleaner in terms of the possible irritant byproducts of combustion (nitrogen dioxide and carbon monoxide). Electric stoves are cleaner than gas appliances. (A wood-burning stove is out of the question for an asthmatic.)

A source of pollution in the home that cannot be easily eliminated, and that can be particularly irritating to asthmatics, is *formaldehyde*. Formaldehyde is released from plywood, from particle board, and from urea-formaldehyde foam (which is used in insulation).

Molds

Molds are almost impossible to eliminate from a household, even if plants are kept to a minimum. They thrive in damp, dark, chilly, poorly ventilated areas, and also grow in some unexpected places. Molds grow in garbage containers and food storage areas, on upholstery, wallpaper, shower curtains, and window moldings, in plaster and wallboard, in damp basements, humidifiers, and air conditioners, and under leaky roofs. The two most effective mold-control techniques are dehumidification (eliminating or reducing dampness) and the use of fungicides (chemicals that kill mold spores).

Any areas—such as roofs and basements—where rain or ground-water leak in should be repaired immediately with a silicone-rubber seal. A basement should also be kept heated and lit in winter and well ventilated during the summer. An asthmatic planning to buy an existing house should avoid one with a sump pump or with water seepage or flood marks on the basement walls.

No matter how free of dampness your current or newly purchased house appears, you can be sure that mold has penetrated the plaster or wallboard. All walls and ceilings should be sealed with shellac or varnish (done, of course, while the asthmatic is not in the house). Then they should be painted with a mold-resistant paint like *Loxon* (by Sherwin-Williams), or with a fungicide—like *Dowicide* or

Captan—added to regular paint (one tablespoon for each quart of paint).

For a new house, have the builders put heavy black polyethylene sheets (which are waterproof) under the basement foundation and outside the foundation walls. Whether the house is old or new, avoid moss-rock fireplaces and grasscloth or burlap wallpapers.

Unavoidably mold-prone areas (refrigerator, garbage containers, shower curtain, humidifier, etc.) should be cleaned frequently with a fungicide. Inexpensive, effective products are readily available in supermarkets: phenolated disinfectants (such as *Lysol*), halogens (such as *Clorox*), and cationic surface cleaners (such as *benzalkonium chloride* and *Zephiran*).

Air Cleaners

No matter how well dust and mold controls have been carried out, some asthmatics will be affected by particles and spores still left in the environment. If this happens, it is time to consider buying an electrical air cleaner. The "Air Cleaning and Purifying" section of your Yellow Pages lists local dealers. Choose one that both rents and sells air cleaners, so that you can try out the machine you are considering before you buy. If the machine that seemed right does not do the job you need, try out a different one.

The best of the electrical air cleaners is the *high-efficiency particulate air (HEPA) filter*, which removes close to 100 percent of airborne particles. It is more effective than the best of the electrostatic air cleaners, which only remove from 70 to 90 percent. Both kinds of air cleaners are expensive, but the electrostatic cleaner also requires high-voltage safeguards and produces ozone, a potential irritant.

A number of small, inexpensive tabletop air cleaners became available in response to public concern about smoke pollution. Manufacturers claim that these devices eliminate all particulate matter in the air, plus odors and bacteria. A large quantity of air, however, must circulate through the machine to filter the air in an entire room effectively. This requires a large motor, and large motors are expensive to buy and operate (as with a vacuum cleaner and an air conditioner). A small, inexpensive unit is unlikely to clean the air often enough.

You need two types of information to help you decide on an air cleaner. One is how quickly a particular machine does its cleaning job, indicated by the number of times an hour it will change the air in your room. The other is how efficiently the machine does its job, which is its ability to remove the particles that trigger your asthma.

To determine how rapidly a machine will clean your room, you must know how much air circulates through the machine every minute (its cubic feet/minute displacement—or CFM—rating), and the amount of air (in cubic feet) contained in the room where the air cleaner will be used. You can learn the CFM from a salesperson or sales brochure; to get your room's volume of air, multiply its length by its width by its height. Then multiply the CFM by 60 to get the amount of air that the machine cleans in one hour. Dividing this hourly total by the cubic room size tells you how many times an hour a particular machine will clean the air in this room. This can all be written in a simple formula to carry with you when you go shopping:

$$\frac{\text{CFM} \times 60 \text{ (amount of air cleaned in 1 hr.)}}{\text{Room L} \times \text{W} \times \text{H (amount of air in room)}} = \begin{array}{l}\text{no. of air changes}\\ \text{per hour}\end{array}$$

Two air changes an hour is the minimum rate acceptable. Four is considered significantly more effective, but going much beyond this rate will not make a real difference. Ten air changes an hour is regarded as overkill.

An air cleaning machine's efficiency rating tells you how well it cleans. The best source for this information is the machine's manufacturer, who will send you (on request) a graph that shows how completely—or not—the machine cleans different types of particles from the air. Because this graph provides much greater detail than any sales bro-

chure can, you will know how efficiently the air cleaner
removes the specific particles that trigger your asthma
symptoms.

Individual room-sized units are adequate for most asthmatics who benefit from cleaner household air. Some
severely allergic asthmatics need to install centralized air-
cleaning equipment, occasionally with an individual unit
added in the bedroom. Although the need for such an elaborate air-cleaning system is the exception, installing it
when appropriate can radically improve the asthmatic's
life.

If you find that your local dealers cannot answer all your
questions, you can consult manufacturers that were recommended to us for this purpose. Techtronic Products, which
makes individual room units, is at 6743 Kinne St., East Syr-
acuse, NY 13057 (1-315-463-0240). Honeywell, Inc., which
makes both room units and centralized equipment, is at 1885
Douglas Drive North, Golden Valley, MN 55422 (mark cor-
respondence to the attention of Consumer Affairs). They can
also be reached at 1-800-468-1502.

Humidifiers and Dehumidifiers

The effect of humidity on asthma seems to be a very individual matter. Some asthmatics do better in humid
weather, while others find themselves more comfortable
in drier conditions. The best indoor humidity range seems
to be between 35 and 50 percent. If the humidity level in
your home is not right for you, a humidifier or dehumidifier should solve this problem. The comfort gained from
a humidifier, however, must be balanced against two potentially important disadvantages. Both dust mites and
molds prefer—and thrive in—humid environments.

There are three types of humidifiers: reservoir, evapo-
rator, and jet spray. The one most appropriate for you
depends on the size and design of your house, the kind of
heating system you have, and the climate of your area.
Whatever you choose must be cleaned regularly and treated

with a mold inhibitor to minimize the chance of contaminating the air with bacteria or mold.

A dehumidifier will do away with excess humidity. But before you buy an expensive machine, try these much cheaper measures. They may reduce the humidity as much as you need. Install a venting fan in the kitchen and bathroom(s) to reduce humidity in these areas. If you have a clothes dryer, make sure that it is vented to the outside. Wrap cold-water pipes in insulation to stop them from sweating. Put plastic sheeting over a dirt basement floor and over crawl spaces to reduce moisture entering the house from outside.

Negative-Ion Generator

Manufacturers and fans of this device claim that it provides a variety of health benefits by filling the air with negative ions. Air always contains a mixture of positive and negative ions. (An ion is a small particle with a negative or positive electrical charge.) Positive ions are popularly regarded as negatively affecting our well-being, and negative ions as positively affecting it.

The hot desert winds—which contain a high proportion of positive ions—have long been regarded as a negative influence. Headaches, irritability, and chest tightness increase during these winds. Best known are the mistral in southern France, the hamseen coming from the Arabian deserts in the Middle East, and the Santa Ana blowing in from the southern California desert. High amounts of negative ions are found near water—beaches, streams, waterfalls, and so on—environments that most people find highly relaxing.

Negative-ion generators do make the air rich in negative ions. They are said to help the respiratory system by neutralizing the effect of positive ions in the air. What little objective information exists—and it is very little—suggests that the benefits may come directly from the negative ions themselves rather than from merely canceling out the positive ions' ill effects.

It is much more likely, however, that this machine's benefits come from its air-cleaning ability. It removes dust particles from the air by electrostatic precipitation. The negative ions released into the air combine with dust particles. Each resulting ion-dust particle carries a negative charge. Because a room's walls tend to attract negatively charged particles, the dust ends up sticking to the walls instead of floating in the air.

OUTDOOR AVOIDANCE/ELIMINATION OF TRIGGERS

Moving to Another Part of the Country

Normally, asthma triggers are much more difficult to control or avoid when they are outdoors. There are rare circumstances in which the asthmatic must move to another part of the country to avoid a localized allergen—such as ragweed pollen—to which he is extraordinarily sensitive.

Any asthmatic considering such a dramatic solution should first take an extended vacation (three to six weeks) in the area he would relocate to. If the possibility is still appealing, there are some cautions to keep in mind when making the big decision. The benefit picture changes over time. Although asthma often improves substantially or even disappears immediately after such a move, experience suggests that it eventually returns. The relocated asthmatic may become sensitive to the new area's local allergens and/or he may become allergic to something familiar that never bothered him before.

So moving from one part of the country to another most often means exchanging one set of asthma triggers for another, with an asthma-free period until the new sensitivities develop. Because the ultimate benefit is often very small, the decision to move should not be made primarily for health reasons. Balance them against the unavoidable financial, psychological, and social stresses of a major move. And do not forget that the most positive-looking move will be useless if you bring your allergens with you, such as an heirloom quilt or your beloved furry pet.

Some Major Outdoor Triggers

The amount of *air pollution* in an area at any particular time results from two factors. One is the amount of fuel-burning activity (as from power plants, factories, automobiles), which produces the pollutants. The other is existing atmospheric conditions, which determine how quickly fresh air replaces the polluted air.

Burning any type of fuel (except for nuclear fuel, which has its own set of problems) produces carbon monoxide and nitric oxide. Nitric oxide converts to *nitrogen dioxide*, which can be highly irritating to the airways. In addition to this, when small hydrocarbons (residue from burning fossil fuels) and strong sunlight come together, ozone and other photochemical products are formed. If there are no winds to disperse them, the result is *photochemical smog*, also called *Los Angeles smog* after the city where it is best known.

London smog is named for the killer smog that caused 3,500 to 4,000 premature deaths in that city in just four days in December 1952. London smog can occur when coal, or oil high in sulfur, is burned in a power plant. This releases *sulfur dioxide* (in addition to carbon monoxide and nitric oxide), which combines with both oxygen and moisture in the air to form *sulfuric acid*, which then combines with ammonia in the air to produce particles of *sulfate salts*. All these sulfur byproducts are potent airway irritants. In December 1952, they stagnated over London in substantial amounts during four windless, foggy days.

When similar pollution and atmospheric conditions existed in 1948 over Donora, Pennsylvania (population 14,000), there were 18 smog-related deaths. Ninety percent of the town's asthmatics reported that their conditions worsened significantly during the smog, and 40 percent of the nonasthmatic population complained of respiratory problems.

In addition to *weather*'s role in creating smog, weather changes of any kind can produce an unpleasant reaction in asthmatics. The humidity and temperature changes that affect asthmatics indoors have the same effect outdoors. A rapid temperature drop seems particularly difficult for asthmatics. (Other outdoor asthma triggers were discussed in detail in Chapter 3.)

Protecting Yourself

There are several ways to protect yourself from outdoor asthma triggers. The simplest is to stay inside while you keep the pollution out. The best way to keep it outside is with a central air conditioning unit with air purification filters. Combining a regular air conditioner with a HEPA air cleaner is much less expensive and does a reasonably good job.

During air pollution alerts, be more disciplined in carrying out your normal daily precautions. Avoid any unnecessary physical activity outdoors. Be especially careful to stay out of rooms filled with smoke or other irritants, and stay away from anyone with a cold or other respiratory infection. Call your doctor to see if you should temporarily increase any of your asthma medications. (He will probably be busier than usual, and so harder to contact.) Make sure you have all emergency telephone numbers close at hand. If the high pollution is expected to continue for several days and you can afford to leave the area during this time, that is obviously the ideal solution.

Masks—ranging in sophistication from a handkerchief to a helmet—are not very attractive, and they are hard to talk and breathe through. But they can form a barrier between you and several kinds of asthma triggers. They can be worn outdoors during high pollution, a high pollen count, dusty conditions, and cold weather. A mask can also prevent you from inhaling respiratory irritants in the work place.

Remember that you need the right kind of mask for the situation, and that it has to fit properly. A surgical mask can protect against pollens and dust, but not against air pollutants. A "nuisance odor" mask, which is a surgical mask with activated charcoal, can help against ozone and other pollutant gases.

A simple surgical mask also protects against broncho-spasm triggered by cold air, because the air you breathe from behind the mask is kept much warmer than the actual outdoor temperature. Some sports shops now carry cold-weather masks made of neoprene rubber. Although we have not yet tested them, the principle is sound. A number of asthmatics have told us that breathing through a scarf held or tied over the mouth on a cold day also warms the air a little before it enters the throat. These asthmatics are much more comfortable on cold days since taking up this habit.

Immunotherapy

If avoiding allergens is impractical or ineffective, asthmatics whose attacks are triggered primarily, or only, by allergens can try neutralizing these triggers. This applies to only a relatively small group of asthmatics.

Although allergic asthma was once thought to be the prevalent form of this disease, current surveys indicate that allergy is a major or sole contributor for only about 25 percent of all asthmatics. As an example, of 234 asthmatics (adults and children) seen at the Scripps Clinic in La Jolla, California, just under 50 percent of the group responded to allergy triggers. But only 25 percent of these asthmatics (59 people) had allergies as the major cause of their attacks, and only 5 percent (12 people) had allergies as the only cause.

In general, 20 to 25 percent of asthmatics are appropriate candidates for immunotherapy, a medical approach that attempts to neutralize the effect of allergens. Immunotherapy consists of a long-term series of injections containing a gradually increasing amount of allergen extract. It does not cure the asthma, but can reduce or do away with the asthmatic's reaction to certain allergens. We will describe the treatment in detail after we explain how it works.

IMMUNOTHERAPY'S BEGINNINGS

Immunotherapy, also called *desensitization* and *hyposensitization*, has been an accepted treatment for allergic disorders for the past 75 years. It was sparked by two separate discoveries in the mid-1800s. One was the realization that seasonal rhinitis (i.e., hay fever) is caused by pollen. The other was the success of immunization in controlling rabies, tetanus, and diphtheria. Then these two developments were linked in an attempt to immunize hay fever sufferers against the effects of pollen.

Early researchers were unsuccessful because they thought that pollen caused hay fever by producing toxins. (A toxin is a poison produced by certain plants, animals, and bacteria.) So they grew grass pollen "antitoxin" in animals for use in humans. Then scientists theorized that a series of injections of grass pollen extract should give immunity to the hay fever sufferer by causing pollen antitoxin to form. The theory was still wrong, but this time the therapy was right. Active immunization for treating grass pollen hay fever began in 1909, with apparently excellent results.

At this same time, work on anaphylactic reactions in animals provided the key to understanding the allergic reaction in general. These experiments attempted to cure animals susceptible to anaphylaxis by desensitizing them to the agent causing the reaction. Results corrected scientists' mistaken view of this extreme allergic reaction. They had initially thought it signified an animal's lowered resistance to the agent's toxins, but soon learned that it actually reflected a heightened sensitivity to the agent (an antigen) from repeated exposures. This realization eventually evolved into the concept of *immunology*, which led to the branch of medical science dealing with the body's response to antigens (involving disease and allergy) and to the recognition of "self" and "not self" (transplant rejections belong to this area).

C. P. von Pirquet, an Austrian pediatrician who practiced in the early twentieth century, contributed to this growing understanding of the immune system with his view of *allergy* as heightened immunological reactivity—what is now called *hypersensitivity*. He was the first to realize that *immunizing* people against grass pollen and *desensitizing* anaphylactically sensitive animals actually reflected the same immunological mechanisms.

The term *desensitization* initially referred to a series of allergen injections in sensitized animals of gradually increasing sublethal doses. Later results with humans, however, led to an additional term for this allergy therapy. Soon after successful desensitization with animals, a report described work with 114 patients with asthma and hay fever linked to pollen hypersensitivity. Unlike desensitized animals, which no longer reacted to the offending allergen in a skin test, humans—even when dramatic clinical improvement occurred after desensitization therapy—still reacted to the allergen in a skin test. Because this antiallergy therapy had not produced complete desensitization, the term *hyposensitization* was coined to describe its use with humans.

HOW DOES IMMUNOTHERAPY WORK?

Despite immunotherapy's successful use for 75 years, how it works is still not fully understood. But the significant elements in the process are known. They are (1) the specific IgE that the immune system produces in response to an allergen, (2) the mast cells and specialized white blood cells releasing the mediators that stimulate allergic symptoms, and (3) *blocking antibodies*. The first two elements have been described in the discussion of the allergic reaction in Chapter 3. Blocking antibodies are produced by the immune system during the injection series. Most of them are of the IgG variety, and a small number are IgA. Found free in the blood, blocking antibodies compete

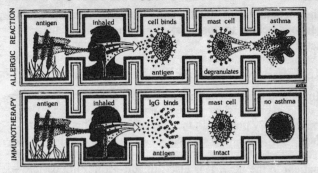

Figure 10.2 How immunotherapy works. *Top*: A typical allergic asthma attack. *Bottom*: Shows the hypothesis that immunotherapy increases IgG (immunoglobin G) production, which prevents the allergen molecules from reaching the IgE–mast cell units.

with the IgE antibodies (which are bound to mast cells) for the allergen after it invades the body (Figure 10.2). By preventing the allergen from reaching the antibody–mast cell unit, mediators are never released. The allergic response is thereby aborted.

Immunotherapy also appears to reduce the levels of specific IgE over time. People with a seasonal allergy normally show a temporary rise in these antibodies during their allergy period, with the level waning over the rest of the year. Several years of immunotherapy reduce both the maximum and minimum antibody levels.

Immunotherapy may also directly affect mast cells in the lungs. After immunotherapy with animals, postmortem studies have been done that combine an allergen either with isolated pieces of lung tissue or with a type of white blood cell that is very similar to mast cells. The same postmortem tissue test is done for allergic animals that had no therapy, and the results are compared. After immunotherapy, these cells are much less responsive to allergens.

The reason why is still open to question. Reduced IgE levels could explain their lessened responsiveness. Another possibility is simply that there are fewer mast cells, or that they no longer bind effectively with IgE. Or per-

haps immunotherapy interferes with the mast cell's biochemical chain of events that culminates in mediator release.

IS IMMUNOTHERAPY EFFECTIVE?

Immunotherapy is an inexact and controversial science
(some even consider it more an art than a science) that
became very popular in the United States. This popularity,
however, has not been echoed in the rest of the world.
The effect of immunotherapy is not consistent from one
patient to the next. It is also difficult—if not impossible—
to know in advance how completely, and for how long, it
will block a new patient's allergic response to a particular
allergen.

The effectiveness of immunotherapy for allergic asthmatics breaks down into two issues: how well does this
therapy work in allergic asthma, and which patients are
most likely to benefit from it?

How Well Does Immunotherapy Work?

Since 1949, more than 20 well-designed studies have examined the effect of immunotherapy on sensitivity to pollen or insect venom (e.g., bees and wasps). Each of these
studies compared results from two groups of patients. One
group was given immunotherapy, and the other was given
injections that did not contain any allergen extract. Only
2 of the 20 studies showed no effect from immunotherapy.
In the others, 60 to 80 percent of the immunotherapy patients improved, but only 20 to 30 percent of the other
patients improved.

Unfortunately, only two of these studies examined the
effects of immunotherapy on allergic asthmatics, and both
of them dealt only with children. Although immunotherapy gave excellent results in both studies, the children participating in these investigations were very carefully
selected. The complete set of data needed to evaluate the
effect of immunotherapy on allergic asthmatics—children
and adults—does not yet exist.

However well-accepted immunology may be in the general treatment of certain allergies, it remains one of the most controversial areas of asthma therapy. For one thing, the degree of improvement is not consistent from one patient to another. For another, it is difficult—if not impossible—to know in advance how much a new patient will actually benefit from an expensive treatment that will last for several years.

Another problem is that some patients unexpectedly develop major sensitivity to an allergen that has not been part of their therapy program. The lengthy aspect of immunotherapy increases this likelihood. If a patient changes jobs during this time, for example, he may well be exposed to new allergens.

A further difficulty is that—despite the treatment's apparent success with children—experts in the field do not recommend subjecting children to several years of regular injections for an outcome that cannot be guaranteed. It is highly unpleasant for them, and whatever benefits they may eventually experience are too far in the future to provide any meaningful comfort in the unpalatable present. The experience too often leaves a child frightened of doctors and ill disposed to cooperating in other aspects of his treatment.

The allergies immunotherapy treats most successfully, compared to the list of allergens that can cause allergic asthmatics severe problems, are few: pollen from ragweed and from certain grasses and trees, and house dust.

Immunotherapy is usually not recommended for animal dander allergies because of the intense reaction to injections. (A new preparation against cat allergies has become available, which appears to have good results.) It also does not seem to be effective with mold allergies. Other allergens are sometimes considered for immunotherapy. Although results may be good in individual cases, specific data have not been published.

If a patient's asthma is strongly allergic in origin, and if his history and careful skin testing support sensitivity to an allergen that responds well to immunotherapy, then there is a good chance that this lengthy and expensive treatment will reduce the frequency and severity of asthma symptoms (but by how much, and for how long, often remains unknown until after treatment). This means that less medication will be needed for asthma control. For the appropriate individual, immunotherapy can be very helpful as an additional tool in treating allergic asthma.

What Kind of Patient Benefits Most?

It bears repeating: The best allergic asthma candidates for immunotherapy are those for whom allergies are a central trigger. The problem allergen(s) should be among those that respond well to this treatment, and should provoke a clear-cut skin test reaction. (Having a family member who has done well with immunotherapy also increases the patient's chance of success with it.)

Within this group is the smaller number of patients for whom the benefits of immunotherapy have the greatest impact. This occurs for any one, or combination, of the following reasons: their asthma is troubling to the point where it diminishes their quality of life; they are unable to avoid the allergen(s)—perhaps they cannot move, or cannot change jobs, or cannot change their living conditions; or they experience unacceptable side effects from their asthma or hay fever medication.

If your doctor feels that you are a good prospect for immunotherapy, no decision should be made until you have thoroughly discussed several issues with him that are raised here in brief. Will successful immunotherapy change the course of your disease enough to make it worth the time, inconvenience, expense, and possible risk of unpleasant (or dangerous) injection reactions? (The next section contains details about this possibility.)

HOW IS IMMUNOTHERAPY DONE?

If your doctor considers you a potential candidate for immunotherapy, and you have agreed after discussing the above questions with him, the next step is careful skin or

RAST testing for the allergen(s) your history points to. If the results for a particular allergen are negative, then immunotherapy for it is not advised. (Also, allergens that provoke a skin-test reaction but have never caused any other allergic symptoms should not be used in immunotherapy.) Combined with a history of specific allergy, a positive skin test—or a strong positive RAST, if skin testing must be avoided—means that immunotherapy can proceed.

When immunotherapy begins, occasionally a patient makes the mistake of thinking it can substitute for his daily efforts to minimize the allergens in his home environment. This treatment is an addition, not a replacement. Beginning immunotherapy does not mean an allergic asthmatic can safely stop these environmental controls, or bring an animal into the house, or disregard pollution alerts.

The first series of injections is on a weekly basis for several months or so. The initial injections contain a very low dose of the substance the patient is allergic to, with the amount gradually increasing over this period until it reaches a prescribed maximum dose—the largest amount of the most concentrated extract that does not cause a large local (that is, around the injection site) or a systemic (involving several bodily systems) reaction. Highly allergic patients are given a longer period for this first series so that the amount of allergen can be increased more slowly.

When the maximum dose is reached, the interval between injections begins to lengthen as soon as asthma symptoms are noticeably less when the patient encounters the allergen. First they are given every two weeks, then every three weeks, then monthly until the patient has been symptom-free, or at least with very easily controllable symptoms, for a predetermined period. Again, how long the patient remains at each stage depends on how allergic he was to start with. And some allergists prefer, as a general rule, to continue monthly injections until the patient has been symptom-free or easily controllable for one full year or more.

What Happens After an Allergen Injection?

Most reactions to an allergen injection occur within the first 30 minutes. The typical reaction is limited to some temporary swelling and redness at the injection site. If a reaction lasts for more than one full day, or covers an area larger than a quarter, tell your doctor at your next appointment. This is a caution sign, meaning that further increases in allergen dose must be made more slowly to avoid a possible systemic reaction.

If a local reaction becomes uncomfortable before it subsides, you can put a cold washcloth or some ice on it. If you prefer, you can take an oral antihistamine (like Benadryl, which is now available without prescription). The discomfort is annoying, but nothing to worry about.

A systemic reaction, on the other hand, is an emergency. The symptoms can include sneezing, chest tightness, hives, throat swelling, difficulty in swallowing, nausea, stomachache, fainting, and a full-blown asthma attack. Because such an emergency demands immediate treatment, a patient should always remain in the doctor's office for the full 30-minute period after each injection. Then, if the patient does have a serious reaction, treatment will not be delayed.

Sometimes an injection of adrenaline, plus antihistamines and theophylline, are needed to stop a systemic reaction from progressing to anaphylactic shock. The doctor may also tie a tourniquet around the patient's arm to slow the allergen's absorption into the bloodstream.

Occasionally a reaction (not a systemic one) occurs 4 to 12 hours after the injection, either a large local reaction or a widespread rash. This delayed reaction sometimes includes fever, headache, malaise, or asthma. An antihistamine, or an anti-inflammatory drug such as aspirin (for asthmatics who are not aspirin-sensitive), will help relieve discomfort.

Just as with an immediate local reaction that is larger, or lasts longer, than usual, your doctor must also be told of a delayed reaction if you have one. Then he can change the pace of your treatment if he feels that your reaction warrants it.

How Long Does Immunotherapy Take?

The duration averages somewhere between three and four years, and is rarely more than five years. Where an individual falls within this range depends on how allergic he is to start with, how quickly his symptoms diminish and how completely they disappear, and on his doctor's particular definition of "longer" and "shorter" time periods.

How Long Do Immunotherapy Benefits Last?

Again, this depends on the individual. Some allergic asthmatics find long-lasting improvement. Others find that symptoms return fairly quickly, but are less intense than before therapy. And some experience increasing symptoms once therapy stops. In this case, injections may have to be resumed.

✧✧ 11 ✧✧

Stress and Anxiety Management

The importance of stress and anxiety in triggering or aggravating asthma episodes has been reported over the centuries. In recent decades, research has taken three different paths in trying to identify and understand the psychological factors involved. One has already been discussed, and the other two are the focus of this chapter.

One research pathway has attempted to link asthma both to stress-producing personality characteristics and with certain stressful family interaction patterns as "causes" of this chronic disease. As emphasized in the introductory chapter and in the discussion of asthma triggers, the development of asthma does not spring from a neurotic mother, a neurotic personality, or any other negative psychological influence. Stress and fear can worsen an asthma episode or even trigger one, but not unless the necessary genes and environmental circumstances have already combined to produce the disease. Experiments carried out in this area were prejudiced from the start. They were designed from the point of view that asthma reflects a psychological disturbance, and so they served only to perpetuate this myth.

Another group of asthma studies attempts to understand the interplay between emotional/neurological, physiological, and immunological elements of the human system in precipitating asthma attacks. We are going to examine this area briefly to set the stage for our primary topic, which is the variety of techniques for reducing the stress and anxiety that are typically so troublesome in asthma.

Asthma, Anxiety, and the Brain

Although it is not yet certain how the brain influences asthma, scientists have come up with hypotheses which let us visualize two possibilities. There are two ways the brain appears to play a significant role—via the emotions—in modulating asthma.

At the simplest level, anxiety can cause many people to hyperventilate. For an asthmatic, hyperventilation aggravates the disease. This worsening increases his anxiety, which increases his hyperventilation and worsens the asthma attack still further, making him even more anxious, and so on. It is a classic vicious cycle.

Hyperventilation due to other causes—such as strenuous exercise—does not continue to spiral. Once the feedback signals reaching the respiratory center indicate that enough excess carbon dioxide has been eliminated, hyperventilation is no longer needed and breathing returns to normal. But anxiety-produced hyperventilation is not under direct respiratory center control or feedback modification. It appears to be driven from the *hypothalamus*, the part of our brain dominantly involved in emotions. When the hypothalamus controls the respiratory system, the usual feedback signals are largely ignored.

Anxiety's effects on asthma may also involve the brain much more directly. The sympathetic and parasympathetic nervous systems—the two branches of the autonomic nervous system—are intimately connected with asthma symptoms. (The sympathetic branch stimulates the production of cAMP, which relaxes the airway muscles. The parasympathetic branch stimulates the production of cGMP, which contracts these muscles.) The autonomic nervous system is controlled by the hypothalamus, which in turn receives information from the cerebral cortex, the thinking part of our brain. The hypothalamus translates thoughts into their emotional counterparts, then stimulates the appropriate branch of the autonomic nervous system.

There are two important points to keep in mind. One is that these branches of the autonomic nervous system achieve opposite effects in every area of the body's functioning that they influence. The hormones that each branch stimulates have opposite effects, immunoglobin production increases or diminishes depending on which branch is involved, the airways constrict or dilate, and so forth. The second point is that these effects are normal. Whether their *consequences* are normal depends on the state of the organ system involved. When stress activates the parasympathetic nervous system and the airway muscles contract, a person with normal lungs does not experience any breathing difficulty. But the individual with lung pathology—such as asthma—has a problem because his airway muscles contract too strongly.

Stress/Anxiety Management and Asthma

A variety of stress and anxiety management techniques are effective with asthma. They include psychotherapy and its branches, relaxation techniques, systematic desensitization, hypnosis, biofeedback, and operant conditioning. The goals for all involve helping the asthmatic become more responsible for his own treatment, helping him cope more effectively with his disease, and diminishing the frequency and severity of attacks. Although the virtues of many of these techniques have been grossly exaggerated—sometimes at the expense, both financial and health-wise, of the patient—they most certainly can be useful additions to the essential basics (medication and asthma-proofing) of asthma treatment.

Caution: These techniques are not inherently harmful, and in many cases they offer substantial help. The danger lies in deciding that—if a particular technique gives you significant benefit—it can be substituted for your medication. The most effective way to treat asthma is by *adding* one or more of these techniques to your medication. If you eventually feel that your asthma has improved enough to let you reduce your medication, we urge you to do this under your doctor's supervision.

It is also important not to be so overly cautious as to rely solely on medication. Drugs can have significant side effects. The reasonable approach to managing asthma is a balanced program that integrates the benefits of medication, self-regulation of stress/anxiety, and exercise. (Exercise for the asthmatic is the next chapter's topic.)

Because the respiratory improvement gained from these techniques is relatively small compared to the changes that result from drugs, some doctors believe these techniques are not worth the effort. But their value is not measured just by the numbers on testing instruments. To whatever degree they allow the asthmatic to reduce drug usage, they are valuable. And even a small improvement, or simply stabilization, of pulmonary function is of great clinical importance if it provides the edge that reverses or lessens a serious attack. Even if there were no direct pulmonary benefits, the calming influence of these techniques substantially decreases the fear and panic that often mushroom when respiratory distress suddenly occurs.

Your Doctor's Support

Ideally, your first encounter with stress management should be informal, occurring during your first visit to your doctor's office. A sympathetic, supportive doctor can alleviate a great deal of the average asthmatic's anxiety by using a nurturing approach to give the asthmatic and his family a thorough, realistic education concerning this disease and how to live with it most effectively. (It is also the treating physician's responsibility to identify any psychiatric problems—especially depression—that may complicate asthma treatment, and refer the patient to a psychiatrist if necessary.)

Psychotherapy

Psychotherapy is said to help asthmatics with two kinds of anxiety problems that—if they exist—can make it very difficult for them to deal effectively with their disease. These personality characteristics do not cause, or result from, the asthma. They are part of some asthmatics' personalities regardless of pulmonary disease and assume importance only if they interfere with the asthmatics' ability to manage the disease well.

One type of personality problem is hypochondria. The hypochondriac's excessive concern about every tiny change in his health, plus his tendency to overmedicate himself, are counterproductive in helping his asthma and quality of life. At the other end is the asthmatic who denies the truth of his condition and so refuses to cooperate in taking medication, monitoring his symptoms, and making appropriate changes in his environment.

A considerable problem with psychotherapy is that its great financial expense makes it inaccessible to a great many of the asthmatics who could benefit from it.

Another helpful form of therapy is group therapy, preferably with others in the same situation (asthmatics, or parents of asthmatic children). Joining others who are in an identical situation forms a *support group*. A support group is invaluable for two reasons. Because the new asthmatic (or parent) realizes that he is not the only one coping with this disease, his sense of isolation and frustration are greatly relieved. Talking out his experiences and feelings

with others who understand his problems firsthand is irreplaceable in building confidence and creating a positive
sense of one's place in the world. A support group also
forms an educational network for the exchange of information and problem-solving solutions of all kinds (such as
good vacation spots, effective mechanical aids, dealing
with a child's school, anticipating and handling a variety
of problems).

One large study of the value of group therapy divided
asthmatics into three different treatment groups. Two of
the groups used different medication combinations, and the
third group added group therapy. In this third group, the
percentage of patients whose asthma improved was three
to four times greater. Unfortunately, the investigators did
not record the asthma severity in the three different groups.
If the patients who improved most had the mildest asthma
to begin with, their hefty improvement rate is not as impressive as it would otherwise be. Better-designed studies
obviously need to be done.

Relaxation Techniques

Relaxation techniques include four overlapping approaches: inducing relaxation by working directly with the
muscles; systematic desensitization; different forms of
meditation; and hypnosis.

MUSCLE RELAXATION

Jacobson's relaxation technique, the most widely used of
the many relaxation methods, bears the name of the man
who developed it in the early 1920s. Edmond Jacobson
was a Chicago physician and physiologist who theorized
that muscle relaxation and psychological stress cannot coexist. A growing body of evidence now suggests that muscle relaxation causes physiological changes that are the
opposite of those occurring with stress and anxiety. Taken

together, these changes are called the "relaxation response."

In theory, if stress cannot exist in a relaxed body, then improving an asthmatic's ability to relax his muscles at will should eliminate whatever role anxiety plays in worsening his bronchospasms. Research with asthmatics indicates that the regular use of a muscle-relaxation technique reduces the intensity of attacks. (It is not clear yet whether attacks also become less frequent and/or medication decreases.)

Jacobson's technique is a prescribed sequence of quiet muscle exercises that alternately tense and relax all the major muscle groups. While one group is being focused on, all the others are to remain as relaxed as possible. A few sessions with a physical therapist are usually all that is needed to learn this technique of progressive relaxation.

Initially the exercises should be done while lying down in a quiet, dimly lit room. Once the technique is mastered, it can be done while sitting in a comfortable chair, or even at work. Start at the head or toes, focusing on each part of the body in order until the end of the sequence is reached. The sequence progresses over seven areas: (1) ankles, shins, calves, knees, thighs, buttocks, lower back; (2) stomach; (3) neck, chest, shoulders; (4) jaws, lips, head; (5) eyes; (6) forehead, biceps, elbows; (7) fingers, hands, forearms, upper arms.

Within an area, each muscle site is tensed individually for 5 to 10 seconds, then relaxed for about 30 seconds. This is repeated several times before continuing to the next group of muscles. With each muscle, the person concentrates on how contraction makes it feel, and how it feels when it relaxes. The entire procedure takes about 30 minutes. Several sessions gradually produce a clear memory of what relaxation feels like, and the ability to control it. You will get out of this program what you put into it, which means that it can work only if you are committed to doing it regularly. Ideally, a specific time each day should be set aside for these relaxation exercises.

SYSTEMATIC DESENSITIZATION

Systematic desensitization uses muscle relaxation to minimize or eliminate a person's anxiety in situations that normally cause him overwhelming stress. There are four steps in this process. One is mastery of Jacobson's relaxation technique. Two is use of an anxiety scale. Three is construction of the individual's "anxiety hierarchies." Four is using muscle relaxation in the presence of visualized anxiety-causing stimuli of increasing strength.

After mastering muscle relaxation, the patient lists all the situations that make him anxious. Then he uses an anxiety scale to evaluate each one, assigning a number from 0 to 100. For example, thinking about getting a parking ticket may be a 20 for him; thinking of having an IRS tax audit may be an 80; being criticized by his boss may be a 65; going to an audition may be a 90; taking a test may be a 40. The phrase "may be" emphasizes that each person's responses will be different, both in the kinds of situations on his list and in the relative amount of anxiety that each one causes him.

Then another list is made, an "anxiety hierarchy." For the asthmatic, this means selecting all the situations he knows cause or worsen asthma attacks for him, and using the anxiety ratings to order them from weakest to most potent.

The final desensitization phase requires the patient to visualize a situation from his anxiety hierarchy while he carries out muscle relaxation. He starts at the bottom of his hierarchy—that is, with the least anxiety-producing situation—and gradually continues up the hierarchy until he can relax his muscles at will while visualizing his most potent anxiety-producing situation. By this time, situations further down on his hierarchy will probably no longer cause him any anxiety at all. His body has learned to associate them with relaxation instead of anxiety.

Systematic desensitization can be thought of as the psychological equivalent of immunotherapy. Just as an allergist starts with a tiny amount of allergen and gradually increases the dose, this technique progresses from low-anxiety situations up to the highest ones to reduce the anxiety response to all of them substantially. Research shows that systematic desensitization improves the asthmatic's pulmonary function during an attack, just as muscle relaxation does. It also appears to make attacks less frequent and to reduce aerosol bronchodilator use.

MEDITATION

The effects of meditation are very real on a physical level. Successful use of a meditation technique actually means that the person has learned to control certain aspects of his central nervous system. This is another way to achieve the relaxation response. *Transcendental meditation* (TM) in particular has been studied extensively, perhaps because of the sudden popularity it attained during the 1960s. TM definitely lowers oxygen use, ventilation, and heart rate. An experiment specifically with asthmatics found TM to lower airway resistance by half and to increase airflow by a small but meaningful amount. But the long-term relation of meditation techniques to mysticism—because of their historical roots in Eastern and Western religions—has kept them from the mainstream of therapy.

Although the different meditation techniques appear to produce the same physiological effects, there are pronounced differences between some of them in actual practice. An asthmatic interested in meditation should learn about these basic differences and choose the technique he feels most comfortable with. His local library or bookstore should have some informative introductory material. Another information source are meditation institutes or centers, which are listed under "Meditation Instruction" in the Yellow Pages.

HYPNOSIS

Hypnosis is a trance state that combines heightened inner awareness with a diminished awareness of one's surroundings. It can be induced artificially (by *hypnotism*), but it also occurs naturally under the appropriate circumstances. Hypnosis is similar to the state reached during daydreaming, and to the experience of being so completely engrossed—such as by music or a theatrical performance—that awareness of one's surroundings temporarily disappears.

Hypnosis can be a therapeutic tool because a hypnotized person is especially susceptible to positive, reasonable suggestions. An unfortunate myth is that the hypnotized person can be ordered to do things he would otherwise refuse to do. For any suggestion to be accepted, it must make sense to the individual and not violate his moral code.

The earliest recorded use of hypnosis in medicine is contained in a three-thousand-year-old Egyptian papyrus. It was of major medical importance in ancient Greece. Priests at the temple of Asclepios (the Greek god of medicine) on the Aegean island of Epidaurus used the hypnotic trance to cure pilgrims seeking help for their medical problems.

The modern use of hypnosis is said to have begun with the Viennese physician Franz Anton Mesmer (from whose name comes the word *mesmerize*) in the late seventeenth and early eighteenth centuries. He introduced the use of hypnosis into Viennese, then Parisian, medical circles. Mesmer thought that magnetism explained the effects of hypnotism, and coined the term "animal magnetism" to differentiate it from magnetism in the physical world. Reports of miraculous cures in Vienna and Paris soon won Mesmer a large popular following and the enmity of both medical establishments. They barred him from practicing medicine. After a stay in England, Mesmer returned to a life of obscurity in Austria and died in 1815.

Hypnotism's popularity was cyclical after Mesmer's death. The lack of interest following its first epidemic use was punctuated with periodic curiosity. The high point in its resurgence was between 1885 and 1910, with smaller revivals after World War I in treating war-related neuroses. The final decline of hypnosis was due to a combination of rejections. The medical profession had never accepted hypnotism as a legitimate tool, and Sigmund Freud eventually rejected it as a tool in the practice of psychoanalysis (which itself was rapidly gaining popularity).

Recent evidence, however, indicates that hypnosis may be valuable in treating asthma. The typical suggestion is: "As you relax, your breathing will become easier and easier." Benefits may be long-term. Two well-designed studies, each using well over two hundred asthmatics, divided their subjects into two equal groups. One group was given relaxation training, the other was given hypnotherapy. Each subject's asthma was reevaluated one year after completing training. In one study, improvement was seen in 50 percent of the hypnotherapy subjects and 42 percent of those using muscle relaxation. The other study showed a more impressive difference between the two groups. Asthma improved in 59 percent of the hypnotherapy subjects, and only 43 percent of the others. In fact, Dr. Margaret Turner-Warwick, professor of thoracic medicine at the University of London, finds that many of her most difficult asthma patients improve when hypnotherapy is added to their treatment.

Many people are highly skeptical about their own capacity to be hypnotized. Except for those with severe mental disturbance, most people can be hypnotized to some degree. (Degree of hypnotizability reflects how long and how hard the hypnotist must work to achieve hypnosis.) This degree is assessed by the amount of white that shows after a person is told to roll his eyes up and keep them there while he lowers his eyelids. The higher the eye remains, the more hypnotizable the person is. This basic potential for hypnosis can be modified by motivation. Actual hypnotizability can be tested by hypnotizing the person to raise his arm, and recording the number of instructions and amount of time it takes. Obviously, fewer instructions and less time go along with greater hypnotizability.

Once hypnotizability and motivation are established, the person is hypnotized, given the appropriate suggestion(s), and taught to hypnotize himself (called *autohypnosis*). Autohypnosis—which should be done daily—induces relaxation and also reinforces the suggestions implanted during the hypnosis sessions.

Operant Conditioning

Operant conditioning—the most popular form of behavior modification—aims to eliminate unwanted behavior and encourage desirable behavior. Adjusting to asthma, as with any chronic disease, is made easier by positive behavior and more difficult by negative actions. Examples of negative behavior for the asthmatic are smoking, overmedication, and disregarding medication. Eliminating ("extinguishing") such negative behaviors and strengthening ("reinforcing" or "rewarding") their favorable opposites should improve the asthmatic's control of his disease.

Operant conditioning focuses on "operant" behavior. "Operant" means that the chance of the specific behavior recurring is influenced by the event immediately following it. If this event is rewarding, the behavior is more and more likely to recur. If the reward is permanently discontinued, the behavior will eventually disappear. This process of changing behavior by identifying and manipulating the specific experience that influences it is technically called "conditioning." We often instinctively rely on this kind of approach with children and animals when we want to encourage or discourage a particular behavior. Applying operant conditioning to change your, or your child's, behavior in the complex kinds of situations involving a chronic disease is often done under the guidance of a behavior therapist.

An example of extinguishing negative behavior involves an asthmatic girl whose life was disrupted by frequent severe coughing episodes that were obviously excessive for the degree of her asthma. A behavior therapist pinpointed the girl's reward as her parents' sympathy and attention following each coughing attack. The number of these episodes dropped dramatically after the girl's parents withheld their sympathy and attention whenever such an attack went beyond what was appropriate for the severity of her asthma.

An example of reinforcing a positive behavior concerns another asthmatic child, a toddler who fought against taking his oral medication. He loved having a plant mister sprayed in his mouth. The child became substantially more cooperative in swallowing his medicine after his mother began giving him this treat every time he cooperated.

The need for *immediate* reinforcement in order to condition the positive behavior makes this technique far more difficult than it first seems. It is not effective to work with a patient only in the limited setting of the therapist's office. It is critically important that reinforcement and withholding be carried out consistently in all settings that are relevant for the patient. This means that the people close to the patient must know about and understand what is going on, and cooperate in carrying it out.

Biofeedback

Biofeedback uses a learning situation to change the nature of a physiological response (heart rate, for example). Electronic or mechanical equipment continuously measures and displays this physiological behavior so the patient can see what happens when he attempts to change it. In this way he learns how to achieve this change. Biofeedback has been used with asthma in two different contexts: facilitating relaxation training and controlling the opening of the airways.

For relaxation training, both skin temperature and the electrical activity in the muscles supply the feedback that helps the asthmatic do a more effective job of reducing his muscle tone (Figure 11.1). Skin temperature and electrical

Figure 11.1 Typical biofeedback setup. The patient is watching a recording of the electrical activity from her facial muscles. Activity falls as she relaxes these muscles. Her target is maintaining the electrical activity below the horizontal line on the screen.

activity both diminish as the muscles relax. (Biofeedback-assisted relaxation training combined with another stress-reducing method has also reduced airway resistance in some asthmatics.)

Using biofeedback to increase the airway openings—using information on airflow or airway resistance—is not an unqualified success. The equipment needed to measure these aspects of pulmonary function is expensive, and the small improvement gained offers no advantage over the far more inexpensive relaxation techniques already discussed. A new feedback device, however, gives promise in this area. The device measures breathing sounds through a stethoscope, and the asthmatic tries to diminish the intensity of these sounds. Preliminary results indicate that working with breathing sounds in this way improves lung function. And asthmatics who have trained with this device report that they feel better and are using less medication. If this simple and inexpensive technique lives up to its initial promise, it will provide an easy and workable approach to asthma self-management.

Perhaps the most intriguing biofeedback research with asthma used facial muscle tone to change pulmonary function. This study found that asthmatics' airway resistance lowers as their facial muscles relax. And nonasthmatics' lung function becomes poorer when they tense their facial muscles! The mechanism behind this is not yet understood, but the implications for relaxation training with asthmatics is clear. Special emphasis should be placed on relaxing the facial muscles.

$\ast\!\ast$ 12 $\ast\!\ast$

Physical Therapies
for Asthma

Today, physical therapy covers more than rehabilitating muscles that were injured or paralyzed. It includes training them so that the heart and lungs can supply oxygenated blood to the body much more efficiently than they could before. Sometimes this is necessary after an acute health problem, such as a heart attack. It can also be of major importance for a chronic condition, such as asthma. That is the focus of this chapter.

First we will examine the more traditional aspects of pulmonary physical therapy: exercises for breathing more effectively with narrowed airways, and postural drainage to clear the airways of tenacious mucus. The remainder of this chapter is devoted to the importance for asthmatics of physical fitness.

Breathing Exercises

Breathing exercises are probably the most widely used of all physical therapy techniques, yet they are the least supported by objective scientific data. It is impossible—except by hypnosis, for some people—to consciously change

221

the tone of our airway muscles. But we do have a great deal of voluntary control over our respiratory muscles. Asthmatics can use this control to improve their respiration by learning the most effective way to breathe through narrowed airways.

The faster you try to force air through a narrow tube, the more resistance the air encounters and the harder you have to work. The asthmatic who breathes rapidly finds breathing much harder and more stressful. Some asthmatics naturally adopt a slow style of breathing. Others, perhaps because of greater anxiety about their disease, breathe much more rapidly than they need to. Because it makes their breathing far more difficult, they become even more distressed and anxious.

This heightened anxiety level in turn increases the tension of their abdominal muscles, which prevents the diaphragm—the primary inspiratory muscle—from moving and functioning properly. The diaphragm is the dome-shaped muscle separating the chest and abdominal cavities. It contracts during inspiration, causing the dome to move down into the abdominal area. To make room, the abdominal contents (such as the stomach and intestines) are compressed and the muscles that form the abdominal wall are pushed outward. But if these muscles are unusually tense, they cannot be pushed completely out of the way. Then the diaphragm does not have enough room to contract fully, which reduces the size of inspirations.

Breathing exercises were developed with two goals in mind. *Diaphragmatic breathing* uses the abdominal muscles, and therefore the diaphragm, properly. *Pursed-lip expiration* slows down the rate of breathing, and may also help keep the airways open. (Because the abdominal muscles are relaxed, these breathing exercises reinforce the results of the relaxation techniques that we discussed in the last chapter.)

Note: Although both components of the breathing exercises are simple to learn and do on your own, it is a good idea to learn them from a physical therapist to make sure that you are doing them properly.

HOW TO DO THE BREATHING EXERCISES

Lie flat on your back with a pillow under your knees, because this position exaggerates abdominal movement. First preference is a carpeted floor, second preference is a firm bed. Keep your mouth closed so that you always breathe through your nose. Rest one hand on the middle of your chest at about your nipple level. Place the other hand on your abdomen, thumb just below your navel. Since your abdomen—not your chest—should move as you breathe, the hand that moves tells you whether or not you are doing the exercises properly.

First concentrate on letting your abdominal muscles relax. As you breathe, you should feel the hand on your abdomen rise and fall while the hand on your chest remains still. When you are ready to add pursed-lip expiration to diaphragmatic breathing, inhale, then purse your lips and breathe out slowly. Your lips should be tight enough so that the air comes out with a hissing sound. You should feel your abdomen moving inward, with no movement in your chest. Make your expirations twice as long as your inspirations. Some people find that a two-second inspiration and four-second expiration work well. A loud clock or a metronome can help to pace your breathing.

Practice this exercise combination for 20 minutes a day. When it has become quite effortless, do the exercise in a sitting position instead of lying down. Once this becomes very easy, graduate to a standing position, and then finally do it while you walk. (Your breathing rate may increase slightly to make up for the added oxygen demands of walking.)

WHY DO THESE EXERCISES WORK?

Everyone agrees on the benefits of the slow, relaxed breathing that diaphragmatic breathing and pursed-lip expiration foster. Discussion continues, however, as to what underlies these benefits. One school of thought claims that making breathing slower allows it to become more coordinated. The other suggests that the pressure developed by expiring through pursed lips actually keeps the airways open. There is also controversy as to the best method for achieving slow, relaxed breathing. Is it diaphragmatic plus pursed-lip breathing, yoga, Zen meditation, learning to play a wind instrument (such as flute or recorder)? Our feeling is that none of these techniques is harmful, and anything that increases an asthmatic's sensitivity to what his respiratory system is doing must be helpful.

Postural Drainage

The asthmatic whose mucus is so tenacious that coughing does not bring it up can benefit from a technique called *postural* or *gravity drainage*. As the name implies, this technique uses gravity to help drain mucus that has been loosened by clapping (technically called percussing), and then vibrating, the asthmatic's chest and back. This is done in a variety of postures (nine at most) for a maximum of 30 minutes. Someone else is needed to do the clapping and vibrating. Most often this is a physical therapist or nurse, but the technique is so easy that a family member can learn it from one of these professionals in just a few sessions.

Postural drainage needs to be done only when a great deal of tenacious mucus is being produced. For some asthmatics this means daily, and for others it is only periodic. Not all asthmatics need to use all nine positions for effective mucus drainage. This point should be checked with the professional who teaches the technique to the asthmatic and his partner.

A large glass of warm water is taken before doing postural drainage. (Asthmatics should always be well hydrated, which means having an ample amount of fluid in one's system. This is especially important for the asthmatic with tenacious mucus.) Nine different positions exist

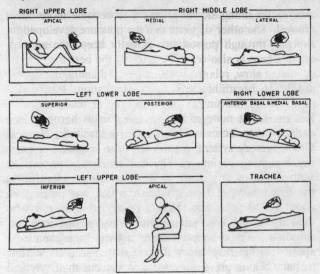

RIGHT UPPER LOBE | RIGHT MIDDLE LOBE

APICAL | MEDIAL | LATERAL

LEFT LOWER LOBE | RIGHT LOWER LOBE

SUPERIOR | POSTERIOR | ANTERIOR BASAL & MEDIAL BASAL

LEFT UPPER LOBE | TRACHEA

INFERIOR | APICAL

Figure 12.1 Postural drainage positions. (Reproduced with permission from A. Haas et al., *Pulmonary Therapy and Rehabilitation: Principles and Practice*. Baltimore: Williams and Wilkins, 1979, p. 127.)

for drainage because the bronchial tree branches in many directions. Figure 12.1 illustrates these positions and where clapping and vibration must be applied to drain each section of the lungs. Although a board is most convenient for the positions lying down, a bed can be used with blocks raising the foot 18 inches higher than the head.

Each position should be held for two to three minutes while clapping and vibration are done. Clapping is done with a cupped hand to produce a hollow—not sharp— sound. Vibrating is done during expiration by quickly shaking the hand on the designated area. Although mucus may be coughed up immediately, some or all of it may take a while to come up.

Precaution: Many elderly people have fragile bones, especially if they have been on steroids for a long time.

An elderly asthmatic with this problem risks rib fractures from the clapping. If there is the slightest question about this possibility, the asthmatic's doctor must be consulted.

Physical Fitness

Asthma has been doubly associated with exercise since earliest times. The word itself is derived from the classical Greek verb describing the normal open-mouthed or panting breathing of intense physical exertion. The earliest written use of this word in Western culture appeared in the first record of Homer's *Iliad*, which was transcribed about 2,700 years ago. Homer described a warrior who died at the end of a furious battle with "asthma and perspiration." The descriptive term "asthma" was eventually applied to the respiratory disease that caused its victims to pant heavily as if they were in the midst of physical exertion.

It was also realized very early that physical exertion can provoke asthma. Aretaeus, the second-century Cappadocian doctor mentioned at the start of Chapter 1, wrote, "If from running, gymnastic exercise or any other work the breathing becomes difficult, it is called Asthma." In 1698, Sir John Floyer wrote the first book devoted entirely to asthma and clearly stated its association with exercise. "All violent exercise makes the asthmatic to breathe short, because their lungs are frequently oppressed with . . . [mucus]; and if the exercise be continued, it occasions a fit. . . . The most agreeable exercise is riding; the greatest [asthma-producers] are sawing, bowling, ringing a dumb bell, swinging, dancing; walking is more vehement than riding but not so great as the others."

In fact, bronchospasm as a response to exercise is so prevalent among asthmatics that it bears its own name— *exercise-induced asthma* or *bronchospasm*. In medical lingo it becomes *EIA* or *EIB*. The estimates of asthmatics who respond to exercise in this way range from 65 to 100 percent. Also, it is suspected that a group of "hidden" (undiagnosed) asthmatics exists who have only EIA symptoms. With this history, it is not surprising that the prevailing opinion—both medical and lay—was that asthmatics should not exercise. Some physicians believed that swimming was the only exception.

(*Note*: Exercise-induced asthma should not be confused with exercise-induced anaphylaxis. The latter is a very infrequent allergic disorder in which exercise produces a rash, hives, tremendous body heat, flushing, lightheadedness, and breathing difficulty. The reaction can become life-threatening.)

Recently, the negative attitude toward exercise for asthmatics has begun to change. The new approach is exemplified in the current article "Comprehensive Approach to Asthma" by Dr. Reuben M. Cherniack, chairman of the department of medicine at the National Jewish Center for Immunology and Respiratory Medicine in Denver, Colorado. "Achievement of maximal physical fitness must be emphasized," he insists, "and patients should be advised gradually to increase their exercise tolerance."

What has caused this abrupt and dramatic change? One factor is certainly the development of medications that can protect against EIA (the albuterol/salbutamol sprays and cromolyn sodium). The second factor is more subtle. The past 25 years have witnessed a movement in this society toward physical fitness. First spurred by this movement, and then contributing to its further growth, is an expanding body of data that links aerobic fitness with a lowered risk of heart disease, and with prevention or better control of diabetes and high blood pressure. The most comprehensive study of the relationship between exercise and longevity was the recent Stanford University study, publicized by *Time* magazine in 1986. Data on students who entered Harvard between 1916 and 1950 dramatically demonstrated that aerobically active people live longer than sedentary people do. We believe that this changing attitude toward physical fitness, with the rapid accumulation of data supporting it, quietly pressured the medical community to examine its traditional approach to asthma and exercise. This assessment generated an explosion of asthma/exercise studies that had been going on for 20 years at the time this book was written.

The 1984 Summer Olympic Games illustrate in a dramatic way the net effect of these new medications and positive attitude. Just over 11 percent of the U.S. team (67 of the total 597) were asthmatic. Forty-one of the team's medals were won by members of this "select" group. They included cyclists Alexei Grawal, Bill Nitts, and Steve Hegg; heptathlon champion Jackie Joyner; sprinter Jeanette Bolden; swimmer Nancy Hogshead; Greco-Roman wrestler Dave Schultz; volleyball player Paul Weishoff; and basketball player Sam Perkins. The 1984 Winter Olympic team included eight asthmatic athletes, the best known being Bill Koch, the premier American cross-country skier (and medalist from the 1980 Olympics).

Interestingly, cyclist Bill Nitts did not know he had developed asthma until after he went to the medical office during training camp because he was suddenly severely short of breath right at the end of his workouts. A stress test confirmed asthma triggered by exercise. Control by medication enabled Nitts to regain his former endurance and win a silver medal.

(On a more sobering note: While asthmatic athletes won medals in the 1984 Olympics, the brilliant English runner—and asthmatic—Steve Ovett collapsed and was hospitalized after his 1,500-meter race. Olympic medical observers attributed his collapse to the combination of Los Angeles's poor air quality, the heat, an existing infection, and his underlying asthma. The asthmatic athlete can realize his athletic potential, but he cannot be guaranteed risk-free competition.)

What We Know About Exercise-Induced Asthma

Although the existence of EIA has been known for at least two thousand years, it has received scientific attention only since the mid-1960s. Now researchers know what happens, but they are still trying to figure out the mechanism behind it.

Except for a small number of atypical asthmatics, the bronchospasm normally does not start during the exercise. It usually develops soon after exercise ends, the point at which nonasthmatics are well on their way to recovering from the respiratory demands of exercise. Without medication, the EIA attack usually peaks from 5 to 10 minutes after exercise and lasts about 30 to 60 minutes.

During exercise, many asthmatics actually find that they breathe more comfortably than when they are at rest. The first observation of this phenomenon was published in 1863. The English physician Dr. Henry Hyde Salter (who was also asthmatic) noted, ''I have seen several cases in which prolonged bodily exertion has been of great benefit, indeed, some in which it has been the best remedy to which the asthmatic could resort. This treatment . . . , of course, . . . must be taken in the intervals of the attacks: but when so taken it seems to have a marvellous efficacy in keeping them off and in giving to the asthmatic a lightness and freedom of respiration to which at other times he is a stranger. Its rationale puzzles me.''

Actually, an asthmatic's improved breathing during exercise is not very startling. The body releases adrenaline during exercise, and adrenaline is a potent airway dilator. (An injection of adrenaline is often the first medication given in emergency asthma treatment.)

It is not yet clearly understood what causes the bronchospasm once exercise ends. At present, there are two hotly competing theories. One is championed by asthma research laboratories in Israel and in Australia. These scientists believe that mast cells release asthma-causing mediators during exercise.

The competing theory was developed by an American research group at the Harvard Medical School. Their view is that airway cooling during exercise explains EIA. During nonstrenuous activity, air is inspired relatively slowly and has time to be properly warmed before it reaches the airways. Breathing air during exercise is like fanning yourself on a hot day. As air circulates over your skin, your skin gives up heat and cools down. The faster the air circulates, the greater the cooling. During the rapid breathing of exercise, air reaches the airways before it has been fully warmed and also travels through the airways more quickly. The airways give up heat as this colder air circulates rapidly over their inner surface. The greater the airway cooling, the greater the EIA. In addition to faster breathing, colder external air temperatures and lower humidity also cool the airways. Air pollution combined with any of the three cooling factors makes EIA worse.

The airway-cooling hypothesis certainly helps explain the long-standing observation that swimming is more acceptable than running as a sport for asthmatics. Because the air breathed in during swimming is consistently warm and contains significantly more moisture than it does during running, there is less airway cooling at the same level of breathing effort.

The major problem with the airway-cooling hypothesis is a missing link. It is true that airway cooling and EIA seem to occur together, but the theory does not explain how airway cooling actually causes a bronchospasm. This theory is also inconsistent with several observations. (1) When an asthmatic exercises, stops, then exercises again, his bronchospasm is always milder the second time around. Airway cooling, however, is the same each time. (2) The bronchospasm first begins several minutes after airway cooling has already started to decrease. (3) The bronchospasm progresses toward its peak while the airway temperature is returning to normal.

Perhaps airway cooling triggers an intermediary mechanism that actually sets off the bronchoconstriction. There is evidence for three such possibilities: a neural reflex, an altered balance in the influence of the autonomic nervous system, and the release of chemical mediators from mast cells. The most convincing evidence favors the mediator-release mechanism. The evidence: cromolyn sodium, which prevents the release of mast cell mediators, also prevents EIA in most asthmatics. (On first examination, this mediator-release mechanism sounds like the theory proposed by the American group's opponents. It really is not, although the intricacies and subtleties of the differences are beyond the scope of this book.)

What usually happens in science when there are good data supporting two or more opposing theories? Eventually another theory will be developed that integrates this initial group of explanations. Then more research will be done to test the more comprehensive theory. If there are still observations that it cannot account for, the new theory will have come closer to the truth, but no prize yet. If the new theory does explain everything that we can observe about EIA, and permits us to control it without exception, then theory transcends to the realm of accepted fact.

But whatever the actual mechanism turns out to be, everyone agrees that the severity of an asthmatic's EIA depends on the intensity of the exercise. This fact brings us to the next part of the discussion.

Aerobic Training

If exercise causes bronchospasm for most or all asthmatics, why are we encouraging asthmatic people to exercise? In part, it is for the same reason that we encourage most people to exercise. The overwhelming weight of the evidence is that exercise is good for you. And, in addition, we believe that exercise is good for your asthma. A small but growing body of highly convincing research—which includes the work in our laboratory—indicates that exercise can directly reduce the impact of certain asthma triggers.

First let us see how our body—in particular, the cardiovascular system—adapts to exercise. The kind of exercise we are referring to is aerobic exercise, which means that the muscles get their energy from oxygen-fueled metabolism. *Training* is the term given to the cardiovascular adaptation process.

During any given bout of aerobic exercise, more and more oxygen must be carried to the exercising muscles. The heart does part of this job by pumping faster, which increases the amount of blood circulating through the lungs to pick up oxygen and increases the amount of oxygen-rich blood reaching the muscles. The other part of the job belongs to the respiratory system, which has to make more oxygen available for the increased volume of blood now coming through the lungs. The respiratory muscles work harder to take in more fresh air with each breath, and to increase the number of breaths per minute.

What happens when this exercise is repeated on a routine (meaning at least three times a week) basis? Training takes place. This does not mean that the heart or lungs become more efficient at their job. It is the muscle tissue that becomes much more efficient at taking oxygen out of the blood circulating through it. As the muscles "learn" to use a much greater proportion of the oxygen available to them, the heart no longer has to pump as much additional blood, and the respiratory muscles do not have to help the lungs bring in as much additional air.

Because the exercise level is unchanged even though the heart and respiratory system are no longer working as hard, the person's maximum exercise capacity is now greater than it was. This means that reaching his maximum heart and lung output will require a higher exercise intensity than it did before. This is another way of saying that training has occurred.

TRAINING BENEFITS FOR THE ASTHMATIC

What does this mean to the asthmatic? Whereas running 25 yards to catch a bus would cause a bronchospasm before training, after training this same sprint will cause little or no breathing difficulty. But there is more to it than eliminating the breathing difficulties that used to occur at the same exercise level.

What happens when an aerobically trained asthmatic is asked to exercise until his heart and respiratory system are working as hard as they once had to before training? In theory, we would expect the same intensity of EIA that the identical level of cardiopulmonary effort had provoked prior to training. After all, ventilation—and therefore airway cooling—is the same, and this higher exercise level is the same proportion of the current maximum capacity as the pretraining level was of the pretraining maximum.

In our work, however, we have consistently found something different. The EIA is less severe than it was before training started. The implication is that the physically fit asthmatic's airways have become less sensitive to stimulation. (Whether this effect carries over to other forms of nonspecific asthma triggers remains to be studied.)

The psychological benefits of physical fitness for the asthmatic are also important. The most universal reaction from the asthmatics who have completed our experimental physical fitness program is that confidence has replaced anxiety in coping with their asthma. Many of these asthmatics find their lives far fuller and their satisfactions much richer because of their increased physical capacity, sense of well-being, and the confidence these changes inspired.

Because the concept of encouraging this level of physical fitness for asthmatics is so new, at the chapter's end we have added some personal statements from three trained asthmatics, a private citizen, and two athletes.

HOW TO EXERCISE: GENERAL ADVICE

Most asthmatics who want to become physically fit do not have a choice between doing it on their own or enrolling in a supervised outpatient program designed especially for people with asthma. The only such program that we are aware of is our experimental project at the New York University Medical Center. A program such as ours certainly makes the job easier for the asthmatic. The discipline of maintaining a schedule and not giving up is easier when exercise is done on a formal basis amid a highly supportive group of people. In addition, a lot of anxiety is alleviated because each asthmatic's heart rate and breathing are continuously monitored and help—should it ever be needed—is instantly at hand.

If you feel confident enough to try an exercise program on your own, the one essential that you need is your doctor's approval. Once you have this, we have some pointers for you that are often helpful in preventing or reducing EIA.

Walking and swimming create less of an EIA problem than running and bicycling do. (Six to 10 minutes of vigorous running or cycling will provoke an EIA in most asthmatics.) A caution about swimming is that some asthmatics develop a bronchospasm from the hydrochloric acid formed by chlorinated pool water.

EIA can be reduced by exercising in a warm, humid environment. A not-too-air-conditioned gym or squash court are good choices. If you plan to exercise outside on cold days, using a cold weather mask to prewarm the air you breathe may help. (On very cold days, however, masks have a tendency to freeze over. This ice buildup may actually obstruct breathing.) Inspired air can also be warmed by tying a scarf over your nose and mouth. There are some commercial heat-reservoir devices, but they are cumbersome and do not seem to do an effective job at higher respiratory demands. We do not find them worth the price. Although your nose is excellent at warming inspired air, its high airflow resistance makes it an impractical solution for all but the lightest exercise levels. Another suggestion for minimizing EIA is a warmup that progresses from light to moderate exercise, but this has not yet been thoroughly tested.

HOW TO EXERCISE: PREMEDICATION

However helpful these precautions may be, in many cases they are not enough to prevent EIA. Then prophylactic— preventive—drug therapy is needed. Do not confuse this with maintenance medication, which does not assure you adequate protection against EIA. Prophylactic medication in this context is preexercise medication or, as it is usually called, *premedication*.

Premedication is obviously needed when severe obstruction exists before exercise even starts. When it is not so clear-cut, the objective means for deciding to premedicate is a PEFR (peak expiratory flow rate) or FEV_1 (amount of air forced out in 1 second) that decreases by 25 percent or more from what it had been before exercise started. This decision, however, does not have to hinge on having a laboratory stress test or using a peak flow meter before and after exercise. It can be made subjectively. If bronchospasm becomes too uncomfortable for you, either while or after you exercise, then it makes sense to premedicate.

Some asthmatics will find that they need premedication only under certain circumstances, such as greater air pollution, temperature and/or humidity changes, and the period after a respiratory infection or flu. If on any given day you find yourself unsure about premedication, it is probably best to do it.

The two drugs that seem to be particularly effective in protecting the asthmatic against EIA are *solbutamol* (also called *albuterol*), marketed under the names *Proventil* and *Ventolin*; and *cromolyn sodium (Intal)*. Whichever drug is used should be taken 15 to 30 minutes before exercising. The drug of choice for any individual asthmatic is the one that works best for him. And sometimes a combination of

both is the best answer. Discuss these drugs with your
doctor before you begin premedication.

In 1972, U.S. swimmer Dick DeMont lost his Olympic
gold medal because the U.S. Olympic Medical Committee
had failed to file for approval of his anti-EIA medication.
Because he did not declare his asthma drugs, he was ac-
cused of "doping." A competitive asthmatic athlete should
always make sure that the appropriate official has been
notified of whatever anti-EIA drug he is using (with the
drug schedule and dosage), and that he has approval for
it. Some international competitions prohibit most types of
beta-receptor stimulators, which would make cromolyn
sodium the only allowable drug. Others are more liberal.
Approved asthma medications for the Olympics include
theophylline, cromolyn sodium, salbutamol (also known
as albuterol), and terbutaline.

HOW TO EXERCISE: ANTI-EIA ROUTINE

- Use cromolyn sodium and/or a beta-receptor stimulator 15 to 30 minutes before you will begin your
  exercise.

- With vigorous exercise, do a warmup 10 to 15
  minutes beforehand.

- If you feel yourself getting "tight" while you are
  exercising, you can try to work through these EIA
  symptoms. If you cannot, or if you are apprehen-
  sive about trying to do this, stop to take some inhaled bronchodilator, then resume your workout.

- If you are exercising in a cold, dry climate (such
  as cross-country skiing), keep a scarf or mask over
  your mouth.

- Follow your workout with a 10 to 30 minute cool-
  down period of slow jogging, stretching, and, if
  you like, light weight-work.

Even with the best precautions and management, some

asthmatics may still experience what they feel are intolerable EIA symptoms. Before giving up on exercise, try switching to another type. If jogging is too hard on your airways, try squash or swimming. Or combine bicycle riding in the spring/summer with swimming for the fall/winter. The primary key is good overall control of your underlying asthma. The freer you are of symptoms from other asthma triggers, the less likely you are to experience the kind of bronchospasm that will force you to abandon exercise.

Postscript

In our long-term experimental physical fitness project for asthmatics (conducted at the New York University Medical Center), we have worked with a large number of volunteers. Once they get past the emotional, endurance, and discipline difficulties of starting an exercise program, most of our volunteers begin to bring us reports of the dramatic benefits from the physical and psychological aspects of their exercise experience. Although these reports are usually verbal, this one was given to us in writing. Because the writer's experience is typical, we are including it here.

Dear Dr. Haas:

It's hard to believe that I've already been in your exercise program for 25 weeks, and I've only been home sick for 2½ days—and that was for the flu, not for an asthma attack.

I am on a completely different plateau of living than I have ever been. What does that mean? Well, I have the energy to put in a long work day, do my exercise, and go out a couple of times a week or take a course at night. For the first time, I see how the asthma has debilitated me even though I wasn't constantly sick with wheezing attacks. I was constantly getting virus infections, was home for at least a week at a time, and was very depressed. Every winter I had one "grand collapse'' of about two to three weeks. This fall/winter has been the first in my life when I haven't been constantly sick; 2½ days is a miracle.

My medication is also down substantially. When I started the exercise program I was on a daily dose of 700mg of theophylline, 4 to 8mg of Ventolin, and my bronchial inhaler as needed. Now and throughout this winter, I have been on only 200mg of theophylline, 4mg of Ventolin, and the inhaler as needed. At particularly stressful times or when I feel I am on the verge of getting sick, I increase the theophylline to 400mg.

Last winter I was still on heavy medication, but walking around breathless. At my weakest times I was literally leaning on pillars in the subway for support. This winter, for the first time I have been able to be out in the cold and not constantly getting wheezing attacks. I have also, for the first time in my life, been able to be out in the cold without the *fear* of getting a wheezing attack, which has been a tremendous relief.

I have also been able to let go of other emotional fears created by the asthma. I was brought up with: ''Oh, Carol, don't push yourself, you'll get sick.'' I was always afraid of pushing myself with physical exercise. I would never take on a challenge because, when the going literally got rough, that tape would go off in my head and I would quit rather than pushing through. Through this exercise program and the progress I see myself making, I now have the confidence to push through difficulties.

When I started your program last fall, I could hardly walk at a slow pace on the treadmill for 25 minutes. Today, I run at 4.4 to 4.7 mph for 18 minutes—that's 1½ miles! I am so excited about this. I could only do a mile a month ago, and I love to see my progress. Now I say to myself: ''Go, Carol. You can do it.'' I have nicknamed myself ''Rockyette.'' Additionally, I now ride the bike and/or row before or after running. Two months ago, I could hardly handle the running. I have seen that even at my longest running time, my heart rate remains low, and if I can continue to build up my wind, I can go much further.

Never before have I had such confidence in my physical capability, enjoyed exercising so much, and been able to laugh at myself in fun about it. This confidence is pervading other aspects of my life.

This fall/winter I have been under tremendous financial and professional pressure, since I am in a new career and on a commission income. In spite of this, I have continued to function very well.

This is the 25th week I have been in this program, and I am proud to say that I have kept my commitment of coming three times a week. This is evidence of how much I believe in the program. I make my schedule of work, traveling, and socializing around getting to the hospital three times a week, which isn't always easy. I've learned a new sense of discipline from this, of keeping going through hard times and bad weather, of being easy on myself on days when I'm not too strong. Consequently, I have learned to monitor myself more carefully.

Another benefit is that, now that I breathe better, I have much stronger sexual feelings—and that sure ain't bad, as they say!

I was fascinated when I made new folders for my 1986 expenses. In 1985, the medical folder was the first I made. This year, my medical folder was only the sixth. This small event said a lot to me about how my being sick is finally taking a back seat to living and enjoying life.

Warmest regards,
Carol Bernton

Following are excerpts from our interview with Virginia Gilden, who was 25 when she won a silver medal in women's rowing at the 1984 Summer Olympics. She has suffered from allergic asthma for many years.

Q: *When did your asthma begin, and how serious was it?*

A: It started when I was 11. Before that I had eczema and was allergic to cats. My brother was already asthmatic, but no one realized that I had developed it too. First my mother took me to an ear, nose, and throat doctor, who said there was nothing wrong with me. But my symptoms didn't go away, and finally I was taken to my brother's allergist. He diagnosed my asthma.

My asthma was serious enough to land me in the emergency room on occasion. When I was younger I had shots [immunotherapy] and I took medication every day. But I didn't like the shots. When I went to high school, I stopped the shots and just used my medication when I had a problem. I didn't begin using daily medication again until 1978, my senior year in college. My attacks had gotten much worse that year.

My last two bad attacks were three years apart, in 1982 and then 1985. I have finally learned to accept and deal with my asthma, control my medication, and become really conscientious about staying away from the things I am allergic to.

Q: *This is a two-sided question. Has your asthma affected you at all as an athlete? And has your sports involvement affected your asthma?*

A: My asthma has certainly not limited me as an athlete. I have had a lot of physiological testing, and I always do as well as other athletes. I don't think it has made any difference in my performance.

Being an athlete has very definitely helped me come to terms with my asthma. There was a period of time when I was denying it completely. When I first started training—in 1975—I had no intention of letting my asthma stop me. But to me at that time it meant not doing anything about my asthma. I was very irresponsible in controlling it. I wouldn't take any medication. So whenever I had an asthma attack, I would end up having a shot of epinephrine [adrenaline]. Each time, the doctor and one particular nurse would say: "Listen, Ginny, there are better ways of handling your asthma." But I kept ignoring them until I had no choice because it had gotten so bad.

Most people have some type of injury or weak link in their bodies, and when you are an athlete you have to come to terms with it as quickly as you can if you want to be strong. So my sports training made me a lot more aware of the fact that I am asthmatic, and that there was no way I could become a super-good athlete without incorporating this awareness in my whole life-style.

Following are excerpts from our interview with Nancy Hogshead who, at the age of 22, won three gold medals and one silver medal in swimming at the 1984 Olympics. Although Nancy suffers from EIA, she was a "hidden" asthmatic for years. In fact, she did not learn that she had asthma until she finished her last Olympic race.

Q: *How long have you had asthma?*

A: For years, except that I only realized it during the Olympics. I had known that something wasn't right with my lungs, but I had no idea it was asthma. Here is the story.

I was swimming competitively for 15 years, and ranked in the top three for 8 years. In 1977 I was ranked number one in the world. At the 1984 Olympics, I had the opportunity to win more [gold] medals than any other female swimmer in Olympic history. I lost it because I missed first place in my last event by seven hundredths of a second. It was a two-minute race, and I almost could not finish it! I finally realized that something serious was wrong, so I went to a doctor. He put me on a treadmill, and diagnosed exercise-induced asthma. The irony is that my father is a physician, and my brother has "regular" asthma.

I used to pass out after some of my races, but I would always accredit that to not being in good shape. When I would come in from a hard practice, I would clutch the wall. All I could think about was breathing in and out, just getting enough air. I always knew that there was a problem with my lungs, that they were the weak link in the chain. But I thought that they simply weren't good at oxygen exchange. I never knew there was such a thing as exercise-induced asthma.

Q: *Do you take medication now?*

A: Yes. I take Ventolin. I'm not swimming competitively any longer, but I run a lot, I play tennis, I get in the water at least once a week, and I do lots of other things. I take the Ventolin inhaler about 30 to 40 minutes before I exercise. I get ready for my exercise during that 30- to 40-minute interval. I put my sneakers and clothes on, braid my hair, do my stretches, that kind of thing.

Q: *Is there anything you would like to tell asthmatic kids and their parents?*

A: Yes. Take your medication, exercise, and don't be afraid of your asthma. The better shape you're in and the more physically healthy you are, the less your asthma will hinder your life.

✹✹ 13 ✹✹

Asthma and Sex

A person's sexual activity and how he feels about it are basic components of his identity and self-esteem. Unfortunately, the individual with sexual problems does not have an easy time in this society. Reverence for physical perfection has combined with the remnants of the Victorian heritage of shame and secrecy about sexual matters—especially sexual difficulties—to make honesty and a search for solutions extremely difficult.

Asthmatics are especially prone to sexual problems because they are vulnerable to an attack during sexual activity. Sex exposes them to a potent combination of triggers: emotional, exercise, and environmental (perfumes, hair spray, cosmetics, etc.). Anxiety about having an asthma attack during sex can make the symptomatic asthmatic even more short of breath. This anxiety—on the part of the asthmatic or his partner—can also bring on sexual failure. The consequence is greater anxiety, often with fear and humiliation. Then sexual activity becomes such a negative experience that one or both partners may avoid it altogether.

Yet there is very little open discussion about the sexual problems that can plague the asthmatic. The prevalence of bronchospasm during sex is reflected by the fact that medical dictionaries list "sexual asthma" as an asthma category. One actually defines it as a "reflex asthma . . . from . . . excessive [*sic*] sexual excitement." In a lighter vein, it has also been termed "sexercise-induced asthma." So medical dictionaries acknowledge it, but that does little to help the asthmatic whose sex life, self-esteem, and intimate relationship(s) are suffering.

If you have encountered sexual problems involving your asthma, you are not alone. Perhaps this fact in itself will provide some reassurance that nothing terrible or unchangeable is wrong with you. For change to occur, these problems should be dealt with on two levels, one psychological and the other pharmaceutical.

Honesty with your partner about your asthma is the first requirement. Then you and your partner must both have an accurate understanding of what asthma is, and what can trigger your bronchospasms. Perhaps a joint session with your doctor is in order, and you might also want to point out the sections in this book that were particularly helpful to you in understanding your condition more clearly. Counseling can help explore and resolve any continuing conflicts. And once your partner knows of your asthma and what asthma is, you can take the two basic preventive measures: *eliminate* and *premedicate*.

Elimination involves applying some of the concepts discussed in Chapter 10. Your partner should stop using anything that is an allergen or irritant to which you are sensitive, such as perfume, hair spray, makeup, or a scented soap. Pillows and bed coverings should also be asthma-proofed.

Premedication is the same principle discussed in regard to EIA. Use albuterol/salbutamol or cromolyn sodium before sex. Keep your MDI on your night table to make it as convenient as possible. The asthmatic who is on medication every four hours should find it fairly easy to schedule the last dose at bedtime. Otherwise, use it when you think you might need it. Just remember that one dose gives you about four hours of protection. If you are both feeling sexy again at a point that would take you beyond this protective range, use your inhaler again.

Fatigue can put a damper on sexual relations. If this is a particular problem of yours, try to set up your schedules so that lovemaking can usually be when you are both well rested. Another aspect to consider is the sexual positions you use. Some asthmatics have told us that any position placing weight on their chest makes them very uncomfortable. If you find this is true for you, discuss it with your partner and find some enjoyable substitutions.

It is also important to know if any of the medications you are taking have a negative effect on sexual drive. Some sympathomimetic drugs—the group that beta-stimulators belong to—can cause urinary retention, which may interfere with sexual arousal. Steroids, and such nonasthma drugs as antihypertensives and antidepressants, can also affect mood, sex drive, and sex performance. Talk with your doctor about this aspect of your medication. If a particular drug you are taking is contributing to sexual difficulty, discuss the possibility of substituting an effective variant that is less likely to cause this side effect.

Despite all these potential problems, the relationship between asthma and sex does have its positive side. The natural release of adrenaline during sexual excitement and vigorous activity causes bronchodilation. The much-quoted Dr. Salter remarked on this effect in the 1860s.

Not long ago I was informed by a patient . . . who had suffered greatly for many years, that however severe an attack might be, venereal excitement would almost invariably cure it. He told me also, that, when a youth, he had been guilty of the practice of onanism [masturbation], and that the unnatural excitement thereby produced had just the same curative effect on asthma. Indeed, he pleaded this effect of it as a sort of excuse for the practice; and assured me that when his breath was very bad at night he used to resort to it for the purpose of curing it. I have known two or three cases in which sexual excitement has had just the same effect.

Appropriate education of both partners, supported by counseling and premedication, should minimize the asthmatic's sexual difficulties. And both the asthmatic and his partner are encouraged to enjoy sexual intimacy as often as they wish.

✳✳ 14 ✳✳

Asthma and Pregnancy

About 1 percent of all pregnancies involve an asthmatic mother-to-be. Several questions emerge when an asthmatic woman becomes pregnant for the first time. The future parents want to know how pregnancy will affect the expectant mother's asthma, and how her asthma will affect the fetus and her experience of pregnancy. Parents and doctor(s)—whether a rural general practitioner or asthma specialist/obstetrician—want to use antiasthma drugs that are effective for the mother, yet safe for the fetus. (This is also an issue for the nursing asthmatic mother.) And if either parent comes from a family with a history of asthma and/or allergy, they will both want to know their baby's chances of avoiding the problem, and what they may do to improve these chances.

Normal Changes of Pregnancy

The ways pregnancy and asthma can affect each other make sense once we understand certain changes that normally occur when a woman becomes pregnant. The growing fetus and uterus eventually press upward on the diaphragm and lungs, hormonal balances change dramatically, and the immune system is profoundly affected. There are also new psychological pressures.

PULMONARY FUNCTION CHANGES

Pulmonary function tests show surprisingly mild changes despite the variety of factors affecting the respiratory system during pregnancy. The basic mechanical influence on respiration occurs as the growing fetus and expanding uterus gradually push the abdominal contents upward, restricting diaphragm movement and giving the lungs less and less room to expand. Although the total amount of air that the lungs can hold does not change substantially during pregnancy, less air than normal remains in the lungs after both relaxed and maximum expirations.

Pregnancy appears to decrease airway resistance, but expiratory airflow during intense efforts does not seem to improve. Although oxygen does not cross as easily from the air sacs to the blood circulating through them, this apparently does not pose any problem for healthy pregnant women.

The amount of air breathed in and out on each breath starts to increase during the first few weeks of pregnancy and continues rising. Even though respiratory rate does not change, the larger breath size means that more air than usual is taken in each minute, that is, ventilation increases. This hyperventilation can slightly increase the amount of oxygen in the blood. It also reduces the amount of carbon dioxide, which makes the blood less acidic than normal.

The big surprise is that some of the changes described above either appear before the fetus has grown large enough to limit the lungs' expansion, or else are out of proportion to the fetus's needs. The reduced amount of air left in the lungs after expiration appears well before the fetus and uterus have grown beyond the pelvic area. For much of the pregnancy, the degree of hyperventilation is much greater than the fetus's oxygen demands. Until relatively late in the pregnancy, then, something other than simple mechanical changes seems most important in affecting the respiratory system.

HORMONE CHANGES

Some of the complex hormonal changes of pregnancy affect the respiratory system. Both estrogen and progesterone rise steadily, starting early in pregnancy. One of progesterone's effects is respiratory center stimulation, and estrogen may act in a similar way. Their increase may explain the normal hyperventilation that accompanies pregnancy.

Progesterone also relaxes smooth muscle, which is the type of muscle encircling the airways. Although the one study in this area found progesterone to lower airway resistance and improve expiratory airflow, there were too few people in the group for any general conclusions to be drawn. The possibility that progesterone acts as a bronchodilator still exists in theory, but adequate research must be done for theory to become fact.

Of potentially greater importance to the asthmatic mother-to-be is the pregnancy-related increase in adrenal corticosteroid production. The actual impact is controversial. Almost all the cortisol—the most anti-inflammatory of the adrenal glucocorticoids—in our system attaches to proteins in our blood. Only the small fraction remaining free is biologically active. Initially, controversy focused on whether the overall cortisol increase included a greater amount of free cortisol. Now that there does appear to be a modest rise in free cortisol during pregnancy, controversy has shifted. Currently it concerns whether certain hormones produced by the placenta may in fact offset the additional free cortisol by making the airways (among other tissues) less responsive to it.

IMMUNOLOGIC CHANGES

Immunologists want to understand more fully why the pregnant woman's immune system does not reject the fetus as a foreign body. The fetus produces proteins, inherited from the father, that should be incompatible with the mother's immune system. Because of this, one would expect the first fetus to be quickly expelled and the mother sensitized to any subsequent pregnancies from the same father. But this is obviously not what happens. Most immunologic studies of pregnancy have been devoted to understanding what takes place to allow the mother's body to accept a fetus.

Most of the immunologic changes of pregnancy seem designed to inhibit maternal rejection of the fetus. These include changes in antibody production. The amount of IgG, for example, decreases. IgE—the antibody closely linked to allergic asthma—shows variable changes. These antibodies consistently become less numerous and less active in areas producing the white blood cells that defend against invading foreign bodies. The overall amount of IgE decreases in non-asthmatic pregnant women and in some pregnant asthmatics. In other pregnant asthmatics, these antibodies become more numerous.

At this point, one can only speculate about the effects of these antibody changes on asthma. There may be a greater susceptibility to respiratory infections that can trigger an attack. Sinusitis, for example, is six times more frequent in pregnant women. The relationship between overall pregnancy-related IgE changes and asthma symptoms was examined in one small study. Asthmatic pregnant women whose IgE decreased tended to have either unchanged or fewer asthma symptoms. Those with more IgE had more asthma symptoms. Much more work needs to be done, however, before any firm conclusions can be drawn.

PSYCHOLOGICAL CHANGES

Pregnancy is a time of heightened psychological vulnerability. The typical pregnant woman is emotional and moody, and has ambivalent feelings about the imminent changes in her life. An altered body image, the physical discomforts of pregnancy that most women experience, large hormonal shifts, and various fears concerning pregnancy, birth, and the baby are all additional sources of stress for the pregnant woman. For those asthmatic women who find that psychological stress makes their asthma worse, the stresses of pregnancy may play a temporary role in their disease.

How Pregnancy Affects Asthma

When we were expecting our first child, we had quite a few questions for "our" obstetrician. He avoided a lot of generalizations in his answers, emphasizing that "pregnancy is different for each woman and, for the same woman, each new pregnancy can be different." It should not be surprising, then, to find that how pregnancy affects asthma differs from one pregnant asthmatic to the next, and sometimes even from one woman's pregnancy to her next.

To sum up all the reports describing pregnancy's influence on asthma: roughly a little less than one-third of the cases improve, slightly more than one-third are unchanged, and the remaining one-third get worse. That any changes always disappear after birth indicates that this variation is not simply a reflection of the random ups and downs that normally occur with asthma. A general relationship has been charted in which women with moderate to severe pre-pregnancy asthma (i.e., symptoms at least weekly) are either more likely to worsen or less likely to improve than women with mild asthma (i.e., symptoms monthly or less). But trying to predict beforehand how pregnancy will affect a given woman's asthma is risky.

And whether a woman's asthma improves, worsens, or remains the same, she can expect the majority of her flareups from weeks 24 to 36 of her pregnancy (the normal pregnancy is about 39 weeks). Many women find that their asthma then improves in the last several weeks before birth.

Only a handful of women actually experience asthma symptoms during labor and delivery. In 1983, the Kaiser-Permanente Medical Center in San Diego, California, published its "Prospective Study of Asthma During Pregnancy" in the professional literature. Of the 120 asthmatic women who were observed for this study, 90 percent of them had no symptoms at all during the birth. Half of the remaining 12 women did not need any asthma medication, and 5 simply used an inhaled bronchodilator. Only 1 woman—less than 1 percent of the entire group—had an attack severe enough to require intravenous aminophylline.

How Asthma Affects Pregnancy

Two large retrospective studies on asthma and pregnancy risk were published in early 1972. "Retrospective" means that data were gathered after the event of interest occurred. In this case old birth records were divided into two groups—asthmatic mothers and healthy mothers—and the birth outcomes were analyzed. This kind of study provides a large number of people in one fell swoop, but often means that not enough background information about these people is available to understand the results adequately. A "prospective" study, on the other hand, starts before the event in question and carefully follows a group of people through it (like the Kaiser-Permanente study just mentioned). This allows the researchers to determine their hypothesis in advance, and then collect all the information needed to prove or disprove it.

These two large retrospective studies indicated that

asthma slightly increases risk to the fetus during pregnancy and/or birth. The risks included premature birth, symptoms of inadequate oxygen, and stillbirth. The problem with these studies is the lack of any information as to how well each of the women involved had controlled her asthma during her pregnancy. In the Kaiser-Permanente prospective study, the asthma was carefully controlled for all 120 women. The results: they had no more complications than a comparison group of nonasthmatic women did.

Comparing these retrospective and prospective studies provides crucial information. The different results emphasize the importance of early identification and appropriate management of asthma for avoiding complications. An uncontrolled asthma attack introduces the major risk factor, which is far too little oxygen reaching the fetus.

The mother-to-be must completely support all the fetus's needs. The mother gives the fetus nutrients and oxygen and receives all the fetal waste products for disposal. The point of exchange is the placenta, which can be thought of as somewhat like the lungs and the blood circulating through them (Figure 14.1). In the mother's lungs, each breath fills and empties the air sacs where gas exchange occurs with capillary blood. In the placenta, spurts of oxygen- and nutrient-rich maternal blood bathe fetal blood vessels. Oxygen and nutrients pass from the mother's blood to the fetus's blood, while carbon dioxide and metabolic wastes pass in the opposite direction.

Hyperventilating exhales more carbon dioxide than usual, so less is carried in the blood, which then becomes less acidic than normal. When hyperventilation occurs during an asthma attack—which can happen even with mild episodes—this state of affairs is only temporary. Because the typical pregnant woman hyperventilates throughout most of her pregnancy, her blood remains less acidic until the birth. If a pregnant asthmatic hyperventilates even more during an attack, the temporarily reduced blood acidity is added to this long-term acid reduction.

This state of affairs has two negative consequences for

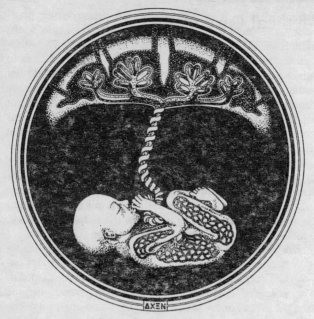

Figure 14.1 Placenta-fetus blood circulation.

the fetus. The loss of acid tends to reduce blood flow to the uterus, which means that less oxygen is available for exchange. In addition, less-acidic blood makes red blood cells (which are the oxygen carriers) hold on to their oxygen more tightly. This reduces even further the amount of oxygen available for the fetus. The fetus may become starved for oxygen. Because asthma-induced hyperventilation can occur even during mild attacks, it is imperative that—during pregnancy—all attacks be prevented.

Medical Care of the Pregnant Asthmatic

Agents that are harmful during pregnancy can damage a fetus in one of two ways. Some can cause severe malformations when they are used from 3 to 10 weeks after conception, the time when specialized tissues and organs are forming. Called *teratogens*—from the Greek word for monster—these agents include radiation, alcohol, and certain drugs. Agents that are harmful after the first 10 weeks act by distorting the growth or function of normally formed tissues and organs.

From current reports, the modern antiasthma drugs—except adrenaline—appear safe for the fetus. The evidence on adrenaline comes from the huge Collaborative Perinatal Project (CPP) that studied the possible teratogenic effect of a variety of drugs—including adrenaline and the older beta-2-stimulators—used in the early part of pregnancy. Information was collected on more than fifty thousand newborn infants and their mothers seen in 12 centers in the United States from 1959 to 1965. CPP results linked adrenaline use with a higher-than-normal number of malformed fetuses. From other research it is known that adrenaline also constricts the blood vessels, reducing blood flow—and therefore oxygen—to the uterus. Adrenaline, then, is the only antiasthma medication absolutely contraindicated during pregnancy unless the pregnant woman's life is endangered without it. It is a teratogen, and it reduces the fetus's oxygen supply.

Theophylline, on the other hand, has a positive side effect. Recent experiments indicate that this antiasthma drug actually increases the flow of blood to the uterus.

Even with this generally encouraging picture, the ideal during pregnancy is still to avoid any pharmacological intervention. For the asthmatic this requires placing greater emphasis on stress-reduction techniques, on environmental precautions, and perhaps on avoiding offending allergens. But if an attack is considered possible despite such measures, any potentially harmful drug effects pose less of a threat to the fetus than depriving it of needed oxygen during an attack.

MAINTENANCE ASTHMA MEDICATION

Concern for the fetus must actually begin before conception. As soon as an asthmatic woman decides to become pregnant, she should tell her physician. Guided by the philosophy of reducing drug intake as much as possible during pregnancy, he may feel that drug substitution is advisable. Because the fetus is most sensitive to teratogenic drug effects during the first three months of pregnancy, such medication changes should be made before the pregnancy actually begins.

After conception, the way pregnancy does—or does not—affect a patient's asthma may permit further drug reduction, or may require an increase. For the fetus, any possible drug effects could not be as harmful as permitting the disease to progress uncontrolled.

For maintenance, the asthmatic expectant mother uses the minimum medication level that controls her asthma. The mildest cases usually do very well with either no medication at all, or inhaled bronchodilator as needed. If symptom control requires more aggressive intervention, theophylline is preferred to an oral beta-2-stimulator because of theophylline's possible benefits to the fetal blood supply. Some patients will be able to restrict their use of theophylline to a few days during occasional exacerbations of their asthma. For more continuous symptoms, a regular theophylline regimen using a slow-release preparation is often recommended.

If this is still not enough medication to control symptoms, the next steps might be cromolyn sodium and/or beclomethasone (an inhaled steroid). Neither of these drugs, however, should be used until the fourth month of pregnancy because—although they have been found very safe in the studies done on them—the FDA has not yet approved them as nonteratogenic drugs.

If the asthma continues to worsen, oral steroids may have to be used. Oxygen deprivation is probably more damaging to the fetus than long-term steroids. Although steroids cross the placenta into the fetus, only rarely has improper adrenal function been reported in an infant whose mother took steroids during pregnancy.

IMMUNOTHERAPY

What should a newly pregnant asthmatic do if she has been undergoing immunotherapy? The literature indicates that it is safe to continue during pregnancy as long as severe systemic responses are avoided. There is general agreement in the professional community to continue immunotherapy with a severely asthmatic patient who had been responding well to it before the pregnancy.

If the effect has been questionable, it seems most reasonable to stop treatment until after delivery. If immunotherapy is being considered when a pregnancy is confirmed, delay it until the pregnancy is over.

ANTIBIOTICS

The asthmatic mother-to-be must avoid infections that could trigger an attack. As with all pregnant women, antibiotics must be used with care. Tetracycline should not be used at all. Sulfa drugs should be avoided from the fourth month on. Penicillins (if there is no allergy), cephalosporins, and some forms of erythromycin appear to be safe during pregnancy.

IF A SEVERE ATTACK OCCURS

If a severe asthma attack does occur during the pregnancy despite all prevention attempts, providing adequate oxygen to the fetus becomes the most critical issue. The expectant mother must be given supplemental oxygen to maintain the fetus's supply. The initial attempt to bring the attack under control is a small additional dose of the inhaled beta-2-stimulator (a sympathomimetic drug) that the patient has been using on a regular or as-needed basis. Now it might be taken by nebulizer instead of MDI. Because this sympathomimetic drug is still being inhaled directly into the lungs, only a negligible amount would enter the bloodstream and reach the fetus. Of equal importance, the amount needed to achieve a particular effect remains smaller than if it were given orally, intravenously, or by injection.

If the patient does not respond, theophylline is given intravenously. (Medication dripped into the vein does not attain the initial high blood level that it would via a subcutaneous injection.) But for the woman who either cannot tolerate inhaled bronchodilators, or does not respond to the theophylline, or is heading into respiratory failure, a subcutaneous beta-2-sympathomimetic (such as terbutaline) can be used.

9Normally, subcutaneously injected sympathomimetics—especially adrenaline—form the first line of acute asthma treatment. During pregnancy, however, they are used only as a last resort. Although the beta-2-selective sympathomimetics are not chemically equivalent to adrenaline, physicians prefer to remain sparing in their systemic use until definitive research proves that caution with the beta-2-drugs is unnecessary. They are not used unless the risks to the fetus from an uncontrolled attack outweigh possible drug side effects.

During an acute episode, asthmatics normally become dehydrated. The large volume of fluid lost through dramatically increased mucus production and heavy sweating is usually not replaced, because asthmatics tend not to drink as much as they should when they are breathless. In pregnancy the body's fluid volume has increased substantially, and a sudden drop in this volume could lead to shock. Hydration (with care to avoid the discomforts of overhydration) is necessary to maintain this fluid level. These liquids should contain glucose for preventing hypoglycemia, as pregnant women are more susceptible to this condition.

Labor and Delivery

Some of the systemic beta-2-stimulators used to treat asthma were—until recently—also the most effective drugs available for halting premature labor. Some major medical centers still rely on them in this obstetric context. All the obstetricians we have spoken to, however, assured us that this group of antiasthma drugs does not delay the process of normal labor. But as we stated before, theophylline is the preferred maintenance drug during pregnancy because of its possible benefit to the fetus.

For the patient who has been taking theophylline (or a beta-2-stimulator), cromolyn sodium, or beclomethasone spray for daily maintenance, the advice in the literature generally suggests continuing this therapy through labor. It is important that steroid-dependent asthmatics be given supplemental steroids to compensate for the body's failure to produce additional steroids during the added stress of labor.

If delivery is by cesarean section, many authorities in the field suggest that the asthmatic patient be given local or regional rather than general anesthesia. This avoids possible upper airway injury from intubation and potential bronchial irritation from anesthetic gases. If general anesthesia cannot be avoided, the physician will select one of the anesthetics that are less irritating to the airways.

Antiasthma Drugs and the Nursing Mother

Some drugs taken by the mother pass to the newborn through her breast milk. When an asthmatic mother plans to breast-feed, her postnatal antiasthma regimen should be tailored with this in mind. For theophylline, somewhat more than two-thirds of the level in the mother's blood appears in her breast milk. This approaches the therapeutic dose of theophylline used to stimulate breathing in newborns who are in danger of apnea (prolonged periods without breathing). Because of theophylline's documented side effects in newborns—digestive upset, restlessness, sleep problems—it should be prescribed with caution for a nursing mother.

The beta-2 bronchodilators are considered safe to use while nursing because they most probably do not pass into breast milk in appreciable amounts. Although neither cromolyn sodium nor beclomethasone have been adequately studied in terms of breast-feeding, they should be safe. The fact that they attain only low levels in the mother's blood suggests that only low levels can pass into her milk. Prednisone appears safe in moderate doses because it does not cross into breast milk in large amounts. Your own drug requirements pose no problem as long as you work out an appropriate regimen with your doctor.

The rules for antibiotics during pregnancy also hold for the nursing mother: no tetracycline, no sulfa drugs, only certain forms of erythromycin. The penicillins are safe as long as the asthmatic mother is not allergic to them.

Asthma Prevention for the Newborn

The infant with a high potential for developing asthma must first be identified before his parents can try to prevent his genetic inheritance from being realized. Because both identification and subsequent preventive efforts are most feasible for infants with the potential for allergic asthma, this section is devoted to allergy prevention/reduction. Doing away with (or lessening) the allergy does away with (or lessens) the asthma.

IDENTIFYING THE ALLERGY
HIGH-RISK CHILD

As stated earlier, the genetic influence on asthma that Maimonides remarked on in the Middle Ages has been well documented in this century. A family history of allergies is known to spotlight the high-risk child. How broad this history is tells a great deal about the child's likelihood of developing an allergic problem, and when it is likely to appear.

If neither parent is allergic, the child's chances of developing an allergy are only about 13 percent. If one parent has an allergic problem, different survey results show the child's chances rising to 29 to 54 percent. When both parents have allergies, the child's chances become 47 to 71 percent. If both parents have the same allergy, their child is likely to develop it, and possibly with additional symptoms. With one allergic parent, a child slated for allergies has only a 20 percent chance (one in five) of developing them before 18 months of age. But having two allergic parents doubles this chance.

There are multiple reasons for this relationship between family history and allergies. Genetics can determine a variety of allergy-related factors, including the amount of IgE production; the amount of mast cells and other relevant mediator-releasing cells, plus the amount of these mediators and the ease with which they release; the number of IgE receptors on these mediator-releasing cells, plus their affinity for IgE; the amount and proportions of two newly discovered products carried in the blood, SFA (suppressing factor of allergy) and EFA (enhancing factor of allergy); autonomic nervous system balance—alpha-adrenergic hyperresponsiveness or beta-adrenergic hyporesponsiveness; and sensitivity of the target organ, such as the airways in asthma.

In addition to what can be learned from a newborn's family history, blood samples from the umbilical cord can be analyzed for the level of IgE. Although some types of immunoglobulin can cross from the mother to the fetus during pregnancy, IgE does not seem to be one of them. If an unusually high level of IgE appears in the umbilical cord blood, this indicates that the baby is already producing his own, and therefore has a high potential for sensitization.

CONTRIBUTING ENVIRONMENTAL FACTORS

Given a newborn's genetic endowment for allergies, can any aspects of his environment increase this inherited potential? Possible environmental factors are exposure to inhaled allergens, microbes, certain drugs, and allergenic foods.

There are a number of studies on the relationship between inhaling potential allergens during infancy and the later development of allergies (including asthma). Although the details are somewhat confusing, the overall picture contains a correlation between certain birth months and the development of asthma and/or hay fever. In a Finnish study of more than two thousand patients with skin sensitivity to birch pollen, for example, many more of them had been born during the birch pollen season (between February and April). An American study of 1,100 college students sensitive to ragweed found that a significant majority had been born between May and September, with a large clustering in September (the high point for ragweed pollen).

The Finnish researchers estimated that if their patients had not been exposed to birch pollen in their infancy, one-fourth of them would never have become sensitized to it. More definitive studies are needed, however, before such strong conclusions can be confirmed.

Infection has been strongly implicated in all forms of asthma. One of the current theories suggests that the simultaneous occurrence of a respiratory tract infection with allergen exposure is necessary for allergic asthma to develop. A study of 11 allergic children (each with two allergic parents) illustrates that genetic endowment alone does not produce allergies. Ten of these children had a documented viral upper respiratory tract infection only one to two months before their allergies appeared. Because an allergic "constitution" and allergic asthma are so closely related, these results strongly suggest that a similar relationship exists for the development of asthma.

A pregnant woman's use of certain drugs has been proven to increase IgE production in the offspring of that pregnancy. Umbilical blood from two groups of newborns—one whose mothers took progesterone during the pregnancy, the other whose mothers did not—was compared. In the progesterone group, more than half the newborns showed high IgE levels. Only one-fourth of those in the no-progesterone group did. In experiments with mice, low-dose radiation to the pregnant mother intensified her offsprings' IgE responses once they had become sensitized to an allergen. (For obvious ethical reasons, this kind of experiment cannot be repeated on humans.) There is also good evidence that the woman who regularly inhales cigarette smoke during her pregnancy increases her child's IgE production.

Breast-Feeding and Allergy Prevention

The basic health benefits of breast-feeding were strikingly demonstrated in a long-term study of 22,500 infants published over 65 years ago (1922). Month by month, the likelihood of any given baby dying of disease was clearly related to the number of months that he had been breast-fed. The shorter the breast-feeding period, the more likely that an infant would die. A 1934 study of infant deaths from respiratory tract infection showed these deaths to be 120 times more common for infants fed cow's milk than for breast-fed infants. Recent variations on these basic studies have echoed and reechoed the original findings.

It has also been learned that this protection against disease is due to *passive immunity*, the transfer of components of the mother's immune system through her breast milk. This temporary protection, however, is only against those agents to which the mother herself is immune. It is not a guarantee that the infant will never become ill during the breast-feeding period.

The therapeutic benefits of breast-feeding—which are many for any infant—may take on additional importance for the infant of an asthmatic parent. If the theory of a virus initiating asthma in a genetically susceptible person proves true, then the antiviral protection given the infant as he receives his mother's disease-fighting antibodies through her milk could be important in reducing his asthma potential. We strongly encourage breast-feeding for any asthmatic mother-to-be whose family (or spouse's family) has a history of asthma.

But the fact that a mother's milk gives her baby passive immunity raises a dark question. Can an allergic mother also transfer allergic sensitization to her child? The answer: most likely not. Although some types of immunoglobulin pass into breast milk, IgE has not yet been detected there. This suggests that *passive allergic sensitization* of the infant via breast milk is highly improbable.

Breast-feeding may actually offer protection against allergies as well as germs. Prospective studies have been done with children whose family history marked them as being at high risk for allergies. Those children who ingested *only* breast milk and whose parents used allergen-avoidance techniques with them developed less severe allergies than the high-risk children on cow's milk and a regular diet. Another study found asthma onset to be later in breast-fed babies than in babies given formula. In a 20-year follow-up study of childhood asthmatics, those who had been breast-fed for more than eight weeks had the better long-term prognosis.

Breast milk may offer direct allergy protection by temporarily eliminating the potential allergens from non-human milk protein. Even if this postpones rather than prevents food allergies, it is suspected that an allergy is less severe the older the child is when it first appears. Experimental evidence suggests that breast-feeding may also offer indirect allergy protection. Newborns are more likely than older infants to absorb ingested potential allergens through their intestines. Research with newborn animals has shown that breast-feeding substantially decreases this allergen absorption. Human breast milk may also keep potentially allergenic molecules from entering the human newborn's blood.

There is also a caution attached to breast-feeding the infant at high risk for allergies. Because elements of the foods that the nursing mother eats transfer to her infant, the infant at high risk for allergies can be sensitized to foods via his mother's milk. A woman who knows that her unborn child will be at high risk should eliminate all highly allergenic foods from her diet before the birth. The list includes milk and milk products, eggs, corn, wheat, legumes (peanuts, peas, soy and other beans), nuts, citrus fruits, chocolate, fish, and shellfish. Oral calcium supplements will provide the large amounts of calcium—normally gained from milk and cheese—that pregnant and nursing women need.

Soy-based infant formulas were initially marketed as an effective substitute for breast milk in terms of retarding allergy development. Although this promise—upon which the soy formula industry was built—is not supported by current experimental evidence (which finds soy products themselves highly allergenic), these formulas are useful for infants who are intolerant of cow's milk.

PROSPECTIVE STUDY IN PROGRESS

A large-scale allergy prevention study is under way in San Diego under the auspices of the Allergy and Clinical Immunology Divisions of the Kaiser-Permanente Medical Center and the California Medical School. Several hundred pregnant women carrying high-risk infants—identified by family history and documented IgE reactivity in the parents—are enrolled in this study to evaluate a strict regimen for preventing allergies. One group of expectant mothers is following the strict regimen, the other is not.

This preventive regimen has three basic components. Part I is designed to minimize prenatal sensitization of the fetus by eliminating the mother's intake of allergenic foods during the final three months of her pregnancy. Part II entails preventing sensitization to food allergens after birth. Mothers are encouraged to nurse for a minimum of six months, and must continue to avoid highly allergenic foods for the duration of nursing. If nursing must stop earlier, or if the infant needs additional food, *Nutramigen* is recommended. This hypoallergenic, enzymatically prepared breakdown product of casein (a milk protein) includes corn oil, carbohydrates, minerals, and vitamins. Part III involves environmental allergen avoidance and elimination from birth on. This especially includes animals, dust and molds, and any unnecessary drugs for both the infant and the nursing mother. Family members who smoke must stop. Every reasonable attempt is made to avoid exposing the infant to contagious viral illnesses.

The initial reports should be available about the same time this book is published. The results are awaited with great interest.

✕✕ 15 ✕✕

Children with Asthma

Asthma is the most common chronic respiratory disease of childhood. An estimated 8 million American children (12 percent) have had at least one episode of bronchospasm, and 2 million of this group (5 percent) have chronic asthma. (Estimates are used because diagnostic confusion—particularly with younger children—makes accurate figures very difficult to determine.)

Childhood asthma takes a heavy toll. Currently it causes 4.5 million doctor visits, 150,000 hospitalizations, and 540,000 days in the hospital. The disease is also expensive. Doctors are paid $100 million a year for treating asthmatic children, hospital visits incur another $35 million, and $50 million more is spent on medication. Childhood asthma is costly in other ways too. It is the single largest cause of school absenteeism, with 6 million school days lost each year. And every year one hundred to two hundred children die of status asthmaticus. This very small number could become even smaller with more aggressive diagnostic and treatment approaches.

This chapter discusses the aspects of asthma unique to children. Because there are also so many similarities between adult and childhood asthma—in fact, many more similarities than differences—parents of an asthmatic child will find that Chapters 2 through 8 also hold a great deal of important information for them. They will also add to your understanding of this chapter.

Asthma's Comings and Goings

The disease usually develops before a child's fifth birthday—most commonly between ages one and three—but it can appear at any age. Only 1 in every 15 asthmatic children becomes asthmatic during his first year of life. One of every 2 asthmatic children develops the disease before he turns two. Seven out of 10 asthmatic children have had their first episode by the time they are three. A very small number become asthmatic during adolescence. Roughly twice as many boys as girls develop asthma as young children, but this sex difference disappears by adolescence. More boys seem to improve spontaneously with age, and more girls develop asthma as teenagers (often after menstruation begins).

It is well known that some children "outgrow" their asthma, but many professionals question how often and how completely this happens. A fairly high number of "former" asthmatics redevelop asthma at some point in adulthood. Because of this, the current understanding is that children do not really outgrow their asthma, but the asthma—for reasons not at all well understood—becomes dormant for an unpredictable length of time. This concept is supported by experiments that expose "former" asthmatics to a methalcholine or histamine airway challenge. These ex-asthmatics still show airway hyperreactivity. It probably makes good sense, then, for former childhood asthmatics to maintain certain precautions even though they remain free of symptoms. They should not, for example, choose a profession that would expose them to high levels of allergens or general irritants.

Despite the scientific controversy as to whether asthma can ever truly be left behind, the weight of the evidence indicates that the disease certainly improves for most asthmatic children. Exactly how much is difficult to say, because each study in this area gives different figures. The proportion of asthmatic children who continue having moderate to severe attacks ranges from 5 to 20 percent. Asthma symptoms decrease substantially in the other 80 to 95 percent. The estimated chance of becoming a symptom-free adult ranges from 22 to 70 percent. The childhood asthmatic with the best chance of "outgrowing" it developed the disease between three and eight years old, is a boy, and does not have additional allergic problems. Chances seem less bright if the asthma appeared before three or after ten, and/or other allergic problems also exist.

Respiratory System Anatomy and Physiology

Asthma causes the same problems in children and adults. Because it obstructs the airways via airway muscle contraction and excessive mucus production, the airways are unable to provide the air sacs with enough oxygen for the blood circulating through the lungs. Within this similarity, however, there are marked differences. The same asthma trigger can provoke different symptoms in children and adults. A child's attack triggered by a viral infection, for example, can cause much more airway swelling, poorer mucus clearance, and less bronchospasm. And differences in the anatomy and physiology of the juvenile respiratory system make children—especially infants and young children—particularly susceptible to airway obstruction.

AIRWAY RESISTANCE

The lungs grow at an enormous rate for the first several years after birth. By four to eight years of age, the number of air sacs and airways have multiplied to such an extent

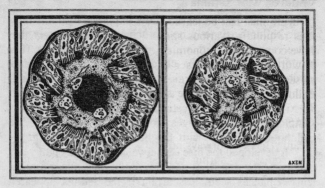

Figure 15.1 Effects of excess mucus on the airway openings of a young child and an adult. *Left*: Adult. *Right*: Young child. With the same amount of mucus produced, the child's airways are much more obstructed.

that the membrane across which gas exchange occurs is 10 times its original size. But airway diameters increase at a much slower pace (especially in the smaller airways), so until about age six they are disproportionately narrow for the amount of air that the lungs handle. Until this disproportion disappears, any condition that narrows the smaller airways raises airway resistance more than it does in adults (Figure 15.1).

Another unique characteristic of the infant's and young child's respiratory system also contributes to greater airway resistance during an asthma attack. Young children have more mucous glands in their larger airways than adults and older children do. It is common for these very young asthmatics to produce substantially more mucus, which worsens their obstruction. (The amount of mucus a young child can produce during an acute episode seems extraordinary—and sometimes frightening—to someone who is not used to it.)

Whether airway muscle contraction occurs in infants is unclear at this point. Early work suggested that children under one year had not yet developed airway muscles, but more recent studies show that these muscles do exist at birth. It must still be learned how the infant's airway muscles respond to various stimuli, and to what extent they have come under autonomic nervous system control. Then it will be known whether bronchospasm occurs—and so raises airway resistance even more—in infants and young children.

GAS EXCHANGE

Healthy infants' airways normally have a tendency to narrow somewhat during expiration. This creates a mild oxygen–blood flow mismatch. Some of the blood that the heart sends through the lungs to pick up oxygen travels through oxygen-poor areas. This means that all infants normally have less oxygen in their blood than older children do. Any disease that reduces airway openings will easily worsen the oxygen–blood flow mismatch. Asthma, then, disturbs gas exchange more profoundly in infants than in most older children and adults.

There is still another complicating factor for these very young asthmatics. Their lungs have not yet developed "collateral" ventilation channels. (Collateral airways are like highway service roads that can be used to detour around a traffic problem.) Adults have these secondary passages between airways and air sacs, which allow incoming air to go around small airway obstructions. The absence of collateral ventilation channels means that any obstruction becomes more likely to cause the collapse of neighboring air sac areas.

THE INFANT'S RESPIRATORY MUSCLES AND SKELETON

A number of factors negatively affecting the infant's inspiratory muscles poorly equip him to cope with the increased breathing work load that asthma creates. One is simply that the muscle fibers of the infant's diaphragm are much more susceptible to fatigue. Another concerns the diaphragm's connections to the body wall. In adults these attachments run at a somewhat vertical angle, allowing the diaphragm to move downward when it contracts. Because these connections are more horizontal in the infant, much of each contraction's force merely pulls in the lower segment of the infant's pliant rib cage instead of moving the diaphragm itself. The amount of air that actually fills an infant's lungs during even normal breathing is further reduced by another set of factors. The inspiratory muscles create a vacuum in the infant's chest cavity, which tends to suck in his entire rib cage. During times of greater respiratory effort, the child uses his accessory inspiratory muscles—those in the neck—to counteract this sucking in and obtain larger breaths. But using these accessory muscles adds even further to the work load placed on the respiratory system.

During normal breathing, these problems are mild. But the asthmatic infant's heightened inspiratory effort during an attack increases the vacuum in his chest cavity to such a degree that even the skin between his ribs is sucked in each time he inhales. Lung hyperinflation—which occurs with all asthmatics during an attack—magnifies the very young asthmatic's various inspiratory inefficiencies because it places all the inspiratory muscles at an even greater disadvantage.

Asthma Triggers

Although the airways remain hyperreactive to pretty much the same triggers throughout childhood, their relative importance changes with age. The major difference between children and adults is that allergic triggers (foods, indoor inhalants, and pollens) are a major problem for about half of all asthmatic children, but for only a minority of adult asthmatics. (In fact, 75 percent to 90 percent of all asthmatic children have specific IgE in their blood, with the more severely ill children having the highest levels.)

The different childhood periods and the relative order of importance for each type of trigger follow. (Key: >>/

much more than; >/more than; =/same as.) The age periods are roughly defined as follows: infancy, birth to 18 to 24 months; early childhood, from approximately two to five or six years; late childhood, from approximately six or seven to twelve or thirteen years; adolescence, from puberty to the end of the teenage years.

Infancy: viral infection >> foods > indoor inhalants > nonspecific irritants. (Pollens appear to have little or no role.)

Early childhood: viral infection = indoor inhalants > nonspecific irritants > foods = pollens.

Late childhood: indoor inhalants = pollens = nonspecific irritants > viral infection. (Food-related asthma is now very rare.)

Adolescence: nonspecific irritants > indoor inhalants = pollens > viral infection. (Food is rarely, if ever, a trigger for asthma unless it is part of a much larger allergic reaction.)

VIRAL INFECTION

A great deal of the wheezing that occurs before the age of three is caused by viral infections. The virus most often responsible in this age group is the *respiratory syncytial virus*, a flu-like virus that affects young children most strongly. The viral triggers in older children are the *influenza viruses* and the *rhinoviruses* (the large group of viruses associated with the common cold).

How viruses specifically cause wheezing is not well understood. They seem to damage cells lining the airways, which would trigger irritant receptors lying underneath. These irritant receptors stimulate wheezing. Viruses also cause changes in autonomic nervous system receptors, which could affect the airways. Recent experiments indicate that a viral infection can generate the formation of an IgE specific for that virus, which suggests an allergic-like component in the overall response.

There is a big question concerning viral triggers and allergic asthma. For a large number of allergy high-risk

infants, their first allergic reaction is preceded—within the
month—by a viral infection. It is not understood, though,
how a viral infection promotes allergen sensitization.

FOODS

Although allergens trigger asthma for both children and
adults, food is an allergy trigger almost exclusively for
children. Behind this difference is the infant's immature
gastrointestinal tract. It cannot yet prevent larger food proteins from being absorbed into the body.

Many different foods can precipitate allergic asthma in
children, but milk and egg proteins appear to be the primary culprits. Even though scientists do not all agree, it
seems a worthwhile precaution to avoid these foods by
breast-feeding for at least six months, particularly for high-
risk children. (The final sections of Chapter 14 discuss
identifying the high-risk child, and suggested precautions.) After one year of age, food allergies start to become less of a worry. By age three, food allergies often
disappear spontaneously.

INHALED SUBSTANCES

Allergies to inhaled substances can occur during the first
year of life, but they are quite rare during this early period.
Sensitization to substances encountered indoors—molds,
dust, animal danders—does not usually occur until early
childhood. Pollen allergies more commonly begin in later
childhood.

NONSPECIFIC IRRITANTS AND
MISCELLANEOUS TRIGGERS

Exercise is the most common nonspecific asthma trigger.
It is so common that an attack caused by exercise has its
own name: exercise-induced asthma, often called EIA.
Estimates for the proportion of asthmatic children whose
airways are hyperreactive to exercise range from 63 to 100
percent. Part of this group is made up of allergic children

whose allergies are *not* asthma triggers, but whose airways are hyperreactive specifically in connection with exercise. In fact, half of all the allergic children without allergic asthma *do* have exercise-induced asthma. Exercise becomes a much more important trigger for older children and adolescents. Whether this reflects a change in activity patterns with age, or a change in the asthma itself, is an open question.

Physicians consider certain kinds of physical activity to be more potent EIA triggers. These are activities that continuously stress the respiratory system, such as distance running or cycling. Sports like basketball or tennis, in which the action is frequently interrupted, are considered less likely to trigger an asthma episode. Swimming is traditionally viewed as the sport least likely to trigger asthma, probably because it involves breathing warm, humid air.

Such irritants as cigarette smoke, fumes, air pollutants, and chemicals can trigger asthma in children. (They often irritate the airways of nonasthmatic children as well. One study found wheezing in 12 percent of *all* children whose parents both smoke, and in 7 percent of those with one smoking parent.) Because children's exposure to many of these irritants is not under their own control, their parents must assume the responsibility of preventing or limiting such exposure.

Although aspirin-induced asthma is primarily an adult problem, some asthmatic children may be susceptible to it. If at all possible, asthmatic children should not be given aspirin or aspirin-like anti-inflammatory drugs. An asthmatic reaction to tartrazine (an azo dye) is as uncommon in children as in adults.

GASTROESOPHAGEAL REFLUX

Gastroesophageal reflux is a medical term describing the passage of stomach contents from the stomach back into the esophagus. (This condition in its mildest form is more commonly known as *heartburn*.) Reflux normally occurs in only 1 of every 500 infants, which is a fraction of 1 percent. Yet 30 to 70 percent (depending on the study) of infants with recurrent pneumonia or chronic asthma also have gastroesophageal reflux. Some physicians believe this condition acts as an asthma trigger.

Gastroesophageal reflux in children is usually not very difficult to treat. For an infant, laying him down to sleep at a 30-degree angle from the horizontal (with his head higher than his feet) and—once solids are added to his diet—thickening his food will help. Older children can take oral antacids and histamine antagonists (such as *Tagamet*) used for gastric disturbances.

PSYCHOLOGICAL FACTORS

Psychological factors obviously affect the course of asthma in some children. Much more important psychological aspects of asthma, however, are this disease's effects both on the child's emotional development and on his relationships with his family and the society in which he must live. These will be discussed in the next chapters.

Diagnosing the Asthmatic Child

We asked the father of an asthmatic child—a 12-year-old who had been severely asthmatic for most of his life—what troubled him most about doctors in connection with his son. He answered emphatically that he could not understand why it had taken so long for their former pediatrician to diagnose his child's asthma. And Virginia Gilden, the Olympic medal winner, recalls her mother's anger when the first doctor who saw her after she had clearly developed asthma (and already had an asthmatic brother) claimed that nothing was wrong with her.

These complaints are understandable. Once a child is correctly diagnosed and his parents eventually learn a lot about asthma, the child's condition seems extraordinarily obvious to them. If their child had been inaccurately diagnosed for some time after first developing asthma, his parents often come to feel very angry about the medical professional(s) who missed what they found so obvious.

But these complaints are not usually justifiable. Although many episodes of childhood wheezing are caused by asthma, the problem is that wheezing in some children is due to other conditions whose symptoms can mimic those of asthma to a perplexing degree. The diagnosis of asthma, especially in the infant, is very difficult.

Bronchiolitis, for example, is a typical wintertime infection that inflames an infant's airways. It is a form of reversible obstructive lung disease, but does not usually lead to asthma. Yet the symptoms are so indistinguishable from asthma that the British call it the "wheezy baby syndrome." Because asthma is very rare in infants under one year old, asthma-like symptoms at this young age tend to be regarded as bronchiolitis. With somewhat older children as well, the diagnosis of bronchiolitis may seem more likely to a physician even though he is actually confronted with asthma. "But," as one allergist we spoke to cautions, "when a child has had three or four episodes of apparent bronchiolitis in the space of several months, especially when the season for bronchiolitis is over, then you should begin to suspect that something else is going on."

Bronchiolitis is not the only pulmonary condition that can mimic asthma so effectively. Other chronic lung infections, diseases such as cystic fibrosis, and even the inhalation of foreign bodies can produce asthma-like symptoms.

THE CHILD'S HISTORY

Because many of the laboratory assessment techniques for diagnosing asthma cannot be used with infants and young children, their history is the physician's single most important diagnostic tool. As this history is usually taken from someone other than the child—usually the mother— a complicating factor is added. The doctor often receives an edited version of the truth because the facts have been interpreted by the person presenting them.

This unwitting tendency to editorialize can be minimized somewhat by writing down observations about your child's symptoms before the first doctor's visit. The doctor will want to know: Does the child's wheezing occur once in a while or often? Is the child ever short of breath? Does he cough? Does he produce mucus? Are his symptoms present all through the year, or just during a particular season? Are his symptoms aggravated by weather changes, by exposure to animals, and so on?

THE CHILD'S PHYSICAL EXAMINATION

For the child who is between attacks when he first sees the doctor, the physical examination tends to be quite normal. During the examination the child may demonstrate the "asthmatic salute"—rubbing his uptilted nose with his fingers and hand. (This "salute" actually serves two purposes: rubbing relieves an itchy nose, and tilting it up lessens nasal airflow obstruction.) The tip of the child's nose might have taken on a slightly pug-nosed tilt (called an "allergic crease") from constant rubbing. Some children have dark rings under their eyes, called "allergic shiners." Abnormal breath sounds are occasionally heard with the stethoscope, especially in severely asthmatic children. The child might have some chest deformities, and lung hyperinflation can sometimes be visualized by X-ray.

The asthmatic child may also be short for his age. Bone density and pubic hair growth are sometimes retarded. This growth retardation is no cause for worry; it will not be permanent. The typical growth pattern for an asthmatic child is for a normal growth rate from infancy until childhood, when it starts to slow down. This slowing becomes more pronounced in adolescence, then growth quickly catches up as the adolescent approaches adulthood. (It is not known whether asthma causes these growth delays, or whether the asthma and the delayed maturation are both caused by a more basic abnormality.)

When a young child is examined during an acute asthma attack, his ribs will pull in instead of expanding when he inhales, and his skin—particularly around his throat and collar bones—will look as if it is being sucked in. (As explained earlier, this is caused by the young child's pliant ribs and intense inspiratory effort.) Many children with acute asthma vomit very frequently because of their incessant coughing and heavy mucus secretion. It is not unusual for them to vomit up cups of mucus during an attack.

X-RAYS

A chest X-ray may rule out heart disease and other lung diseases as the cause of wheezing. It can also be useful during an attack to detect complications. A common complication is *recurrent atelectasis*. Atelectasis refers to the collapse of a localized area of air sacs because of mucus plugs. In this case, the collapse is frequently in the middle lobe on the right side of the lungs. In fact, it is called *right middle-lobe syndrome*. Other possible complications are pneumonia, fractured ribs (from prolonged, intense coughing), and pneumothorax (collapse of one side of the lungs from air entering the space between the lungs and chest wall).

PULMONARY FUNCTION TESTS

Although technically it can be difficult to obtain satisfactory test results from a child before he is six years old, these tests should be an integral part of every initial evaluation. They are also useful for knowing if a child's airway obstruction responds to bronchodilator use, and if a child's airways are hyperreactive to an exercise airway challenge. In fact, airway hyperreactivity due to exercise is so common among asthmatic children that its appearance during an exercise challenge is considered diagnostic of the disease.

ALLERGY TESTING

If allergies are suspected, the child's doctor may want RAST or skin testing done. RAST is the usual choice for the child under three because it is so difficult to do skin testing with such young children. RAST is also used for any child with the potential for a severe systemic or anaphylactic allergic reaction. Skin testing is done whenever possible because the results are more reliable, they are immediate (RAST results take about one week), and the test is less expensive.

A TEST WARNING TO PARENTS

A parent's responsibility to his asthmatic child includes avoiding unnecessary diagnostic tests. It is your right as well as your responsibility to avoid them. It is important that all the tests needed for your child's accurate diagnosis be done, but beyond this, testing should stop. Overtesting is an unnecessary expense, and it will most likely turn doctors' visits into a negative experience for your child.

Even for tests that must be done, your child's comfort remains paramount. The child's doctor should carefully explain to you every test that he feels your child should undergo. This explanation must include the nature and frequency of side effects. If you suspect that a particular test will cause your child an unacceptable degree of discomfort, ask his doctor about alternative or intermediary tests that can be tried first.

One example of easy intermediary tests involves the diagnosis of gastroesophageal reflux. If this condition is suspected in your child, an elaborate diagnostic test is not immediately needed. First try dealing directly with the symptoms by giving your child an antacid. If his heartburn and/or asthma symptoms improve after several days, expensive, time-consuming tests can be avoided.

Do not let yourself be bullied into accepting tests for your child that you believe—after learning all the facts—are inappropriate. Try your best to avoid the unwarranted sense of insecurity that a great many lay people feel in regard to doctors. Do not forget that you know your child better than anyone else does. Because of this, you may know more than a doctor does in certain situations. *Trust yourself.* (This is not simply our advice. It comes from our many conversations with parents of asthmatic children, as well as doctors who care for them.)

A related area for this kind of parental right/responsibility concerns the use of your child in an experiment. We recently met a mother whose child's doctor wanted to hospitalize her for a five-day evaluation procedure for gastroesophageal reflux. This was despite the fact that the child had no gastric symptoms indicating that reflux was a possible asthma trigger for her. This five-day procedure turned out to be part of an experimental study. The physician was concerned more with gathering data than with the possible effects of the experience on the children involved.

As researchers ourselves, we know as well as anyone that scientists cannot carry out their investigations without volunteers to study. Any new treatment must eventually be tested on humans, but this does not permit a physician to withhold information from a parent because he needs "volunteers" for his research project. It is of the utmost importance that you be told when a test—even a routine one—is truly necessary, and when it is simply desired as part of a scientific investigation. We all have the assurance that any research involving human beings has to have passed through a very harsh review procedure to ensure little or no risk of side effects. But it is still *your right to decide* whether you want your child to participate.

✵✵ 16 ✵✵

Treating the Asthmatic Child

When treatment is considered, the child with asthma cannot be viewed in isolation from his family. Although the nature and severity of a child's asthma determine the starting point of treatment, his doctor may modify this basic plan as he gets to know the family and their living circumstances. He will want to know the family's economic resources and physical environment, who is primarily responsible for the asthmatic child's care, and whether one or both parents live at home. He will try to determine the parents' and child's knowledge of, and attitudes toward, asthma. The doctor will also try to evaluate the parents' inherent resources for managing asthma in terms of motivation, energy, intelligence, maturity, and the amount of emotional support they are able to offer their child.

Parents of an asthmatic child—whom we call asthma parents—must realize what is required of them. Finding a competent physician for their child is only the first step. Successful treatment also requires their own involvement and—as soon as possible—the child's direct participation, too. (In fact, many doctors who work well with asthmatic children also regard the child's parents as their patients.) But achieving effective therapy for the asthmatic child is more than parents and child carefully following the doctor's instructions. It is very much a cooperative, give-and-take effort. Each team member has something to teach the others.

These next sections on treating childhood asthma are thus concerned as much with the family as with the child's doctor and medication. To make the material easier for the reader to absorb, we have divided it into two chapters. This chapter contains the material that most immediately affects your child's treatment. The next chapter highlights the common elements in parents' experience of having a child who has developed asthma, their responsibilities to their child, and various suggestions for carrying them out as effectively as possible. And—because some asthmatic children have a brother or sister—we also discuss the impact of asthma on the healthy sibling.

We have divided this material for the sake of convenience. Because much of it is really part of the same fabric, you will find that Chapter 16 cannot completely avoid discussing parental involvement and asthma's impact on the family. And Chapter 17 does not eliminate mention of treatment.

Choosing Your Child's Doctor

Deciding on an appropriate physician is not a clear-cut matter, since a number of specialties overlap in treating childhood asthma. Chest physician, allergist, pediatrician, and general practitioner—each of these specialists is confident that he can treat the asthmatic child adequately by himself with, at most, occasional consultation with one of the other specialists. And to the extent that he sees a large number of asthmatic patients and keeps up with medical advances in the field, he is probably right.

Many parents automatically look for an allergist to treat their child's asthma because of the common belief that childhood asthma is always caused by allergies. Most allergists these days are familiar with pulmonary medicine.

And—in the United States, at least—a large number of allergists also have pediatric training.

Allergies, however, are a major problem for only half the children with asthma. The child's pediatrician seems a logical initial choice to be his primary asthma physician because he knows the whole child, and will be familiar with the various management problems that can arise. And if he finds the need for it, he will either refer the child to an appropriately trained allergist or chest doctor, or call him in as a consultant. Some families' choice will, of course, be limited by the medical resources available where they live. Then the nearest urban medical center can provide additional expertise, if needed, on a consultant basis.

Most important in choosing the doctor who will treat your child's asthma is not the medical specialty, but the essential combination of knowledge with concern for your child and family. If doctor and family are working successfully together in controlling the child's asthma, your choice of doctor was a good one.

Note: If you disagree about something with a doctor whom you basically respect, do not discuss the problem in front of your child. It is very important that your child's confidence in his doctor's competence not be weakened. Do not ignore your differences, but simply bring them up with the doctor out of your child's presence.

When choosing a doctor, know what to avoid in making your choice. The following list summarizes part of what we learned from many parents we met who have a child suffering from asthma. They discovered the hard way what to avoid in choosing a doctor for their child. Do *not* continue a relationship with any doctor who:

- has little or no time for your questions

- does not prepare you for the possible side effects of prescribed medication

- offers little emotional support

- blames you for the existence or severity of your child's asthma

- makes you feel incompetent and negligent as a parent

- regularly leaves you in the waiting room for long periods

- regularly sends you to the emergency room instead of equipping you to treat nonemergency episodes at home

- does not listen to or belittles your observations and suggestions

- is unwilling to try newer medications that seem appropriate

- threatens you with dire consequences for your child if you do not obey his orders

- knows in advance that your child's asthma will never improve.

These asthma parents also discovered that arrogance and lack of concern are as common in major cities as in small towns. They learned that becoming involved with such a doctor is usually of little help to the child, and is painful and debilitating to the entire family. We—and they—hope that this distillation of their hard-won education will help other parents spare themselves and their child needless emotional pain and physical suffering, and the waste of time and money.

Medications

The mainstay of asthma treatment is the use of pharmaceutical agents to prevent airway obstruction from developing, and to relieve obstruction when preventive efforts fail. Although children and adults use the same medications, some of their characteristic problems are different.

One problem unique to medicating asthmatic children occurs because the childhood years are a period of great developmental change. This growth process will probably alter the disease's severity and the child's responsiveness to different antiasthma drugs at some point(s) during this time span, but the nature of these changes in an individual child is unpredictable. No one can know in advance whether the child's disease will ease or worsen (although most children improve), whether he will need his drug dosage raised or lowered, or whether he will need a different drug altogether.

A currently appropriate drug regimen may no longer be ideal at some point in the future. This means that a drug's effectiveness must be kept under constant surveillance. One way to accomplish this—and also to observe the natural history of your child's condition—is to *keep a diary* and *use a peak flow meter* (more on these meters after the various medications are discussed). This diary should include the following kinds of observations (individual doctors may want additional items, and some may have a preprinted form for you to use):

- symptoms ("Woke up two times during the night with wheezing and coughing, but no mucus brought up")

- any notable daily activities ("Had to stay home because of symptoms," "Was able to play the entire basketball game")

- type of drugs used and doses actually taken

- peak flow measurements right after waking up and before going to sleep

- miscellaneous relevant comments ("Weather turned unexpectedly cold," "Went to Susan's birthday party").

Another problem is that the physiological systems of infants and children are less tolerant of medication than are the systems of older patients. This can show itself in the sudden occurrence of nightmares and/or sleepwalking and/or frequent waking, and in such behavioral changes as hyperactivity, irritability, or loss of concentration. A couple whose preteen son recently stopped taking theophylline after six straight years observed with pleasure that "he is suddenly a nicer kid, much less argumentative, and he sleeps more than he used to." There is some question as to whether antiasthma medication interferes with the retention of learned material, which could hamper school performance.

Aside from any problems involving the drugs directly, simply getting a very young child to cooperate in taking his daily medication can be a major problem. Grape juice can help disguise an unpleasant-tasting oral medication. Spraying a plant mister into a child's mouth—which many children adore—can add fun to the medication routine. To gain cooperation in using a nebulizer, a parent must often become more inventive than he thought possible. Make it into any kind of game that works. One mother we spoke to gives her toddler a prized ride in a cardboard box for each deep breath he takes through his nebulizer mask. Another recommended technique is inviting over another asthmatic child—one who uses the nebulizer well—to teach an uncooperative child how to use it. Some children sleep so deeply that the nebulizer mask can be placed on them during a nap and when they fall asleep at night, assuring at least two good nebulizer sessions.

Before we describe the different types of antiasthma drugs that children use, we should define the descriptive terms that everyone uses to indicate age ranges. Except for birth, there are no sharp or rigid demarcations, so these definitions are fairly rough. "Infant" means from birth up to 18 months to two years of age. "Young child" ranges from about two to five or six years old. The "older child" covers from six or seven to twelve or thirteen. "Adolescence" refers to the teenage years.

BETA-ADRENERGIC DRUGS

Most children under 18 months old do not respond very much to adrenergic bronchodilators. Current thinking is that infants either do not yet have beta-receptors in their airways, or these receptors are immature. Because different children develop the capacity to respond to beta-adrenergic drugs at different rates, some will have this capacity between 12 and 18 months. If there is any suspicion that a child in this age range has become able to benefit from these drugs, a test trial is in order.

Although oral beta-2-stimulators are effective and safe for children, they can cause behavior problems (such as hyperactivity, distractability, irritability), tremor, headaches, anxiety, and heart palpitations. Using an inhaled preparation greatly reduces these side effects, but until recently a metered-dose inhaler (MDI) required more coordination than a young child could manage. The development of "spacers" has made coordination far less important in using an inhaler properly. Now children as young as three—and even some two-year-olds—can be taught to use an inhaler without difficulty.

For children who cannot yet manage the MDI, an aerosol of any of the inhaled agents can be made by a compressor-powered nebulizer such as the Pulmo-Aide (by DeVilbiss) or Maxi-Myst (by Mead Johnson Pharmaceutical). Aerosol nebulization is used both for the acutely ill hospitalized child and for routine daily management at home. The aerosolized medication begins to work within minutes, and the effect can last from four to six hours. The nebulizer's primary drawback is the difficulty of keeping a young child calmly in one spot for the five to ten minutes needed for its use.

THEOPHYLLINE

Although theophylline has been used for at least 40 years in treating asthma, the development of new preparations and a better understanding of how theophylline works have created a new surge of interest in this drug. It is now the drug of choice in the United States for all but the mildest forms of asthma.

Liquid theophylline preparations are convenient for young children, but many of them have a relatively high content of alcohol (to hide the bitter taste and increase the drug's solubility), dye, sugar, and preservatives. *Slophyllin 80 Syrup* (William H. Rorer, Inc.), *Theoclear-80 Syrup* (Central Pharmaceuticals, Inc.), and *Aquaphyllin Syrup* (Ferndale Laboratories, Inc.) do not contain any alcohol, sugar, or dyes. Liquid theophylline preparations have two disadvantages. They are relatively short-lasting, and measuring the dose exactly is often difficult with a liquid. The more concentrated liquids—although there is less for a child to swallow—are even more prone to dosing error. Even a small measuring error can cause a large error in the drug's blood level—especially in a small child.

Because theophylline is removed from a child's blood faster than from an adult's, stable blood levels of the drug are more difficult to achieve in children. Sustained-release preparations—which come in capsule and tablet form—minimize this problem. Because they also require less frequent dosing, children tend to be more cooperative in taking them. Most children over the age of four can be taught to swallow capsules and tablets. For those who cannot, and for younger children, the theophylline beads in the *Theo-Dur-Sprinkle* capsule (Key Pharmaceuticals, Inc.) can be removed and sprinkled on a spoonful of applesauce (or whatever else the child enjoys eating).

Theophylline, which belongs to the same drug family as caffeine, does have side effects. In addition to possible gastrointestinal disturbances (nausea, vomiting, and heartburn), theophylline can interfere with sleep (insomnia, sleepwalking, nightmares). Its stimulatory properties can make a child hyperactive and irritable and impair school performance. Finding the lowest effective dose of the drug and maintaining a stable blood level are very important in keeping these effects to a minimum.

Theophylline normally has a narrow range of effective blood concentrations before it becomes toxic. Recent experimental evidence indicates that combining a less-than-full-strength theophylline dose with a reduced beta-2-stimulator dose gives much better symptom relief and morning peak airflows than using either drug alone at full strength. Lowering the theophylline dose reduces the drug's typical side effects.

ANTICHOLINERGIC DRUGS

Atropine, an anticholinergic drug, has been used in asthmatic children to block the component of bronchospasm stimulated by the vagus nerve. (The vagus nerve belongs to the parasympathetic nervous system, where stimulation occurs via the chemical acetylcholine.) The most recent atropine preparation is ipratropium bromide (brand name *Atrovent*), which had not been released for sale in the United States by the time this book was completed (early 1987).

In aerosolized form, this drug achieves bronchodilation in almost half the infants under 18 months old (the age when the beta-stimulators are relatively ineffective) who have tried it. In a preschool group of asthmatic children, this drug equaled a beta-stimulator in the amount of bronchodilation produced. The drug's side effects are minimal. Further studies are needed to establish ipratropium bromide's place in the treatment of childhood asthma.

CROMOLYN SODIUM

In Great Britain, cromolyn sodium is the first-choice preventive drug for childhood asthma. It has not yet found this degree of favor in the United States, even though studies in both countries show a similar range of success rates (effective in 50 to 90 percent of the children taking it).

Part of the reluctance to it here stemmed from the Spinhaler, the awkward—and until very recently the only—system for taking it. We know several people who stopped using cromolyn sodium because of the inconvenience and difficulty involved in breaking the foil wrapper to get a capsule out, placing it just right in the Spinhaler, then inhaling the powder. And the powder often made them cough. More recently, cromolyn sodium became available in a nebulizing solution. And in March 1986 it became available in an MDI, which avoids the problems of the Spinhaler and the nebulizer.

The overwhelming advantage of cromolyn sodium is its safety. It causes few or no side effects. Cromolyn sodium is shorter acting than other drugs, however, so it must be taken four times a day (although some people believe that twice a day is effective). Because it is a preventive, it must be taken continuously even when the child is asymptomatic. Its availability now in an MDI makes these disadvantages much less troublesome than they had been.

CROMOLYN VERSUS THEOPHYLLINE

A well-designed study carried out jointly by Great Britain and the United States showed both cromolyn sodium and theophylline to be equally effective in preventing asthma attacks in moderately ill children. There are differences in their use. Because cromolyn must be taken four times a day, one dose must be given at school. Also, the child must master use of the MDI or the Spinhaler. Although a long-lasting oral theophylline preparation need be taken only twice a day, the child must learn either to swallow whole tablets, or take the gritty little granules without chewing them. Liquid theophylline tastes terrible, is prone to measurement problems, and must be taken every six hours around the clock (meaning that the child must be awakened at night to take it).

Cromolyn's side effects are virtually nonexistent. Theophylline's side effects are few when the drug is properly used and monitored. Cromolyn is more expensive. One month's supply in New York City currently costs three to four times as much as theophylline.

CORTICOSTEROIDS

Steroids are unique in their ability to reverse the pathology of an asthma attack. Steroids are also prescribed when maximum doses of the other kinds of drugs cannot control symptoms. Steroids must be used with caution, however, because of their side effects.

Short-term use (less than two weeks) of injected or oral steroids rarely causes significant side effects, but a child may have lowered blood potassium, mood changes, weight gain, and/or gastrointestinal discomfort. Long-term daily doses can have serious consequences, such as growth suppression, loss of calcium from the bones, and cataract formation. Using an oral steroid only every other day, or switching to an inhaled steroid if possible, minimizes these side effects, and reverses them in patients who have been on daily tablets for some time. A recent report suggests that alternate-day therapy does not suppress growth, so it should be used whenever possible. The dose should be taken before 8:00 A.M. to coincide with the body's time of peak steroid production.

A prednisone syrup is available (*Liquid Pred* by Muro Pharmaceutical, Inc.). Its characteristics are similar to those of the tablet, although peak blood concentration occurs more quickly because the liquid, unlike a pill, does not first have to be digested. Dexamethasone—which is more powerful than prednisone—is available in a suspension (powdered particles in a liquid medium). Dosing is unpredictable, because the number of particles present in a teaspoon of the liquid depends on how vigorously the bottle was shaken.

When beclomethasone, an inhaled steroid, can be substituted for all or part of an adult patient's steroid dose, oral steroid dependence decreases. Beclomethasone, however, is available only in an adult formulation. Although children over the age of six benefit from this formulation in much the same way adults do, a small overdose (which happens only rarely) in these young patients can cause some suppression of adrenal and pituitary gland function. As with oral steroids, the inhaled preparation should be tapered to the lowest effective dose. Although children under six can also benefit from inhaled steroids, the drug is not available in a nebulized form. Using a spacer with the MDI, though, means that children as young as three, and even some two-year-olds, can use beclomethasone.

Whether a child requiring steroids should use alternate-day oral prednisone or daily inhaled beclomethasone depends on the individual. The child who is obese or diabetic, or who suffers from an immunologic disorder, may do better with the inhaled steroid. The child who is unable to inhale medication, or responds poorly to the inhaled steroid, or whose family cannot afford the inhaled preparation, obviously must use the alternate-day oral drug.

HANDLING AN ATTACK AT HOME

Antiasthma medication is used in two different contexts. As a preventive, it is taken on a regular maintenance schedule. When drugs are used to reverse an asthma attack, their use is not so simple and clear-cut; but with enough experience and professional guidance, parents can learn to handle most of their child's nonemergency episodes by themselves.

Dr. Thomas F. Plaut, pediatrician and author of *Children with Asthma: A Manual for Parents*, identifies the three stages of parents' ability to cope with an attack at home. Beginner: Parents recognize that their child is in the midst of an asthma attack and can follow the physician's written or verbal treatment instructions. Intermediate: Parents can judge the severity of an individual attack, can communicate clearly with their child's doctor, can handle each attack well with the doctor's help, and are able to evaluate the progress of an attack and adjust medication accordingly. Advanced: Parents understand the usual course of their child's attacks and can manage most of them without having to consult the doctor. They are also able to give the doctor well-reasoned suggestions on improving their child's treatment.

PEAK FLOW METER

Although it is difficult for either you or your child to sense very early changes in lung function, you need to be aware of them for two reasons. One is to know whether a particular medication or dosage is still effective. The other is to know that an attack is beginning early enough to try and head it off. An objective tool exists to tell you what your senses cannot. It is the *peak flow meter* (Figure 16.1) which some physicians advocate using.

Peak airflow measurements are made upon waking up in the morning, and just before going to sleep at night. Because a sudden decrease in your child's usual numbers is the earliest possible warning that an attack may be coming on, medication can usually be used to head it off. Nipping an attack in the bud, as opposed to trying to reverse a full-blown episode, makes life easier for everyone.

Two such devices are the mini-Wright Peak Flow Meter (about $60, purchasable from Armstrong Industries, 1-800-323-4220), and the much cheaper but less accurate Pulmonary Monitor (about $15, purchasable from Vitalograph Medical Instruments, 1-800-255-6626).

They are used in the following way: Set the pointers at zero, stand the child up, and make sure you are not covering the opening at the end. Tell the child to take as big a breath as he can, place the mouthpiece in his mouth (he must know not to cover it with his tongue), and tell him to blow out hard and fast, but not to force out all his air. You want to see how fast he can make the air come out, not how much will come out. Repeat the procedure twice more (resetting the pointers to zero each time), then record the highest number in your diary.

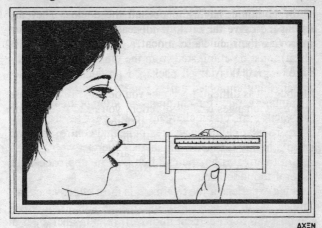

ΔΧΞΝ

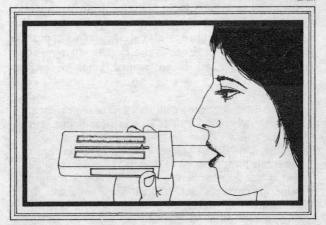

Figure 16.1 Two popular peak-flow meters. *Top*: Mini-Wright meter. *Bottom*: Vitalograph Pulmonary Monitor.

Avoiding/Minimizing Triggers

As emphasized in Chapter 9, exposure to asthma triggers must be kept to a minimum. This includes a ban on smoking in the house, and asthma-proofing the house if allergy testing indicates the need. If food allergies trigger an infant's attacks, then those foods (e.g., eggs, cow's milk, wheat) must be eliminated from the child's diet. Read the list of ingredients for all packaged products, and do not buy anything unlabeled unless you know what is in it.

Immunotherapy for children—an attempt to minimize the reaction to certain allergens that trigger severe attacks in a particular child—is an area of heated controversy. We asked a highly respected Manhattan allergist who specializes in treating asthmatic children how he approaches the issue of immunotherapy.

In his experience, the treatment is most effective against pollens (90 to 95 percent of his treated patients improve) and dust (80 to 85 percent improve). Immunotherapy is at best a stopgap against mold allergies, and has no place with food and animal allergens. (Recently, the allergist has learned of a new serum against cat dander that appears to be effective.) His readiness to use immunotherapy with a particular child depends on several kinds of circumstances.

> I use immunotherapy with very few of the children I treat privately, and I wait as long as I can before starting these few. There are two important reasons for waiting. One is that putting a young child on regular injections turns them off to doctors. Even more important is that immunotherapy has only limited treatment value for most younger children. Since asthma is dynamic and may disappear spontaneously, I prefer to rely on medication at first and see where the asthma goes. And as children get older, their allergies are better characterized. By the time the child is six I usually know if there is going to be an allergic component involving inhaled pollen, dust, or whatever. Then I will use immunotherapy for the child who develops nasal allergies, and for the child whose parents refuse to alter their home environment to remove dust and animal dander.
>
> I use immunotherapy much more frequently for my

clinic pediatric patients because the burden of coping with asthma is much greater for families who live in poverty. They have problems enough with the difficulties of eking out a living. It is unfair to ask them to go through the gymnastics and expense of asthma-proofing, and it's often impossible for them to do so anyway. In this situation, immunotherapy becomes an indispensable alternative.

Educating Your Child

The importance of properly educating the asthmatic child is emphasized in the literature and was stressed by everyone we spoke to—both parents and professionals—who care for asthmatic children. Education involves two phases. In addition to informing your child about his disease, he must learn to take age-appropriate responsibility for his own care.

It is very, very important to tell your child that he has asthma, and to help him understand what that means for him. Hiding the existence of his disease will not protect him or his self-image. Because childhood asthma is usually a daily problem, the asthmatic child is going to realize very quickly that he has difficulty with breathing that other children do not have. As one physician who works with a large number of asthmatic children commented: "A child has got to be really dumb not to realize that something is going on."

Tell your child before he starts learning to read. Many parents who have not spoken openly with their asthmatic child about his disease become frantic when the child is about six. What will they do when the child sees a Lung Association commercial about asthma on television, realizes that it is describing his breathing problems, and can read the name of his disease? Your child's doctor can help you decide when and how to start your child's education.

Most important, your child should eventually become responsible for managing his own asthma. The sooner you can help your child learn what his triggers are, what medicines he takes, and when and how they should be taken, the better off everyone will be. When your child is old enough, he should be put in charge of his medication. The child who understands his disease and is able to participate in handling it will have an important sense of control over it. And the child who learns early on to be responsible for his asthma care will be far better prepared as an adult to deal with these same problems if they continue or reappear.

A variety of formal teaching programs have been created, all based on the principle that the child is an active participant in preventing and controlling his symptoms. One such program is *Asthma Care Training (ACT) for Kids*, developed by the departments of Medicine and Pediatrics at the UCLA School of Medicine. It was meant as a supplemental educational tool to help 7- to 12-year-old children develop self-management skills and to give their parents the information and support that will help them guide their child toward this goal. Preliminary reports on the program's effectiveness indicate that children become much more cooperative in taking medication and avoiding triggers, emergency room visits are much less frequent, and hospital stays are substantially shorter.

ACT for Kids involves five weekly one-hour meetings during which parents and children spend 45 minutes in separate groups going over the same material, then share their perceptions for the remaining time. The five sessions are: (1) What is asthma, and how does it affect my body; (2) Why do I have asthma, and what sets it off; (3) What to do, and when to do it; (4) How to decide; (5) How to balance my wants and needs. Throughout the sessions, an analogy is drawn between maintaining health and driving a car. ACT for Kids is designed to be taught by teachers and health professionals, and is administered by the Asthma and Allergy Foundation of America. (Their address is in Appendix A.)

The American Lung Association's *Superstuff* is a self-help program that was developed for children with serious asthma. It is designed for parents and child to use at home. Superstuff includes a large illustrated book with supplementary materials, including a record, for your child. The content is presented with a child's point of view and sensibilities in mind, and includes the use of games, stories, puzzles, and other activities that children enjoy. Parents receive a news magazine. Superstuff is available either from the American Lung Association (see Appendix A for their address) or from your local Lung Association for a voluntary $10 contribution to defray printing costs.

Physical Management

PHYSICAL THERAPY

Physical therapy can be important in helping school-age (and occasionally younger) children cope effectively with asthma. The control that a child learns from breathing and relaxation exercises can help break the panic cycle that often accompanies an acute attack. When a chest infection occurs, postural drainage can help bring up mucus that would otherwise clog the airways. (Chapter 12 describes all these procedures and how to learn them.)

EXERCISE

When the author William Golding created a symbol of intellectual, rational influence in *Lord of the Flies*, it was in the person of Piggy, the short, fat, bespectacled boy whom "Auntie" had always told not to run or swim or blow hard because of his "assmar." This description enshrines the traditional philosophy of forcing the asthmatic child to avoid any exertion for fear of inducing an attack. The asthmatic's biggest problem is fitting in with his peers, and probably no other area has traditionally isolated the typical asthmatic child from his peers so much as his inability to participate in common games and sports.

In the mid-1970s, Australian researchers involved 46

asthmatic children in a vigorous organized sport and studied the various effects. These children, whose asthma ranged from mild to severe, participated in a five-month swim training program headed by professional swimming coaches. Training, which began with three sessions a week, increased in intensity, duration, and frequency until each child swam vigorously for one hour, five times a week. Pulmonary function tests before and after the training program showed if there was any respiratory improvement. Questionnaires filled out by children and parents showed any impact of the experience on their lives.

After the five months, the children had all gained weight, yet had decreased their body fat. Symptoms were less severe, and the children used less medication. Parents had better insight into their child's asthma. Because of this they also became less protective, giving their child substantially greater freedom, particularly for participating in physical and social activities.

Rather than being dissuaded from physical exercise, asthmatic children should be encouraged to participate in sports. Swimming has traditionally been the sport recommended by the minority of doctors who encouraged physical activity for asthmatics. The warm, moist air of the swimming pool seems to prevent bronchospasm. Now the availability of medication that effectively prevents exercise-induced bronchospasm (described fully in Chapter 12) permits children to participate in any sport—including running and cross-country skiing—without fear.

The Asthmatic Child at School

So far, we have discussed treating the asthmatic child with the underlying assumption that the child is always with a parent or other primary caretaker. This is obviously not the case once a child begins school. Until recently, most asthma episodes, no matter how minor, were dealt with at home. But the frequency of school absenteeism for asthmatics has become a serious concern. Severely asthmatic children are estimated to be as much as one full year behind their age-mates in academic achievement. Asthmatic children should remain in school as much as possible, which means returning to school more quickly after an attack—sometimes during the end stages—and staying in school during minor episodes. To accomplish this, however, the school staff must be educated and cooperative.

APPROACHING THE SCHOOL

You should discuss your child's condition with the appropriate school staff: principal (or director), teachers—especially the gym teacher—and school nurse. Then each of these staff members should be given detailed written instructions, that include possible triggers, your child's medication schedule, what to do and whom to call in the event of an attack. (Your child can carry similar instructions when he visits friends or takes a vacation without you.) Sometimes a phone call or a letter from your child's doctor can be helpful with school personnel who have not yet dealt with an asthmatic child.

Following are two sample instruction letters, one for teachers and the other for the school nurse. They have been adapted from Dr. Thomas Plaut's *Children with Asthma*.

Information for Teachers:
  My son/daughter (name) has asthma. An attack is most often triggered by _____ .
Ordinarily there are no restrictions on his/her physical activity. During an attack, however, strenuous physical exercise and playing outside in cold weather should be avoided. If you see any behavior that is inappropriate in this regard, please let me know.
My child takes the following medicines:

_____ .

The possible side effects are _____ .

Information for the Nurse:

My son/daughter (name) has asthma. An attack is most often triggered by _____ .
Unless he/she is in the middle of an attack, my child can participate fully in class activities and should not be restricted in any way.

During an attack, exposure to cold and engaging in strenuous physical activity should be avoided.

The following medicines are to be taken at the following times: (list medicines, doses, and times).

In case of any questions, I can be reached at (telephone number). If you cannot contact me, call (name) at (telephone number). If neither of us can be reached, please call Dr. (name) at (telephone number) for advice.

MEDICATION SCHEDULE

Adhering closely to a medication schedule is much easier at home than outside. Outside, however, problems are minimal for the child who needs medication only twice a day. Morning and evening doses mean that he does not have to worry about taking medication at school. But sometimes the asthma or the type of drug used requires more frequent use. Because junior and senior high school students frequently find it cumbersome or embarrassing to stop in the middle of an activity to report to the school nurse, they should be able to carry—and be responsible for—their own medication. For younger children, the school nurse should hold all medications and make sure that they are taken appropriately. For asthmatic students of any age, the type of medication, dose, and schedule should be on record in the school's health office and/or in the student's file.

Summer Camp and the Asthmatic Child

Those in the forefront of treating asthmatic children are increasingly concerned with finding the means to help them live in a relatively normal environment and enjoy the same kinds of activities as nonasthmatic children their own age. One such activity that has become accessible to asthmatic children is summer camp.

A well-chosen camp usually provides a highly beneficial experience, particularly for the child who—out of necessity—has been very dependent on his family. He has an environment in which he will find new friends and develop an invaluable sense of confidence and independence. The family benefits from this separation, too. Camp gives them a respite from the otherwise daily need for vigilance, and their child's summer success reassures them that he can be safe away from home.

The severely asthmatic child, because he requires professional medical supervision, can take advantage of camps that are set up specifically to handle the child with asthma (see Appendix B for a list). Less severely ill children will do well at a regular camp as long as the camp staff and the child have been appropriately educated. Certain kinds of precautions are also necessary. Because campfire smoke, for example, can be very irritating to the airways, an asthmatic child—or, to avoid singling him out, his entire group—should always be seated upwind of a campfire. And the camp chosen should, of course, be one that avoids or minimizes exposing the child to his asthma triggers. The child allergic to animals, for example, will be much better off at a water sports camp than one where farm animals are cared for. An appropriate camp, educating the camp's staff, plus attention to details can make the asthmatic child's experience exciting and rewarding.

When is a particular child ready for camp? The decision should be made jointly by the child, his parents, and his doctor. If you are presently considering camp for your child, some of the important questions are: Can your child fall asleep at night without being tucked into bed? Does he brush his teeth and wash himself without help? Can he dress and bathe without assistance? Has your child ever been away from home and family before?

Residential Programs

Despite the medical advances of the past 35 years, there remains a group of asthmatic children whose daily medical needs are either beyond what can possibly be provided at home, or so substantially beyond their family's resources that caring for the child leaves no time for earning an adequate living (as with many single parents and a severely ill child). Residential asthma facilities meet the need created by both these circumstances.

The second of these two needs has become predominant over the past 15 to 20 years. In fact, we thought about titling this section "The Single Parent with an Asthmatic Child." The National Jewish Center for Immunology and Respiratory Medicine in Denver, Colorado, notes, for example, that only 15 percent of their residents were from a single-parent family in 1970, but by 1979 this proportion had climbed to a majority. Sending an asthmatic child to live in a residential facility is more and more often a solution born of economic desperation. Because the consuming demands for daily care do not have to be met by the parent for an extended time, the mother or father is able to work and support the family. And the parent (or his medical insurance company) can share treatment costs with the institution and the state.

ONE PARENT'S STORY

The story of a single parent we met—her husband had left because he could no longer stand their infant asthmatic daughter's constant coughing—starkly illustrates this desperation.

> I have a 10½-year-old daughter, an asthmatic. She's had 52 bouts of pneumonia, she's had a pneumothorax, she's had 104 acute admissions to hospitals. She was in an asthma residence for a year and a half when she was four, for another year when she was nine, and she was admitted again eight months ago for another year.
>
> I'll tell you why my little girl is living away from me. I have a B.A. and my typing and shorthand skills are great, but I cannot keep a job. I've had 72 jobs in 10 years. Whenever my daughter was sick, I would be in the hospital with her every night and then try to do my job—on much too little sleep—during the day. And when she wasn't in the hospital, so often I'd get to my desk and find a note that the sitter had called: "Come home. She's had an attack." You tell the corporations that you have a daughter who is a chronic asthmatic and you are in the hospital with her all the time. They are sympathetic for a while. Then the bosses stop believing you.
>
> The first time I had to send my daughter away, we were living in a cold-water apartment in the far reaches of Brooklyn, because that was all I could afford. Then I lost another job. I couldn't pay the rent. I could not buy food for another day's meal. I could not buy my daughter's medication. Because we were still entitled to my husband's insurance, I could not be accepted for welfare. If I gave up the insurance to be eligible for welfare, I would not be able to pay for my daughter's medical care.
>
> I could no longer survive economically. I had to send my daughter away so that we could both survive. Otherwise I could not hold a job long enough. I had no choice. At least now a New York State law requires that parents be able to visit their children as often as they wish. The first time that I had to leave her there,

parents were only allowed to visit for four hours once a month, and we were allowed two telephone calls each month. The staff told me it was for my child's good. They said that the child needs to be separated from the parent, because asthma is all in the head.

Even with unlimited visiting and phone calls now, it is so lonely. And I see so many other lonely women there when I go to visit my daughter.

WHAT A RESIDENCE PROVIDES

The philosophy that guides these residences' operation has changed radically over the years. The former National Asthma Center (NAC) in Denver, Colorado, America's first residential asthma facility, was founded in the 1940s. The impetus for its existence was Dr. Murray Peshkin's belief that intractable asthma sprang from the parents' damaging psychological influence on their child. "Parentectomy"—removal of the parents—was considered the essential treatment. The concept of parentectomy has only recently become a relic of the past.

The more humane and realistic program eventually developed by the NAC became the model for other residential centers. The NAC had 25 beds for children from infancy to 17 years of age. Children were accepted for a maximum of 18 months. The four basic goals of such a program are achieving control of asthma in patients whose disease could not be controlled at home; encouraging the child's sense of responsibility and self-care; effectively treating psychological issues; and allowing the child to lead a normal life by de-emphasizing asthma as its central focus. The facility provides medical support, health education, psychological intervention for the child and his family, and complete school and recreational programs. Because there are not many long-term residential facilities across the country, the distance between such an asthma center and a patient's home can preclude his family's regular participation in the center's programs.

These asthma treatment residences fill a critical need for certain asthmatic children and their families, yet over the past several years more and more have either closed down or stopped offering such long-term treatment. The staffing required by these facilities to carry out their program makes them very expensive to run. In trying to update existing lists of residential facilities, we spoke with administrators from quite a few that no longer provide residential treatment and with several that still do. We learned that residential centers have been forced to close down completely or discontinue this service because recent restrictions on medical insurance reimbursement have created a crippling financial burden.

First, the government's Diagnostic Related Groupings (DRGs) regulation severely limited in-hospital expenses that can be reimbursed through Medicaid and Medicare. Even more of a problem is that private medical insurance companies have begun to dictate how long a patient should stay in the hospital. These "third-party payers," as they are called, now set a very strict and arbitrary limit on hospital stays and will not reimburse health care fees occurring beyond this artificial deadline.

The effect has been dramatic. All of the residential facilities in California, for example, have had to shut their doors. The center in Chicago, Illinois, just discontinued its residential service as this book was completed. Now 10 days is usually the longest they keep a severely asthmatic child.

The situation is currently in such flux that we found it impossible to provide an updated list of residential facilities that is likely to remain accurate for any length of time. Anyone wishing to learn of the residence facility nearest him, or of one that accepts out-of-state patients, should call his local Lung Association (listed in the White Pages).

Of the few remaining asthma treatment residences, those with substantial philanthropic resources coupled with an aggressive skill at gaining Medicaid assistance for their patients appear to have the best prospects for surviving this very shaky period. It is unclear at this point how the others will be affected by the U.S. government's, and private medical insurers', miserly attitude toward the health-care needs of those who are unable to assume the required economic burden. The basic conclusion expressed by administrators we spoke with is that third-party payers in particular are fooling around with people's lives. They are playing God, and it is dangerous.

❈❈ 17 ❈❈

Asthma Parents

Until your child is old enough to assume complete responsibility for handling his asthma care, you must shoulder the burden that he cannot yet manage. You must take whatever steps are necessary to avoid your child's exposure to his major triggers. You must be unrelenting—and sometimes marvelously inventive—in giving him his medication. If you are attentive to the subtle signs that herald an imminent attack, you will be able to modify your child's medication to prevent—or at least minimize—many of them. And you must be able to decide when a particular episode is beyond your ability to handle at home.

You should also be astute observers of any changes in the signs and symptoms of your child's asthma. Such changes may indicate the need for a shift in type or amount of treatment. Another parental responsibility is educating your child about the nature of his disease and the care it requires, then helping him share this care. And, while meeting the various and continuous demands that coping with childhood asthma places on a family, you should help your child to as normal a childhood as possible.

This list may seem overwhelming to parents who are newcomers to childhood asthma, or who have not had adequate help in adjusting to these circumstances. Do not

panic. The good news from the professional community
is that, by and large, families cope well with asthma. Parents and children rise to the occasion. Parents must re-
mind themselves that the logic and clarity of this list of
responsibilities, as well as self-confidence in their ability
to assume them, take time to materialize.

Before discussing the nature and need for this parental
education, some very basic emotions—mourning, guilt,
anger, and fear—must be dealt with. All asthma parents
face at least some of them at the beginning. An honest
confrontation is essential for your child's and your family's
health.

Childhood Asthma's Emotional Impact

MOURNING AND ITS RESOLUTION

Every parent of a chronically ill child goes through a period of mourning after they first learn of his disability.
They mourn their loss of a perfect child. Mourning is a
dynamic process, potentially progressing through five
stages: shock, panic, denial, grief, and resolution.
Achieving resolution—which translates to acceptance of
your child as he is, not as you wanted him to be—productively concludes the mourning process. Accepting this loss
frees you to marshal your resources for coping aggres-
sively and lovingly with your child's disease.

Why do parents mourn this loss of perfection? Such
mourning would seem to be an unavoidable side effect of
medical progress. Years ago, the roster of dread diseases
that killed many children at birth or soon afterward made
the experience of being a parent very different than it is
now. Parenting involved a great deal more illness, disap-
pointment, and loss. And because such experiences were
the norm, parents and the community at large were far
more understanding and accepting than they are now of

what are relatively minor imperfections. When parents worried about a catastrophic disease robbing them of their child overnight, something as manageable as asthma was not seen as a major handicap for the child or his family.

Today the catastrophic diseases of childhood are a nightmare of the past. Everyone expects to deliver perfectly healthy children and expects them to remain perfect until they eventually absorb some of society's imperfections. In an era that considers perfection the norm, the child with a chronic disease is viewed as damaged goods. From this emotional viewpoint, asthma looms as a far greater burden than it once did.

Mourning in itself is not a problem. If it concludes with acceptance of what cannot be altered and a determination to master your child's disease as much as possible, your experience has been a healthy one. The problem arises if you get stuck at an intermediary stage of the mourning process.

Sometimes parents' emotional stagnation is manifested as anger at all the doctors their child has seen so far. These parents need someone to blame for their child's asthma, and doctors make a very handy target. So it is always the doctor's fault that their child's asthma is not dramatically better, and they drag the child from one doctor to another. Other parents who have become stuck in the mourning process treat the asthma as a burden out of all proportion to the disease's actual severity. They overprotect their child to a degree that often leads to eventual problems in social adjustment. Another stagnation response is denial of the problem: ignore it, and it will not really exist.

GUILT AND ANGER

Guilt commonly follows learning that asthma usually develops in someone who has inherited the genetic predisposition for it. The parent with a family history of allergies and/or asthma is obviously the one most likely to feel guilty. The other parent sometimes reacts with anger, particularly if he or she was never made aware of this history.

Some asthma parents also feel anger because the asthma has suddenly made life so difficult for them and their child.

It is extremely important for both parents not to let their guilt or anger shape much of their behavior to their child or spouse. Keeping both these emotions in perspective prevents them from hurting the child or the family.

FEAR AND ANXIETY

Fear and its companion, anxiety, are present in varying degrees and contexts from the first asthma attack on. We hear typical asthma parents describe their initial response in such terms as: "The fear at that time was like a shock." "We were freaked out." "The first time she had asthma, I thought she was going to die, and I thought she was going to die for the entire first year."

At the beginning, much of the fear comes from not yet understanding the disease adequately. Not fully knowing what goes on during an attack or how to control/prevent symptoms makes a parent feel frighteningly inadequate. And there is no accumulated experience yet to reassure you that your child will survive each new attack. This sense of helplessness and dire uncertainty makes your child's experience of breathing difficulty terrifying to watch.

Parents who are in the midst of these early fears can comfort themselves with the knowledge that their asthmatic child is not going through a similarly frightening experience. One would expect a small child who suddenly cannot breathe well, and does not understand what is happening to him, to be terrified. But everyone we spoke to—physicians, "old hand" asthma parents, child psychologists—emphasized their consistent observation that the most stabilizing influence in the family of an asthmatic child is the child himself. He will eventually feel anxious and overwhelmed only if his parents cannot finally conquer their own fears.

Even once this initial terror dissipates, a thread of anxiety usually remains woven through an asthma parent's consciousness. It rises and falls, but it does not fully disappear. Rather than being primarily a response to an attack, however, this anxiety occurs when anticipating a possible attack. In the words of one father whose daughter's serious allergic asthma was finally under effective control: "It's almost like having a new child. We feel that we're moving forward in a way that we didn't for the past year. Things have really turned around for us. [Pause] And on the other hand, she sneezed this morning before I left for work. I counted them. There were seven in a row. [A long row of sneezes usually means "allergy" rather than "sniffles."] I immediately wondered what I was going to come home to in the evening."

For the parents of younger asthmatic children, winter—with its colds and flus—tends to be an anxious season. As the child becomes older, anticipatory anxieties are aroused by a variety of other concrete threats. There are friends' birthday parties, for example, which mean a cake made with who knows what ingredients, perhaps a dog or cat in the house, possibly adults who smoke. Sleepovers hold the same anxiety-producing possibilities.

A third source of worry—particularly for the parents of an allergic asthmatic child—is his future. What if his allergies and exercise-induced bronchospasm become so severe that they prevent him from any kind of normal peer relationships and social activities? Many parents become fearful that their child will end up sitting at home in a sparse and sterile environment, deprived of most or all pleasurable foods by a greatly restricted diet, and watching through the window as other children play outdoors. They understandably do not want their child banished to such an impoverished existence, constantly reminded that he is not like the other children on the block.

Asthma parents' fears and anxieties are normal. As with mourning, these emotional reactions become a problem only for parents who are unable to integrate them and move beyond them. When this happens, these emotions dictate how parents handle their child's asthma, significantly diminishing the parents' ability to cope well. Fear and anxiety may short-circuit parents' best intentions for treating their child's asthma appropriately and helping him to the best quality of life available to him.

A thorough parental education will minimize this problem. The essential prerequisite is a knowledgeable, caring, and available physician. The education itself takes place gradually. Some of it is formally introduced during doctors' visits. Some of it results from the direct experience of handling a variety of situations and problems. And some of it comes from the confidence that eventually grows as parents realize how much they have learned, and how much they are able to help their child.

The doctor can often gauge the progress of this education by the number and nature of the parents' phone calls. He may be inundated with calls at first as the family seems to stagger from one crisis to the next. Then calls become less and less frequent until they dwindle to a monthly status report and an occasional question.

Parent Support Groups

In addition to feeling frightened, anxious, guilty, and angry, asthma parents tend to feel very isolated and desperate for effective practical advice in handling their child's asthma. Much of this information is not readily available, particularly for the lay person. A great deal of frustrating misinformation partially fills the vacuum.

Some typical asthma parents in New York City and its suburbs have discovered a support group that is irreplaceable in dispelling their loneliness, battling disabling fear and anger, and learning an extraordinary amount about coping with childhood asthma in general, and one's own child in particular. In fact, the allergist treating many of their children—who also participates in the group (and has an asthmatic child as well)—finds that he has learned more about childhood asthma since the group began in April

1983 than he had learned in all his preceding years of practice.

The group's composition changes gradually over time as "old" asthma parents leave and "new" ones come, but the group retains a good mix of experienced and neophyte parents. Experienced asthma parents provide support and information to newcomers, who are eventually able to give of themselves in this way too. Support is available for different needs: getting through the initial terror; learning to treat attacks at home; dealing with—or leaving—an insensitive physician; defining and obtaining one's rights within the medical establishment. And everyone is able to share. They share their angers, fears, guilts, doubts, and joys; they share a great variety of experiences involving their children; they share good and bad times with doctors, emergency rooms, schools, friends, and relatives; they share good vacation spots, practical advice, equipment recommendations; and so on.

These parents are able to give each other something that no physician can provide, no matter how caring he is and how thoroughly he educates his patients' parents. Every parent in this group lives with an asthmatic child every day and every night. Each newcomer discovers a group of peers who know exactly what he is going through because they have all been through it themselves. New asthma parents are no longer alone in this strange world they have suddenly been shifted to. And the experienced asthma parents, who have successfully established themselves in this world, have a powerful desire—and much to give—to help others achieve this.

We were invited to one of the support group's monthly meetings while we were writing this book. There was a great deal to listen to—factual, emotional, philosophical, personal, general. We met parents who felt they owed to the group most or all of their success in coping well with their child's disease. We also met parents who had learned much from the group after getting off to a good start on their own. And we listened to parents there for the first time describe their anxiety, anger, and bewilderment. Help was available in whatever form it was needed.

The group—which informally calls itself "the support group" or "the parents of asthmatic and allergic children"—began in the intensive care unit at St. Vincent's Hospital in Greenwich Village. Two mothers of severely asthmatic sons—one who had already dealt with the disease for seven years—began talking with each other during their vigils in the waiting room. Their exhilarating discovery of many shared feelings and experiences (including the same allergist for their sons) prompted them to meet several weeks later. They were joined by the mother of another asthmatic boy in this same allergist's care. The meeting culminated in their decision to form a support group.

The group has met monthly—except summers—ever since. The subject matter includes individual experiences and problems, general asthma-related topics (such as the questionable value of chiropractic for asthmatics), and an occasional meeting with a professional in the field. Each meeting is attended by about 20 members, although the membership list is appreciably larger than that.

The founders advised us that starting a support group is easy; the only real work involves notifying members when and where each meeting will be held. Ideally, two couples should share this responsibility. It is extremely helpful to have a physician who specializes in childhood asthma associated with the group so that factual questions can be answered. It is ideal if the physician is able to attend the group's meetings. Otherwise, questions can be submitted to him and the answers given at the next meeting. For recruiting members at the beginning—or if the group eventually thins out—notices can be sent for posting to local public and nursery schools, hospital emergency rooms, pediatricians' and allergists' offices, and churches.

Living a Normal Childhood

The child with asthma does best when he can experience as normal a childhood and upbringing as possible. This means the same responsibilities, as well as privileges, as other children his age. This is not always easy to achieve when your child cannot do as much as his older brother or sister or the kid down the block did at that age. Part of what it takes to get around this barrier is educating your child about his disease and helping him to participate in his care.

You must also de-emphasize your child's asthma. In part this means that his maintenance care becomes just another of his daily routines instead of the focal point of family life. Asthma parents must have their own perspective in hand, because their perspective—whether realistic or out of control—will eventually communicate itself to their child.

In trying to provide a relatively normal childhood, asthma parents walk a fine line in balancing their ''No's'' and ''Yes's.'' A ''No'' should be realistic, not motivated by anxiety. And a ''Yes'' should not risk putting your child in danger because you do not want him to feel different from his age-mates. Parents must think their answers through, and then ask their doctor (or support group) for help if they suspect they are needlessly denying their child the rights and freedoms that they would easily give a nonasthmatic child of that age.

Another problem with some asthma parents' ''Yes's'' is not inappropriateness, but timing. These parents take so long to conquer their own anxieties about their child participating in a particular activity that when their ''Yes'' finally comes, children have already gone on to something else. These parents feel proud about permitting their asthmatic child to do everything his friends do, yet their okay is so late that they force their child to be out of step with his peers. Normal activities at an abnormal time does not make a normal childhood.

Talking to other people about your child's asthma is particularly critical in helping your child and the rest of the family to a normal existence. Many asthma parents are afraid to let friends and relatives know of their child's disease. They fear publicizing their child's "imperfection." They are also anxious about being blamed for the disease, because so many people are still convinced that asthma reflects a disturbed mother-child relationship. The well-educated mother of a friend of ours, for example, constantly advises her daughter to take the grandchild—who has severe allergic asthma obviously inherited from her father's highly allergic and asthmatic family—to a psychiatrist instead of wasting time with an allergist. Most adults who cling to this inaccuracy feel free to express their evaluation. Many new asthma parents run into the comment: "My goodness! What have you been doing to your child!"

Encountering this attitude of blame does make it difficult—at first—to tell others that your child has asthma. But it is vitally important for you and your child to overcome your initial reluctance. Start with one person at a time, perhaps the parent of a child the same age as yours. It can be your answer to the frequent question: "How is your child?" It also comes up very appropriately when you plan to visit someone else's home and must make sure that your child will not be exposed to major triggers. Know in advance that making your child's story public will probably be hard and exhausting at first. But practice sooner or later makes it easy, and then it becomes routine. And you decide for yourself how you want to handle the various people who may blame you for your child's asthma.

The Sibling of an Asthmatic Child

Among our friends with an asthmatic child (the number is up to four at this point), one has two children, a nonasthmatic son of five and an asthmatic daughter of two who developed her disease when she was 10 months old. Our friend told us of her son's angry wish that he had asthma so she would pay more attention to him. We thought this highlighted something important, so we asked two professionals how asthma affects the nonasthmatic sibling.

The pediatric allergist we spoke with finds that an inordinately large number of asthmatic children do not have siblings. If a firstborn is asthmatic, parents usually decide not to have any more children because of the unexpected demands of caring for the first one combined with the fear of having a second child with asthma. The parent support group confirmed this observation. Few members over the years have had more than one child.

When there is a sibling, the allergist calls him "the forgotten child." During family office visits, he and his staff quite frequently hear siblings voice the wish that they, too, had asthma.

We also spoke with a well-respected psychologist who specializes in working with children and their families. She, on the other hand, finds that most asthma parents give a fair deal to all their children. Neglecting the healthy child is the exception, and occurs only when parents' reactions to the asthma are abnormal. Either they have not resolved their own problem feelings about the asthmatic sibling's disease, or have become stuck in grieving his loss of "perfection," or have embraced the outmoded concept of the asthmatic child as a totally infirm creature.

In explaining the healthy sibling's jealousy of asthma, she finds that the important word is *jealousy* rather than *asthma*. Jealousy is simply part of the normal experience of being a sibling. A sibling always feels that the other child gets more from their parents, and will find something to blame for this. It can be because the other child is older or younger, it could be the color of his eyes, his height, his sports ability, his intelligence or lack of it—or his asthma.

So if parents regard their child's jealousy of his asthmatic sibling as a general developmental issue and accept the fact that their children need to work out rivalries, they will not feel pained and responsible when their nonasthmatic child screams at his sibling: "You're so lucky that you have asthma!" He does not really want to have asthma, he simply wants at that point to torture his sibling. It is part and parcel of living in a family with more than one child.

And kids are likely to say mean things to others, too. "I hate you," they tell their mother, or "I wish you were dead," or "You ignore me because my brother has asthma." They do not literally mean what they are saying. It is simply part of growing up. The psychologist we spoke with advises parents to take what the sibling says with a large grain of salt, unless the asthmatic child's condition is very atypical, with many emergency room trips or hospitalizations.

During a typical crisis in which the asthmatic child has to be taken to the emergency room, obviously parental attention is temporarily devoted to the sick child. Parents cannot superhumanly be all things to all children all the time. Admittedly it is not easy for the other child to come home from school to find that his grandmother will be substituting for his parents for a few days, or to be shipped off to an aunt and uncle for the interim.

But even under these conditions, children cope remarkably well if their parents acknowledge them and their concern. They like to feel that they can do their part, no matter how small, in a family crisis. This means not leaving them temporarily in the dark about what is happening, and not relaying a message through a baby-sitter. All it takes is a brief telephone call as soon as the asthmatic child is stable, thanking the other child for cooperating and telling him how his sibling is doing. Calling him directly shows that you care, and know that he cares. Then he does not feel left out or neglected. And once the crisis is over, most parents are aware of the attention that they had to divert from the healthy child, and do their best to make it up to him.

✖✖ 18 ✖✖

Final Thoughts

What does the future hold for people who are born to suffer from asthma at some point in their lives? We can try to catch a few glimpses in several directions—understanding asthma better, improved treatment and prevention, more widespread education.

From medical research in the near future, we expect to see a greater understanding of the factors causing asthma. This improved understanding will then refine the diagnosis of asthma. Greater specificity in asthma diagnosis should allow medication regimens to become more individualized once more refined medications are available.

For drugs that prevent an attack or short-circuit one in progress, we do not expect theophylline and the beta-2-stimulators to be replaced anytime soon. We do, however, foresee improved formulations just over the horizon. A once-a-day dose of theophylline is becoming a reality. Beta-2-stimulators that are even longer acting and more specific than the formulations currently used here should be accepted in the United States before too long. By the time you read this book, both fenoterol and the atropine-like drug ipratropium bromide (*Atrovent*) may well be available.

The most substantial drug improvements will involve

prophylactic medication. Cromolyn sodium is currently the most widely used preventive drug. Ketotifen, which can be taken orally and is similar to cromolyn sodium, is available in Europe and should be approved for the U.S. market sometime soon. And more efficient generations of these drugs are already being developed. Antileukotriene medication is about to undergo its first clinical trials. (Leukotrienes are the potent bronchoconstrictors released by basophils, specialized white blood cells that participate in producing an asthma attack.) This drug represents an entirely new class of antiasthma medication.

More effective nonpharmaceutical tools should become available to deal with asthma as biofeedback and various other stress-management techniques evolve further. These will be important in allowing asthmatics to enjoy a normal life-style without fear.

In terms of eventually being able to prevent asthma from developing at all in susceptible people, at this point IgE-mediated asthma is potentially far more vulnerable than other types. This is because the pathway from allergen trigger to asthma symptoms is clearly understood compared to the other forms. Allergic asthma's development could be prevented by appropriate interference with any of its three major components. In broad theoretical terms, such interference would involve either changing biological inheritance by altering the parents' or infant's genes, manipulating aspects of the immune system (e.g., changing antibody production, influencing mast cells, reducing airway muscle sensitivity), or reducing the environmental allergen load on the infant.

Altering gene structure—called genetic engineering—in humans still belongs more to the realm of science fiction. In terms of altering immune system mechanisms, we have heard of techniques now being designed selectively to destroy mast cells. Until the role that mast cells play in the body's ecology is fully understood, such an approach is premature. Further into the future will be drugs designed to increase the newly identified *suppressive factor of allergy* (SFA) that the body produces. Because this factor suppresses IgE formation, increasing it could limit IgE levels to those found in nonallergic people. Finally, new desensitization methods should reduce the impact of allergens on susceptible infants. Long-term immunotherapy will most likely be avoided by the evolution of new and more refined serum extracts and inhaled extracts, and by starting treatment at a to-be-discovered critical time in infancy.

In terms of asthma's psychosocial impact, we believe that people in general will become better educated about the facts of asthma. As this knowledge becomes more widespread, the myths—especially the ones maintaining that asthma is in one's head and so needs a psychiatrist to cure, and that it reflects a disturbed parent-child relationship—that have dogged most asthmatics' lives will finally be forgotten.

The future for asthma also has its negative side, at least in the United States. With the continued cutbacks forecast in the government's domestic spending, particularly in health care and in environmental pollution controls, we foresee an increase in asthma incidence and severity. This will happen especially among the poor, who will not have access to the best medical treatment available.

The U.S. government has also made major, and ill-advised, cutbacks in funds for medical research. The limited pool of money now available for research projects has forced those who decide which projects are funded to consider only those certain to deliver immediate and practical results. There is no room for exploring uncharted paths that may—or may not—lead to a profound breakthrough. So the scope of today's research is usually narrow and the dimensions tend to be small.

This is in addition to the millennia-old tendency to accept only research that falls within the intellectual and philosophical boundaries of the day. Sometimes the judges of acceptability belong to the scientific community, and sometimes it is politicians and/or society at large that renders the verdict. The Church forced Galileo to recant his more accurate astronomy theories because they contradicted the religion-dominated view of the universe held during the Renaissance. Quite recently, the scientist who discovered that genes are made of DNA (which is not a protein) refused to believe his own results because they contradicted the prevailing view that proteins were the building blocks of genes.

The government funding pressures that cut the soul out of research are postponing to the unforeseeable future the major breakthrough that can make asthma a disease of the past. Although the various aspects of treatment described in these chapters now permit the asthmatic to live essentially a normal, challenging, satisfying life, he cannot permit himself the luxury of ignoring his disease or what is necessary to control it. Until that dreamed-of breakthrough finally materializes, the succinct comment of a 12-year-old asthmatic boy we met summarizes this situation: "Asthma stinks!"

Appendix A

Additional Sources of Information

American Academy of Allergy
611 East Wells Street
Milwaukee, WI 53202

Professional society of allergists; publishes *Journal of Allergy and Clinical Immunology*.

American Academy of Pediatrics
P.O. Box 1034
1801 Hinman Avenue
Evanston, IL 60204

Professional society of pediatricians; publishes various guides and handbooks.

American College of Allergists
2141 14th Street
Boulder, CO 80302

Professional society of allergists; publishes *Annals of Allergy*.

American College of Chest Physicians
911 Busse Highway
Park Ridge, IL 60068

Professional society of chest physicians and surgeons; publishes *Chest*.

American Lung Association (ALA)
1740 Broadway
New York, NY 10019
(212) 245-8000

The major national lung organization; publishes many pamphlets. Regional ALA chapters exist in most areas.

American Thoracic Society
1740 Broadway
New York, NY 10019

The medical section of the ALA; publishes *American Review of Respiratory Diseases*.

Asthma and Allergy Foundation of America (AAFA)
1717 Massachusetts Avenue, N.W., Suite 305
Washington, DC 20036
(202) 265-0265

Publishes *The Asthma and Allergy Advance*.

Asthma Project
National Heart, Lung and Blood Institute (NHLBI)
National Institute of Health
Building 31, Room 4A21
9000 Rockville Pike
Bethesda, MD 20205

NHLBI is the major government sponsor of research in respiratory diseases. It has developed four programs for health professionals to use in teaching asthma self-management skills to asthmatic children and their families. They are administered through local ALA organizations.

Asthma Research Council
12 Pembridge Square
London W2 4EH
Great Britain

The British version of the ALA, with branches throughout the country. This can be a good source of information if you are traveling in Great Britain and your asthma acts up.

National Foundation for Asthma/Tucson Medical Center
P.O. Box 42195
Tucson, AZ 85733

Publishes booklets for the public.

National Jewish Center for Immunology and Respiratory Medicine
1400 Jackson Street
Denver, CO 80206

Large referral hospital for difficult asthma cases. Publishes two quarterly newsletters: *New Directions* (for the lay public) and *Update* (for the physician). Also runs Lung Line, a free telephone information service, from 8:30 A.M. to 5:00 P.M. (800-222 LUNG, or from inside Colorado 303-398-1477).

Appendix B

Summer Camps for Asthmatic Children

ARIZONA
Civitan Camp, General Delivery, Williams, AZ 86046
(602) 635-2944
Friendly Pines Camp, Senator Road, Prescott, AZ 86301
(602) 445-2128

ARKANSAS
Medical Camps at Aldersgate Road, 2000 Aldersgate Road,
Little Rock, AR 72205

CALIFORNIA
Asthma and Allergy Foundation of America
(Running Springs, Calif.; 8 to 14 years of age; male and
female; moderate to severe asthma; no charge)
Location: Running Springs, Calif. Boys Club, #365
Campsite.
Contact: A.A.F.A., 8540 Sepulveda Boulevard, Los An-
geles, CA 90045

Camp Scamp
   (Running Springs, Calif.)
   Contact: Lung Association of Orange County, 1717 North
      Broadway, Santa Ana, CA 92706

Camp Wheez
   (Belmont, Calif.; 1-week program)
   Contact: American Lung Association of San Mateo
      County, 2250 Palm Avenue, San Mateo, CA 94403

Camp Wheez
   (San Jose, Calif.; 1-week program)
   Contact: American Lung Association of Santa Clara–San
      Benito Counties, 277 West Hedding Street, San Jose,
      CA 95110

Los Angeles Lung Association Asthma Camp
   (9 to 14 years of age; male and female; moderate to
      severe asthma; no charge)
   Contact: American Lung Association of LA County,
      1670 Beverly Boulevard, Los Angeles, CA 90026

Orange County Lung Association
   (9 to 14 years of age; no charge)
   Contact: O.C.L.A., 1717 North Broadway, Santa Ana,
      CA 92706

Running Springs
   (Pasadena, Calif.)
   Contact: American Lung Association of San Bernardino,
      Inyo, and Mono Counties, 371 West 14th Street, San
      Bernardino, CA 92405 or Lung Association of River-
      side County, 4750 Palm Ave., Riverside, CA 92501

San Diego County Lung Association Camp
   (mild asthma)
   Contact: S.D.C.L.A., 16766 Bernardo Center Drive, San
      Diego, CA 92128

Santa Cruz Mountains Camp
   Contact: Allergy Foundation of Northern California, 141
      Camino Alto, Mill Valley, CA 94941

Scamp Camp
   (Running Springs, Calif.; 1-week program)
   Contact: Lung Association of San Diego and Imperial
      Counties, 3861 Front Street, San Diego, CA 92103

Summer Camp for Children with Lung Disease
(Running Springs, Calif.; 1-week program; 10 to 14 years of age)

Sun-Air Home for Asthmatic Children Camp
(1-week program; 6 to 9 years of age)
Contact: American Lung Association of Los Angeles County, 1670 Beverly Boulevard, Los Angeles, CA 90026

Summer Camp at Running Springs California
Contact: Asthma and Allergy Foundation of America, 6245 Halm Avenue, Los Angeles, CA 90056 (213) 645-1616

Sun-Air for Asthmatic Children
(6 to 8 years of age)
Contact: Children's Hospital of Los Angeles, 4650 Sunset Boulevard, Los Angeles, CA 90027

COLORADO
Champ Camp
(Estes Park, Colo.; 1-week program)
Contact: American Lung Association of Colorado, 1600 Race Street, Denver, CO 80206

CONNECTICUT
Hemlock's Outdoor Education Center, Jones Street, Amston, CT 06231 (203) 228-9496

FLORIDA
Camp Lake Swan
(Melrose, Fla.; 1-week program)
Contact: Florida Lung Association, 5526 Arlington Road, Jacksonville, FL 32211

Camp Sunshine Station (Lake Swan Camp)
(Melrose, Fla.)
Contact: Florida Lung Association, P.O. Box 8127, Jacksonville, FL 32211

ILLINOIS
Camp Tapawingo
(Peoria, Ill.; 1-week program)

Contact: American Lung Association of Illinois, 1 Christmas Seal Drive, Springfield, IL 62703

INDIANA

Julia Jameson Health Camp for Children, Inc., 1100 West 42nd Street, Indianapolis, IN 46208 (317) 923-3925

IOWA

Camp Superkids, YMCA Camp
(Boone, Iowa; 1-week program)
Contact: American Lung Association of Iowa, 1321 Walnut Street, Des Moines, IA 50309

KENTUCKY

Camp Kysoc, 1902 Easterday Road, Carrolton, KY 41008 (502) 732-5333
Camp Sdikrepus, University of Kentucky Medical Center, Lexington, KY 40536
Camp Weasel, University of Kentucky Medical Center, Lexington, KY 40536
Green Shores, Star Route One, Box 74, McDaniels, KY 40152 (502) 257-2508

MICHIGAN

Camp Michi-Mac, 23023 Orchard Lake Road, Farmington, MI 48024 (313) 478-6300
Camp Sun Deer
(Battle Creek, Mich.; 1-week program)
Contact: American Lung Association of Southeastern Michigan, 28 West Adams Street, Detroit, MI 48226 or American Lung Association of Michigan, 403 Seymour Avenue, Lansing, MI 48914

MINNESOTA

Camp Superkids, YMCA Camp Ihduhapi, Loretto, MN 55357 (612) 871-7332
Camp Superkids
(Minneapolis, Minn.)
5000 West 39th Street, Minneapolis, MN 55116

MONTANA

Camp Huff 'n Puff

(Elliston, Mont.; three 1-week programs; by age group)
Contact: American Lung Association of Montana, Christmas Seal Building, 825 Helena Avenue, Helena, MT 59601

NEBRASKA
Camp Superkids
(1-week program)
Contact: American Lung Association of Nebraska, 7363 Pacific Street, Suite 212, Omaha, NE 68114

NEW HAMPSHIRE
YMCA Camp Foss
(Center Barnstead, N.H.; 1-week program)
Contact: New Hampshire Lung Association, 456 Beech Street, Manchester, NH 03105

NEW MEXICO
Camp Superkids
(Santa Fe, N.M.; 1-week program)
Contact: American Lung Association of New Mexico, 216 Truman Avenue, N.E., Albuquerque, NM 87108

NEW YORK
Asthmatic Children's Foundation of New York, Spring Valley Road, Ossining, NY 10562
Camp Massawixie, Adirondack Mountains
Contact: Boy Scout Council of Monroe County, 474 East Avenue, Rochester, NY 14607
Camp Superkids
(Utica, N.Y.; day camp; 1-week program)
Contact: American Lung Association of Mid–New York, 23 South Street, Utica, NY 13501
Camp Vacamas, 215 Park Avenue South, New York, NY 10003
Wagon Road Camp
Contact: Children's Aid Society, 43 Quaker Road, Box 47, Chappaqua, NY 10514 (914) 631-3283

NORTH DAKOTA
Camp Superkids, Triangle Y Camp, Lake Sakakawea
(Garrison, N.D.; 2-week program)

Contact: North Dakota Lung Association, 212 North 2nd
Street, Bismarck, ND 58501

OHIO
Camp Superkids
Contact: Southwestern Ohio Lung Association, 2330
Victory Parkway, Room 400, Cincinnati, OH 45206
(513) 751-3650

Steppin Stones
(day camp)
5650 Given Road, Cincinnati, OH 45243 (513) 831-4660

OKLAHOMA
Camp Superkids
(Sapulpa, Okla.; two 1-week programs)
Contact: American Lung Association of Green County,
Oklahoma, 5553 South Peoria, Tulsa, OK 74105 or
American Lung Association of Oklahoma, Inc., 2442
North Walnut, Oklahoma City, OK 73105

OREGON
Camp Christmas Seal
(two 1-week programs; 9 to 13 years of age)
Contact: Oregon Lung Association, 1020 S.W. Taylor,
Suite 830, Portland, OR 97205

VIRGINIA
Holiday Trails, Route 1, Box 356, Charlottesville, VA
22901 (804) 977-3781

WASHINGTON
Children's Orthopedic Hospital and Medical Center Camp
(Seattle, Wash.)
4800 Sandpoint Way, N.E., Seattle, WA 98105 (206)
634-5423

WEST VIRGINIA
Camp Bronco Junction, R.D. #1, Red House, WV 25168
(304) 755-7621; or 306 May Building, Charleston, WV
25301 (304) 343-5427

(Reprinted with permission from M. S. Scherr, "Summer camps for asthmatics—why and where," *The Journal of Respiratory Diseases*, Vol. 3, p. 39, 1982.)

Appendix C

Further Readings

PAMPHLETS

Available from the American Lung Association,
1740 Broadway, New York, NY 10019.

For Parents

Controlling Asthma (ALA #1125)
The Asthma Handbook (ALA #4002)
There Are Solutions for the Student with Asthma (ALA #
   0083)
What Happens When a Child Has Asthma (ALA #0069)

For Schools

Asthma Alert for School Nurses (ALA #6014)
Asthma Alert for School Administrators (ALA #6016)
Asthma Alert for Teachers (ALA #6013)
Asthma Alert for Physical Education Teachers (ALA #6015)

Available from the National Foundation/Tucson Medical Center, P.O. Box 42195, Tucson, AZ 85733.

Alpert, Linda. *Asthma Fact and Fiction*

Alpert, Linda. *Dust 'n' Stuff* (dust control and allergy-proofing)

Available from the American Academy of Pediatrics, 611 East Wells Street, Milwaukee, WI 53202.

Captain Wonderlung: Breathing Exercises for Asthmatic Children

BOOKS FOR THE LAY PERSON

Asthma and Allergies: An Optimistic Future. U.S. Department of Health and Human Services, NIH-Publication #80-388, March 1980. (More allergy than asthma.)

Butts, Karen R. *Breathing Exercise for Asthma*. Springfield, Ill.: Charles C. Thomas, 1980.

Lane, D. J., and A. Storr. *Asthma: The Facts*. Oxford, England: Oxford University Press, 1979. (Well written, although slightly technical. The book is written from the British point of view, and so offers a different perspective on the treatment of asthma.)

Parcel, G., et al. *Teaching Myself About Asthma*. Available by mail from Health Education Associates, 14 North Lake Road, Columbia, S.C. 29208. The book costs $8.95, plus $1.00 for postage and handling. (This book was written for children with 4th- to 5th-grade reading ability; it comes highly recommended.)

Plaut, T. F. *Children with Asthma: A Manual for Parents*. Amherst, Mass.: Pedipress, 1983. (Invaluable for parents of an asthmatic child. The individual anecdotes written by parents serve as a mini-support group.)

Young, S. H. *The Asthma Handbook: A Complete Guide for Patients and Their Families*. New York: Bantam Books, 1985. (Covers the subject of asthma completely, but from an allergist's point of view.)

WRITTEN FOR PROFESSIONALS, BUT UNDERSTANDABLE BY LAY READERS

Dawson, A., and R. A. Simon, eds. *The Practical Management of Asthma*. Orlando, Fla.: Grune and Stratton, 1984. (A very complete and concise book for the professional, but the abundance of useful tables makes it understandable to lay people willing to make the effort.)

Wilson, J. D. *Asthma and Allergic Diseases*. Sydney, Australia: ADIS Health Science Press, 1983. (Although written for the professional, this is one of the clearest and most easily understood books on the subject we have read.)

FOR THE EXPERTS

Clark, T. J. H., and S. Godfrey, *Asthma*, 2d ed. London: Chapman and Hall, 1983. (A complete, well-written text expressing the British view of asthma.)

Middleton, E., Jr., C. E. Reed, and E. F. Ellis, eds. *Allergy: Principles and Practice*, 2d ed. St. Louis: C. V. Mosby, 1983. (A two-volume textbook of chapters contributed by leaders in their field. Although generally highly technical, three chapters in Volume 2 stand out for the lay reader. Chapter 37 by E. R. McFadden and J. B. Stevens on the history of asthma is a pleasure to read. Chapter 43 by M. Schatz et al. clearly covers the topic of pregnancy and nursing. Chapter 52 by R. Patterson et al. covers the topic of immunotherapy; the last several pages answer questions of direct concern to the patient.)

Weiss, E. B., M. S. Segal, and M. Stein, eds. *Bronchial Asthma*, 2d ed. Boston: Little, Brown and Co., 1985. (A striking technical compilation of conference papers describing the latest thinking on asthma.)

PERIODICALS

There are a number of professional journals dealing with asthma research, most of which are highly technical. The *Journal of Asthma* includes several features for lay readers: reviews of nontechnical books on asthma, lists of devices that may be useful for the asthmatic, and autobiographical narrations by people with asthma.

Asthma Update is a lay newsletter that carries summaries of research articles, notes new devices, contains practical advice, and includes anything else that may be of interest to those with asthma. For information contact D. J. Jamison, 123 Monticello Ave., Annapolis, MD 21401.

New Directions is a quarterly lay newsletter published by the National Jewish Center for Immunology and Respiratory Medicine (listed in Appendix A).

The MA Report, the newest entry, is a very well done monthly newsletter in support of parents of asthmatic children. Put out by a group of asthma mothers, it addresses the practical aspects and relevant issues of raising an asthmatic child. This group has also begun a "Phones Across America" effort to help isolated parents find each other and to provide a support system for those who do not have access to a local support group or asthma program. For information on either project, contact Mothers of Asthmatics, Inc., 5316 Summit Drive, Fairfax, VA 22030.

DRUG INFORMATION

Physicians' Desk Reference for Prescription Drugs. Published yearly by the Medical Economics Co., Oradell, NJ 07649.

Facts and Comparisons Drug Information. Updated monthly, and published by the Facts and Comparisons Division, J. B. Lippincott Co., 111 West Port Plaza, St. Louis, MO 63141.

United States Pharmacopeial Convention. One-page, easy-to-understand descriptions of medications. The page covers proper use, interaction with other drugs, side effects, how each drug works, and a list of generic types. For asthma these include:

Adrenergic Bronchodilator (Aerosol Inhalation)
Adrenergic Bronchodilator (Oral/Injection)
Adrenocorticoids (Aerosol)
Adrenocorticoids (Inhalation/Oral)
Cromolyn Sodium (Inhalation)
Xanthine (Theophylline) Bronchodilators (Oral)

DICTIONARY

Dorland's Illustrated Medical Dictionary. Philadelphia: W. B. Saunders. (We find this book relatively easy to use.)

Glossary

Words in quotation marks within a definition are also defined in the Glossary.

Accessory muscles of respiration: These muscles of the neck and shoulders help the main respiratory muscles during strenuous exercise and when it becomes difficult to breathe. Their contraction lifts the rib cage, which makes it larger. The severity of an asthma attack can be judged by how much these muscles bulge out during breathing. The right-hand section of Figure 2.4 shows the most important accessory muscles.

Adrenaline: Also called *epinephrine*, this is a hormone released by the adrenal glands during stress. It is also the drug typically used in the emergency room to reverse a severe asthma attack or anaphylactic shock (see "Anaphylaxis"). (Also see "Adrenergic.")

Adrenergic: Pertains to three related items: (1) the group of "hormones" produced by the inner segment of the adrenal glands, (2) the receptors in other organs that these hormones stimulate to achieve their effects, and (3) the drugs that stimulate these same receptors. Adrenergic drugs dilate the airways.

Aerosol: A spray of fine particles that can be inhaled. Antiasthma drugs that can be prepared in liquid form can be taken this way. The aerosol is created with either a "nebulizer" or a "metered-dose inhaler."

Airway hyperreactivity: A response characteristic of the airways of some people—particularly asthmatics—to constrict when exposed to a stimulus that does not affect other people's airways.

Allergen: A substance that causes an "allergy." For asthmatics, the most worrisome substances are carried in the air (e.g., pollens). They are called *aeroallergens*.

Allergy: A hypersensitive "immune system" response to a substance the person has already been exposed to at least once. People without this allergy are unaffected by the same substance. This response appears in one or more of the following ways: rash, "hives," runny nose, itchy eyes, swelling, asthma.

Allergy shots: See "Immunotherapy."

Alveolus: One of the millions of air sacs in the lungs, located at the ends of airways. The *alveoli* (referring to more than one) are surrounded by "capillaries." The exchange of "oxygen" and "carbon dioxide" occurs through the membrane separating the alveoli and capillaries. (Also see "Capillaries.")

Anaphylaxis: The most serious form of allergic reaction (see "Allergy"), it involves the entire body. There are generalized swelling and "hives," the airways close, and the cardiovascular system can collapse. In its most severe form, anaphylaxis can result in death.

Antibodies: Also called *immunoglobins*. They are a group of five structurally related proteins (IgA, IgD, "IgE," IgG, IgM) produced by the "immune system" when the body is invaded by foreign proteins. Antibodies are produced during the first encounter with a particular invading protein, and then help to destroy them during future invasions. Each antibody type reacts to a different kind of foreign protein—bacteria, "allergens," etc. Within each antibody type, a specific antibody is created for each different foreign protein.

Arterial blood gases: The two gases carried in our blood are "oxygen" and "carbon dioxide." The concentrations carried in our arterial blood—blood freshly oxygenated and cleansed of excess carbon dioxide by the lungs—are referred to as arterial blood gases.

Asymptomatic: A disease period during which the patient does not experience any symptoms. In asthma this is the time between attacks, a period when the patient has no problems breathing.

Atelectasis: Collapse of a small or large area of the lungs because all the gas in those "alveoli" has been absorbed and not replaced. ("Pneumothorax" is also a collapse, but is caused by a different process.)

Autonomic nervous system: This part of the nervous system regulates the various organs in the body over which there is no voluntary control. Its two branches are the *sympathetic* and *parasympathetic nervous systems*. In asthma, stimulating the sympathetic branch causes the airways to dilate, and stimulating the parasympathetic branch causes "bronchoconstriction."

Basophil: A type of white blood cell involved in allergic (see "Allergy") reactions. Basophils are similar to "mast cells" and contain chemicals whose release can cause "bronchoconstriction."

Beta-2-receptors: One type of receptor that is stimulated by "adrenergic" "hormones" such as "adrenaline." Activating beta-2-receptors causes bronchodilation, and stops "mast cells" and "basophils" from releasing their "bronchoconstricting" chemicals.

Breath sounds: Sounds heard through the stethoscope as air moves in and out of the lungs. Certain breath sounds are characteristic of particular lung problems (see "Wheeze").

Bronchi: The larger airways (meaning a diameter of more than 1/12 inch or 2mm). They are the most affected in asthma (see Figure 2.1).

Bronchioles: The airways, smaller than the "bronchi," that branch off to the "alveoli."

Bronchiolitis: An airway infection, usually in young children, that is indistinguishable from an acute asthma attack.

Bronchoconstrictor: Any substance that causes the airways to narrow.

Bronchoconstriction: Narrowing of the airways from one or more of the following causes: "bronchospasm"; swelling of the tissue lining the airways; excessive mucus clogging the airways.

Bronchodilator: Any substance that reverses "bronchoconstriction."

Bronchospasm: Narrowing of the airways from contraction of the muscles surrounding them. It is the most typical event in asthma attacks.

Capillaries: The smallest blood vessels, and the site of gas exchange throughout the body. In the lungs, capillary blood picks up "oxygen" from the "alveoli" while it discharges "carbon dioxide." In other tissues, oxygen leaves the capillaries while they pick up carbon dioxide.

Carbon dioxide: Abbreviated as CO_2, this gas is a waste product (the other being water) of energy metabolism. It is important in maintaining the proper acidity of the blood, and is the major regulator of "ventilation."

Chronic obstructive pulmonary disease: Abbreviated as COPD. Sometimes called COAD, with *airway* substituted for *pulmonary*. A class of lung diseases that primarily affect expiration, COPD includes chronic bronchitis, emphysema, bronchiectasis, and cystic fibrosis. Not everyone includes asthma in this group. We do.

Cilia: Microscopic hair-like structures on the cells lining the inner surface of the airways. They sweep particles out of the lungs after they are trapped in mucus. Inhaled cigarette smoke damages this sweeping mechanism.

Cyanosis: The bluish tint that appears around the lips and under the fingernails when there is inadequate "oxygen" in the blood.

Diaphragm: The major muscle of inspiration. This large,

thin, dome-shaped muscle separates the chest and abdominal cavities (see Figure 2.4).

Dyspnea: The subjective feeling of not being able to catch one's breath.

Edema: Excess fluid in the tissues, often from inflammation. In more severe asthma attacks inflammation causes fluid to accumulate around the airways, which compresses them and so narrows them further.

Epinephrine: See "Adrenaline" and "Adrenergic."

Expectorant: Any drug or other product (e.g., garlic) that helps to move and get rid of airway secretions.

Extrinsic asthma: A convenient term (but of limited use) for a form of asthma in which the trigger is known, usually an allergen (e.g., birch tree pollen).

FEV_1: The volume of air that can be forcefully expired from a maximum inspiration during the first second. This is a traditional test for evaluating how well the lungs are working. Because an airway obstruction reduces this volume, it is always smaller during an asthma attack.

FVC: Forced vital capacity, which is the total amount of air that can be forcefully expired from a maximum inspiration. Whether it is reduced during an asthma attack depends on the attack's severity.

Generic drugs: Drugs that do not carry a brand name and instead are called by their common chemical name. They are usually cheaper than their brand-name counterparts.

Genetic: Referring to the inheritance of biological traits.

Histamine: A chemical contained in "mast cells" and other cells. It causes nasal stuffiness, swelling, and dripping in hay fever or a common cold; red, itchy skin blotches in an "allergy" reaction; and "bronchoconstriction" in asthma.

Hives: A rash caused by an "allergy" reaction. It is more technically called a *wheal*.

Hormone: A substance released by one organ in the body that travels to another organ to act. "Adrenaline," for example, is released by the adrenal glands and then carried by the blood to the various organs it acts on. One organ is the heart, which it speeds up; another is the airways, which it dilates.

Hyperventilation: "Ventilation" that brings more "oxygen" to the lungs than the body needs. Although very little of this additional inhaled oxygen actually enters the blood, "carbon dioxide" is removed from the blood at a much faster rate. Hyperventilation is technicaly defined as a reduction below normal in the amount of carbon dioxide in arterial blood.

Hypoventilation: The opposite of "hyperventilation," it is the inability to "ventilate" enough to meet the body's metabolic demands for "oxygen." It is technically defined as an increase above normal in the amount of "carbon dioxide" in arterial blood, and a fall below normal in arterial blood's oxygen content.

Hypoxemia: Inadequate "oxygen" in the blood, usually due to lung disease or a problem with the blood's oxygen-carrying capacity (such as anemia).

Hypoxia: A more general term for inadequate "oxygen," it can be due to heart disease, lung disease, anemia, or high altitude (where there is not enough oxygen in the air). "Hypoxemia" and hypoxia are often used interchangeably.

Immune system: All the mechanisms involved in protecting the body against disease.

Immunoglobins: See "Antibodies."

IgE: Immunoglobin E. This type of "antibody" is normally found only in small amounts. Although its exact non-pathological function is not clear, it seems to be involved in protecting the body against parasites. In people "genetic"ally predisposed to "allergies," IgE is the major intermediary in these reactions. They tend to have much higher amounts of IgE than normal.

Immunotherapy: Also called *desensitization, hyposensitization,* and "allergy" shots. An antiallergy treatment that injects extracts of those substances to which an individual is allergic to produce tolerance or immunity. The treatment takes several years and follows a careful chronological sequence.

Incidence: The rate at which something occurs (e.g., 10 percent of Americans have asthma). This term is sometimes confused with "prevalence."

Intravenous medication: Medicine injected directly into a vein.

Intrinsic asthma: A convenient—but often incorrect—term for a type of asthma in which the external cause is not known.

Local: See "Systemic."

Mast cells: These cells play a pivotal role in asthma. They are extensively distributed throughout much of the body, particularly at surfaces in contact with the external environment. They are especially numerous in the mouth, airways, skin, and digestive tract. They contain powerful "mediators" such as "histamine," which can cause asthma when released in the airways.

Mediator: Any chemical that can activate a biological response.

Metered-dose inhaler: Also called by its abbreviation, MDI. It is a hand-held device that uses medication in liquid form to dispense a fixed dose via "aerosol."

Nebulizer: A device that converts a liquid into a fine spray that is inhaled with a mask.

Oxygen: The gas that allows energy to be released from the food we eat. *Metabolism* is the process by which this happens.

Parasympathetic nervous system: See "Autonomic nervous system."

Pneumothorax: This technical term for *collapsed lung* literally describes the presence of air (pneumo-) between the lungs and chest wall (the thorax). Air entering the thorax breaks the vacuum that otherwise prevents the lungs from completely collapsing, so this collapse occurs. Because the right and left sides of the chest cavity are isolated from each other, a pneumothorax usually involves collapse of only one side of the lungs.

Prevalence: The number of disease cases existing in a specific population at a particular time (e.g., 20 million Americans currently have asthma). This term is sometimes confused with "incidence."

Prophylactic: Preventive. In asthma, for example, cromolyn sodium is a prophylactic medication because it prevents asthma attacks, but it cannot reverse an attack once it is started.

Prostaglandins: A group of "hormones" that serve many functions in the body. It is thought that some of them may play a role in asthma.

Provocation test: A diagnostic test for asthma designed to provoke "bronchoconstriction" in susceptible people when a clear-cut diagnosis of asthma has been impossible. Exercise, cold air, methacholine (a "bronchoconstricting" chemical), and "histamine" have all been used to provoke this reaction.

Pulmonary: Dealing with the lungs and breathing.

Pulmonary function tests: A series of tests designed to evaluate the health of the lungs (see Figures 5.2, 5.3, and 5.4).

RAST: Radioallergosorbent test. A blood test that measures the various amounts of "IgE" specific to substances to which a patient may be allergic (see "Allergy"). It measures, for example, the amount of IgE that recognizes ragweed pollen.

Reflex: An involuntary response to a stimulus. One asthma trigger works via reflex. Stimulating the airways' irritant receptors increases activity in the vagus nerve (part of the parasympathetic branch of the "autonomic nervous system"), which culminates in "bronchospasm."

Respiratory tract: The system of tubes that pass air from the mouth and nose to the "alveoli" (see Figure 2.1). It is divided into two sections. The upper respiratory tract runs from the mouth and nose to the end of the "trachea'' (windpipe). The lower respiratory tract goes from the end of the trachea to the ''alveoli'' entry points.

Retraction: The ribs are sucked in instead of expanding during inspiration. This happens with adults only when the airways are obstructed. Very slight retraction is normal in infants, and airway obstruction can increase it substantially. In all cases, the degree of retraction indicates the degree of obstruction.

Sign: Something that is observed about a patient, such as the bluish tint around the lips from inadequate ''oxygen.'' This stands in contrast to a *symptom*, which is something the patient notices or complains about. An example is a tight feeling in the chest after exercise.

Sputum: Also called *phlegm*, this is material coughed up from the lungs. It contains mucus and cells, cellular debris, bacteria, etc. (see Figure 5.1).

Sympathetic nervous system: See ''Autonomic nervous system.''

Symptom: See ''Sign.''

Systemic: Pertaining to the entire body. A systemic drug is taken orally or by injection, because these routes distribute the drug throughout the body. A local drug is administered at the site where it is needed. When a certain concentration of a bronchodilator drug is needed in the airways to be effective, a systemic preparation must be given in a larger amount than a local preparation. This is because a systemic preparation becomes diluted as it spreads through the body, whereas all of a locally used drug reaches the desired area.

Trachea: The main windpipe connecting the mouth and nose to the lungs. It begins just below the Adam's apple and ends where it divides into the main right and left ''bronchi'' (see Figure 2.1).

Trigger: The cause of an asthma attack.

Vaccine: A substance usually derived from live disease organisms which, when injected into animals or people, protects them from developing that disease.

Ventilation: The amount of air that moves in and out of the lungs. It is usually measured for a given time and recorded in liters per minute (called *minute ventilation*).

Wheeze: This "breath sound" indicates the presence of airway obstruction. It is a high-pitched whistle usually heard during expiration, but sometimes during inspiration. This sound is the turbulence of the air as it passes around an obstruction.

❖❖ Index ❖❖

About the Authors

DR. FRANCOIS HAAS earned his Ph.D. in pulmonary physiology from the Department of Physiology at the New York University School of Medicine. He has been on its faculty since then, and is also director of Pulmonary Function Laboratory at the Medical Center. Dr. Haas studies lung mechanics and exercise-induced asthma, and recently completed an NIH-funded project on how aerobic fitness affects asthmatics. His work is widely published in professional journals.

DR. SHEILA SPERBER HAAS earned her Ph.D. in psychology from the Personality Program at the City University of New York's Graduate School and University Center. There she studied the relationship between personality types and breathing styles. She writes on a variety of medical and science topics for professional and lay audiences.

The Drs. Haas live in New York City with their two young children.